1000 Dreams

THE *Nature* OF DREAMS

People whose experience is of dropping every night into a deep and uneventful sleep, a black nullity, might be surprised to discover that, in all likelihood, everybody dreams. Although many of us forget most or all of the dreams that have visited us during the night, normally we dream for about one fifth of the time that we are asleep. Freud, Jung and other pioneers of the unconscious have helped us to understand that the scenarios of our dream life are not just random mental "noise". Far from being meaningless, they constitute a vivid inward show of the preoccupations that stir within our minds at the deepest levels of our being. Dreams, in many ways, are windows into our true, uncensored selves.

Dreams through History

All through history we have sought to fathom the meanings of our dreams. Intrigued by their strange images, and by their apparent cargo of symbolism, we have searched them ingeniously for insights into our present lives and for clues about our future.

The most ancient civilizations believed that dreams carried messages from the gods. Cuneiform tablets from Assyria and Babylon dating from the end of the fourth millennium BC depict a society whose priests and kings received warnings in their dreams from the deity Zaqar. The *Epic of Gilgamesh*, the great tale of a Mesopotamian hero-king written in the Akkadian language during the first millennium BC, is full of dream accounts, many replete with divine omens of danger or victory; in one a nightmare creature leads the hero Enkidu to the "Land of Dust" where the souls of the dead live in perpetual darkness.

Ancient Jewish tradition anticipated modern dream theory by recognizing that the life-circumstances of the dreamer are as important in interpretation as the dream content itself. The Babylonians revered the Jews as dream interpreters, and in the sixth century BC they summoned the Israelite prophet Daniel to interpret one of King Nebuchadnezzar's dreams, whereupon he correctly predicted the king's imminent seven years of madness (Daniel 4: 535). The Egyptians were also respectful of the Jewish tradition of dream interpretation. Joseph, sold into slavery in Egypt by his brothers, was able to rise from poverty to a position of considerable power by correctly interpreting the Pharaoh's dream that foretold seven plentiful and seven lean years in the ancient kingdom (Genesis 41: 138).

The Ancient World

The Egyptians themselves did much to systematize dream interpretation during the years of the Middle Kingdom (2040–1786 BC), and their methods (as recorded in the Chester Beatty papyrus) have echoes in present-day dream directories. Dreams were understood in terms of meaningful opposites: thus, apparently happy dreams presaged disaster, while the worst nightmare could stand for better times to come. Individual dream symbols were fathomed either through rhyming similarities between word sounds, or through the modern method of association.

It was believed that dreams contained messages from both good and evil spirits. By ingesting herbal potions or reciting spells, a dreamer would attempt to induce the good spirits and deter the bad. Thus prepared, the subject would sleep in the temple, and then upon awakening would submit his or her dreams to the temple priest for interpretation.

The Dreamtime

In Australian Aboriginal myth there is a creation period called the Dreamtime. It is believed that during a primordial epoch the ancestors travelled across Australia shaping the landscape and determining the forms of society. The Dreamtime is a time of origins yet it is also a kind of alternative dimension, in parallel with the everyday world.

As a state of being the Dreamtime remains accessible to Aboriginal people through wandering the landscape and through ritual. Episodes from the Dreamtime are re-enacted at sacred sites in which the participants briefly become the ancestors whose journeys they recreate.

The ancient Greeks borrowed extensively from the Egyptians, and built more than 300 shrines to serve as dream oracles. Mortals in these shrines were subjected to the soporific power of Hypnos, god of sleep, as he fanned them with his wings. Once they had passed into slumber, the god Morpheus could communicate with his adepts, passing warnings and prophecies to them in their dreams. Many of these shrines became famous as centres of healing. The sick would sleep there, hoping for a visitation from Aesculapius, the god of healing, who provided remedies for physical ills, sometimes effecting immediate cures, while the dreamer lay asleep surrounded by harmless yellow snakes. Aesculapius is also said to have summoned sacred snakes to the shrines to lick the wounds of the afflicted in their sleep, and so heal them. The caduceus – a device consisting of two snakes entwined around a rod – is still widely used to represent healing in Western symbolism.

Plato, writing in the fourth century BC, took a less mystical view, believing the liver to be the seat of dreams. He attributed some dreams to the gods, but others to what in *The Republic* he called the "lawless wild beast nature which peers out in sleep", anticipating Freud by more than 2,000 years when he explained that dreams were a place where a person's bestial desires run riot, unless the "well-governed soul" is able to replace baser instincts with reason, in which case dreams equip us to come "nearer to grasping the truth than at any other time". His pupil Aristotle, on the other hand, foreshadowed twentieth-century scientific rationalism by arguing that dreams were triggered by purely sensory causes. He said that the insights available from dreams were like objects reflected in water: when the water is calm, the forms are easy to see; when the water is agitated (that is, when the mind is emotionally disturbed), the reflections become distorted and meaningless. The more the mind can be stilled before sleep, said Aristotle, the more the dreamer can learn.

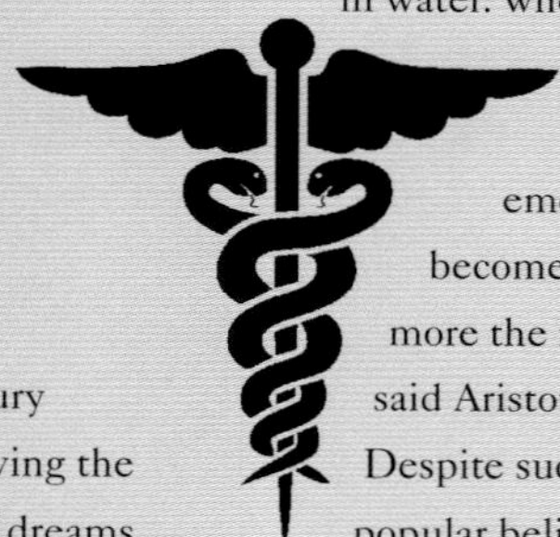

Despite such cautionary voices, however, popular belief in the divinatory power of dreams remained widespread, and allegedly affected the course of Roman history: both Hannibal's epic journey across the Alps and Caesar's invasion of Rome were prompted by divine dream encouragement.

In the second century AD the Sophist philosopher Artemidorus of Daldis (who makes two brief and enigmatic appearances in Shakespeare's *Julius Caesar*) drew together the wisdom of earlier centuries, much of it already collected in the great library of the Babylonian King Asurna at Nineveh. His researches appeared in five highly influential dream books,

collectively entitled the *Oneirocritica* (from the Greek *oneiros*, meaning "a dream").

Although many of his interpretations sound somewhat quaint to present-day ears, Artemidorus was surprisingly modern in some respects. For example, he identified the importance of the dreamer's personality in dream analysis, as a primary factor in determining significance; and he observed the nature and frequency of sexual symbols. In his formulation that a mirror in a dream represents the feminine to male dreamers and the masculine to female dreamers, he even anticipated the Jungian concepts of the Anima and Animus (see page 103).

Eastern Traditions

Oriental dream traditions also offer rewarding perspectives. Generally, they lay more emphasis upon the dreamer's state of mind. Chinese sages recognized that consciousness has different levels, and when interpreting dreams they took account of the physical condition and horoscope of the dreamer, as well as the time of year. They believed that consciousness leaves the body during sleep, and travels in otherworldly realms: to arouse the dreamer abruptly, before mind and body are reunited, could be highly dangerous.

Indian *rsis*, or seers, also believed in the

multi-layered nature of consciousness, recognizing the discrete states of waking, dreaming, dreamless sleep and *samadhi*, the bliss that follows enlightenment. A passage on dream interpretation in the *Atharva Veda*, a philosophical text dating from *c*.1500–1000 BC, teaches that in a series of dreams only the last is important: the suggestion is that dreams work progressively in solving problems or revealing wisdom. Hindu tradition also emphasizes the importance of individual dream images, relating them to a wider symbolic system incorporating the symbolic attributes of gods and demons. The Hindu belief that some symbols are universal while some are personal to the dreamer foreshadows the work of both Freud and Jung.

Islamic and Christian Traditions

In the West, little progress was made in the study of dreams in the centuries after Artemidorus, as it was thought that he had made their mysteries plain. The Arabs, however, influenced by Eastern wisdom, continued to explore the dream world, producing dream dictionaries and a wealth of interpretations. Muhammad rose from obscurity to found Islam after a dream in which he received his prophetic call, and dreams afterwards came to the forefront of religious orthodoxy. In the Koran, the angel Gabriel comes to Muhammad in a dream, leading him on a silvery mare to Jerusalem and then up to heaven, where he meets Christ, Adam and the four evangelists, enters the Garden of Delight and receives instructions from God.

The belief that dreams could be divinely inspired persisted during the early centuries of Christendom, and in the fourth century AD was part of the teaching of Church fathers such as St John Chrysostom, St Augustine and St Jerome. However, Christian orthodoxy was moving away from dream interpretation and prophecy. The dreams of the New Testament were seen as straightforward messages from God to the disciples and other founders of Christianity. Prediction was redundant, because the future was believed to be in God's hands. By the Middle Ages, the Church even discounted the possibility of divine messages to the average believer, because God's revelation was only in and through the Church itself. The Dominican theologian Thomas Aquinas summed up the orthodox position of the thirteenth century when he advised that dreams should be ignored altogether. Martin Luther, who broke from the Roman Catholic Church to initiate the Protestant Reformation, taught that dreams, at most, simply showed us our sins.

However, dream interpretation was too strongly rooted in popular consciousness to be so readily dismissed. With the increasing availability of printed books in Europe from the fifteenth century onward, dream dictionaries proliferated, mostly based on the works of Artemidorus. Despite their naivety, such dictionaries filled a useful role in taking dream interpretation away from the seers and priests and placing it, empoweringly, in the hands of the individual.

Even though the scientific rationalists of the eighteenth century believed that dreams were of little consequence, and that their interpretation was a form of primitive superstition, at a popular level the interest in dreams gathered strength. Moreover, dreams began to feature as prominent themes in literature and art, as the new Romanticism, led by visionaries such as William Blake and Goethe, rejected the claims of the rationalists and placed a new emphasis on the importance of the individual and the creative power of the imagination.

The 19th and 20th Centuries

In nineteenth-century Europe even philosophers such as Johann Gottlieb Fichte (1762–1814) and Johann Friedrich Herbart (1776–1841) began to regard dreams as worthy of serious psychological study, and thus the way was prepared for the revolution in dream theory that began at the end of the century with Sigmund Freud (1856–1939).

In 1899, in his mid-forties, Freud published his monumental work *The Interpretation of Dreams*. His studies as a neurologist had led him to search for the causes of neuroses in the unconscious mind, and after a lengthy course of self-analysis he became convinced of the role that dreams could play in providing access to these inner depths. For Freud the unconscious, or id, was primarily the seat of desires and impulses, mostly of a sexual nature, that are usually repressed by the conscious mind. Most dreams, he believed, are simple wish-fulfilments, or expressions of repressed ideas that force their way into our consciousness when our egos relax control during sleep. He argued that dreaming preserves our sleep by preventing our wishes and desires from waking us up.

The Swiss-born psychologist Carl Jung (1875–1961) worked closely with Freud between 1909 and 1913, but found himself increasingly distanced by Freud's emphasis upon the underlying sexual content of dream symbols. Jung's views on dreams and on the operations of the mind in general form an important counterpoint (and, many psychologists would say, corrective) to those of Freud. More and more, Jung allowed the non-rational side of his nature (powerfully expressed in his childhood fantasies and dreams) to emerge, and through a process of self-discovery he came to develop his highly influential theory of the "collective unconscious" – the belief that the mind contains a vast internal

reservoir of symbolism drawn upon by men and women, across all cultures, in their dreams and their deepest imaginings. Stored in the collective unconscious are the "archetypes" (see pages 96–109), the resonant images and themes that inform the world's myths and religious and symbolic systems, as well as populating our most universally meaningful dreams.

Although many new techniques of dream interpretation have sprung up to supplement those pioneered by Freud and Jung, psychoanalysis and Jungian analysis continue to be at the core of psychological investigation.

The great breakthrough in dream studies in the second half of the twentieth century was the discovery in 1953 of REM (Rapid Eye Movement) sleep, when the most vivid episodes of dreaming occur (see page 41). This opened the way for research. Much work remains to be done before we can construct a fully fledged science of dreaming. In the meantime, through dream workshops and other forms of analysis, we are building up a corpus of case studies for the dream scientists of the future.

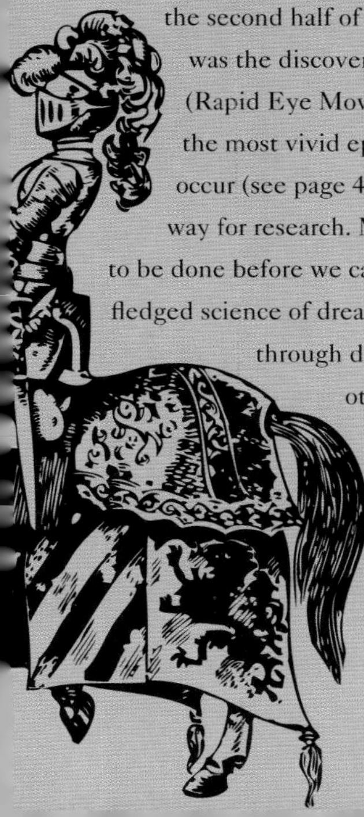

Your Own Temple of Hypnos

In ancient Greece the Temple of Hypnos was the place where people went to experience prophetic and healing dreams. You can create your own dream temple by establishing the bedroom as a special environment conducive to meaningful dreams – not just a utilitarian sleeping-place but a chamber of mystery and meaning.

Establish the mood by careful use of floaty fabrics and soft lighting. Undress and get ready for sleep in pools of light, rather than in the glare from a pendant. Imagine that the spirits of meaningful dreaming are readying themselves in the shadows.

Play gentle music in your bedroom before you retire and use it as the accompaniment to meditation – or at least relaxed, contemplative thoughts. If you find this difficult, just think of a tranquil scene where you were happy and at peace.

Project yourself hopefully into the future as you lie in bed – you are a time traveller. Next morning examine your dreams to see if they offer any clues about your destiny.

Jung on Dreams

No one has been more illuminating in the history of our attempts to understand the dreaming mind than the pioneering psychologist Carl Jung, whose revolutionary work brought out the hidden depth and poetry of dreams, relating them to myth and imagination.

Carl Gustav Jung (1875–1961), the founder of analytical psychology, was born near Basel in Switzerland, and after qualifying as a medical doctor at the local university spent most of his life in private psychotherapeutic practice at Kusnacht on Lake Zurich. Like Freud, with whom he worked closely from 1909 to 1913, he believed in the role that the unconscious plays in neurosis and psychosis, and in the important part played by dreams in uncovering the sources of unconscious problems. Jung departed from Freud, however, in his realization that the common themes running through the delusions and hallucinations of his patients could not all emerge from their personal unconscious conflicts but must stem from some common source. He began to explore correlations that he found among the various dreams of different people and noticed that the individual delusions of his different psychotic patients exhibited remarkable similarities, and that they echoed the themes of myths from all over the world.

His extensive knowledge of comparative religion, mythology and symbol systems such as alchemy convinced him that similar common themes run across cultures and across the centuries, and thus was born his belief in the collective unconscious, a genetic myth-producing level of the mind common to all men and women, and serving as the well-spring of psychological life. Jung gave the term "archetypes" to the mythological motifs and primordial images that emerge from the collective unconscious. He saw these as making

symbolic appearance over and over again in the great myths and legends of the world, and in our deepest and most meaningful dreams.

Jung is often regarded as an early and ardent disciple of Freud who eventually decided to part company with him. In fact, Jung was already well on the way to developing his own theories before he met Freud in 1907, and although he continued to pay generous tribute to the older man after their rift in 1913, there was a measure of scientific disagreement between them from the start.

Ernest Jones, Freud's biographer, writes of Jung's "tendency to occultism, astrology, and ... mysticism", but makes it clear that the ultimate reason for Jung's break-up with Freud was his rejection of Freud's insistence that life energy is primarily sexual. The implications of this disagreement for dream interpretation were profound. Jung saw the sexual symbolism that emerged in dreams as symbolic in turn of a deeper, non-sexual level of meaning, while Freud chose to interpret the sexual content literally. For Jung, "grand" dreams (that is, those stemming from the collective unconscious) were not coded messages alluding to particular desires, but gateways to a mythic world, "the vast historical storehouse of the human race".

Jung also differed from Freud in his method of exploring the unconscious through dream interpretation. Rejecting Freudian free association, he favoured instead the technique of direct association. Jung criticized Freud's method because it allows the mind to freewheel, following a chain of association that leads away from the original dream image and often ends up in some far distant place. Through direct association, Jungians concentrate upon the dream itself, preventing the client's train of thought from wandering by returning it again and again to the original image. Jung conceded that free association leads to valuable psychological insights, but thought that these insights often bear no connection with the message contained in the dream. One might as well take a word at random from the dictionary, and use that as a starting-point.

For Jung, psychotherapy is not a quest to discover the dark secrets of our past by delving into childhood traumas, but a process of discovery and self-realization. Jungians believe that by being in touch with the mythic themes of our collective unconscious, we gradually integrate the disparate and sometimes conflicting aspects of our selves, developing our full potential as we pass in turn through life's successive stages.

Objective and Subjective

Jung suggested that there are two basic approaches to the analysis of dream material: the objective and the subjective. The first approach is literal. If you have a dream about your reprobate sister, who is idle, jobless and sponging off her friends and family, then the dream might be pointing to aspects of your sister's behaviour that you find troubling. However, according to the subjective approach, everyone who appears in the dream represents an aspect of the dreamer. On this reading the sister might represent your own tendencies to opt out of social responsibilties. A more graphic example would be a dream of being pursued by a violent attacker, where the hidden reference might be to the dreamer's own aggressive impulses. Jung argued that the subjective view tends to be much more difficult for the dreamer to accept. A good therapist will encourage the client to recognize the truths of a subjective interpretation, in a way that provides insight and leads to increased self-awareness. Gestalt therapists later extended the subjective approach, applying it even to inanimate objects in a dream.

Whereas Freud attempted to narrow down his dream interpretations by approaching them with rigid theoretical presuppositions, Jung favoured the amplification of dream symbols, drawing out their deeper meanings imaginatively by placing the symbols in their broader mythic and symbolic contexts.

Jung's analysis revealed numerous connections between individual dream symbolism and medieval alchemy. Alchemy was not merely a mystical forerunner of chemistry, but a precursor of the modern study of the unconscious, and of techniques for transforming the base matter of psychic conflict and confusion into the gold of personal wholeness.

Jung saw alchemy as a powerful undercurrent to Western religion and philosophy, much as the dream is to consciousness: "just as the dream compensates the conflicts of the conscious mind, so alchemy endeavours to fill in the gaps left open by the Christian tension of opposites".

Jung not only drew parallels between dream symbols and their alchemical counterparts, but also found in alchemy a symbolic representation of the very process of Jungian analysis and the development of the human psyche. In their search for the powers of self-transformation, alchemists strove to unify opposites such as white and black, sulphur and mercury, heat and cold, sun and moon, life and death, male and female, thus creating the Philosopher's Stone. This was the single unifying principle that also served as a source for certain of the myths surrounding the Holy Grail.

Jung found in these symbolic alchemical transformations a complex metaphor for the union of male and female, Anima and Animus, conscious and unconscious, matter and spirit, that in his view led to wholeness within the human psyche itself – a process described by Jung, borrowing an alchemical term, as individuation.

With his emphasis on the importance of present experience (in contrast to Freud's preoccupation with childhood), Jung saw each stage of life as carrying developmental significance, and stressed that we have a capacity for growth and self-actualization even into advanced old age. The aim of psychotherapy, and thus of dream analysis, was to give the individual access to the personal and collective unconscious – not in order to learn the dark secrets of the past, but rather to discover and integrate each aspect of the self into psychic wholeness. In the course of such integration, men and women not only reconcile conflicting sides of themselves, but also free an often repressed religious function. Jung discovered through his work with his clients that this function is at least equal in strength to the Freudian instincts of sex and aggression. The religious function has nothing to do with creeds and dogmas, but is an expression of the collective unconscious that inspires us toward spirituality and love.

Complexes

Carl Jung used the term "complex", or "feeling-toned complex of ideas", to refer to a "node" in the unconscious – a tangle of unconscious feelings and beliefs that can form as a psychic disturbance and manifest itself in unaccountable behaviour. He initially found evidence for complexes in word association tests in the first decade of the twentieth century, working at Zurich University. At the centre of any complex, he believed, is a universal pattern of experience, or archetype (see pages 96–109) – typically, we might have a complex about our mother or father, or about our brother or sister. A complex has a vitality that is not harmful in itself, but when complexes conflict or are out of balance within ourselves, they can undermine our intentions and disturb our memories, our dreams and our mental effectiveness in waking life. They can damage our inner peace by usurping power from our controlling identity, the ego.

Psychoanalysts will often work with a client on their dreams to discover the roots of a complex – a practice that operates by progressing together in a spirit of discovery.

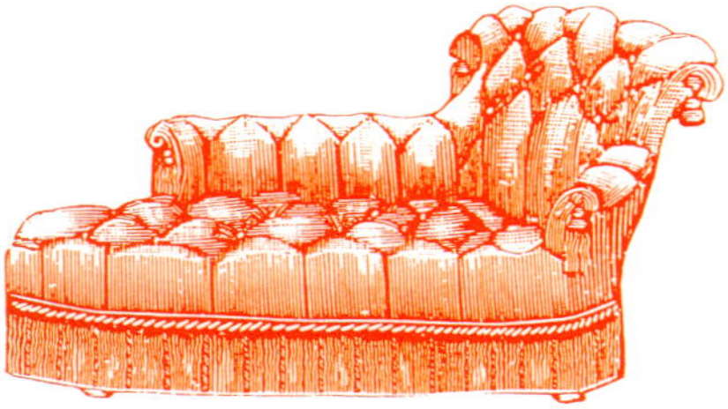

Freud on Dreams

Sigmund Freud is still a highly controversial figure. Some believe that his voluminous works are more important as literature than as a record of scientific discovery; certainly, they are saturated in imaginative power. His insights into the mind are fearless, uncomfortable, thought-provoking and profound.

Sigmund Freud (1856–1939) began his classic work *The Interpretation of Dreams* with what was for 1899 a revolutionary statement: "I shall bring forward proof that there is a psychological technique which makes it possible to interpret dreams." Modern dream psychology was born in this sentence.

The Interpretation of Dreams sold only 351 copies in the first six years, but eventually ran through numerous editions, and became one of the very few books to have changed our way of looking at ourselves. Freud was born in Freiburg in Moravia (now in the Czech Republic), and trained in Vienna as a medical doctor under the noted neurophysiologist Ernst Brücke. From Brücke, Freud derived his deterministic belief that all living phenomena are shaped by the laws of cause and effect, a view which later predisposed him to recognize dreams as subject to these same laws.

Later, while working in Paris with the renowned neurologist and medical hypnotist J.M. Charcot, he concluded that neuroses are caused by psychological rather than by physiological factors, and on his return to Vienna he developed (partly with the help of psychiatrist Josef Breuer) the technique of free association for identifying what these factors might be. The results of this work with free

Free Association

Freud's famous technique of free association can be adapted as an easy way to explore the possible meanings of any recent dream you have had.

Take as your starting point a dream that is still fresh in your mind. Ideally, you should try this exercise in the morning, soon after waking. You will need a pen or pencil and a sheet of blank paper; or alternatively use a page in a special dream notebook.

To unpack the various possible meanings of the dream, take each object, person and situation that played a significant part in the experience, and free-associate around the words for them, one at a time. Let your imagination rove freely. Jot down, anywhere on the sheet of paper, whatever comes to mind; and don't censor or edit anything out. From the first word, follow mental chains of association that arise, and then let one word or image trigger another. You may end up some distance from the original word, but intuition will tell you when to stop. Then go back to the key word and explore another pathway.

For example, free association starting from a dream image of a bicycle might run: bicycle, pedals, shoes, boots, policeman, authority.

The basic idea behind free association is to trick yourself into unconscious revelations. You have deliberately lowered your guard, and it is in these circumstances that you are most likely to hit upon unexpected truths. You may suddenly come to a word or memory that causes you to experience a lightbulb moment.

Do not be concerned if nothing of interest reveals itself this time. But do try more than once, and revisit your free-association notes from time to time to see if you missed any insights the first time around.

association convinced him that many of them lie below the level of the conscious mind, and are associated with the emotional damage caused in early childhood by the repressions and distortions of the life instinct, specifically of the sexual urge, in response to the need for social and parental approval. Recognizing that this revealed the crucial importance of the unconscious, Freud then undertook a lengthy course of self-analysis, and as a result of his discoveries he became convinced of the role that dreams can play in providing access to the mind's hidden material.

Freud famously described dreams as "the royal road to the unconscious", and firmly believed that he had unravelled their full mystery. Many of his conclusions are now disputed, but we owe him a profound debt for recognizing the questions that we should be asking about the meaning and purpose of dreaming, and about the insights dreams give us not only into the contents of the unconscious but also into the role that the unconscious plays in our mental life as a whole.

Underlying Freud's understanding of dreams was his belief that the mind processes its material at different levels. His study of his own dreams, and those of his patients, led him to distinguish between what he called the "primary process" which operates in the unconscious, dreaming mind, and the "secondary process" which characterizes conscious thought. The former process differs from the latter in that it lacks organization and coordination, and consists only of instinctive impulses, each pressing toward its own fulfilment. Freud believed that the primary process takes unconscious impulses, desires and fears, and turns them into symbols; these are linked by associations that have no regard for categories such as time and space, or right and wrong, as the unconscious is unaware of the logic, values and social adaptations of conscious life.

The secondary process, on the other hand, works by subjecting thoughts to the laws of logic, just as language is governed by the rules of grammar.

Freud maintained that unconscious instincts dwell in a kind of primitive chaos, each seeking gratification independently of the others in an animalistic and amoral way. He used the term id (literally, "it") to describe the primary part of the mind, and argued that it contains "everything that is inherited ... [and] is present at birth" – in other words, it contains the primordial instincts that have motivated us since the beginnings of the human race, specifically the instincts for self-survival and for the survival of the species.

Freud's Dream of Irma

Freud had this famous dream in 1895, and it was the first that he submitted to detailed interpretation. It concerned Irma, a young widow and family friend whom Freud was treating for "hysterical anxiety".

The dream: Freud received Irma and other guests in a large hall. He took her to one side and reproached her for rejecting his "solution" to her anxiety problems: "if you still get pains, it's really only your fault". She complained of "choking" pains in her throat, stomach and abdomen. Alarmed, Freud examined her throat, in case he'd missed an organic cause for her problems, and found a large white patch as well as "some remarkable curly structures", like "bones of the nose". Dr M. repeated the examination and confirmed Freud's findings. Freud decided the infection was caused by an injection given by Otto, a doctor he knew, probably with an unclean syringe. In Dr M.'s opinion, Irma would soon contract dysentery; and the toxin would be eliminated.

The interpretation: Analyzing the dream, and subjecting key parts of it to free association, Freud became aware that it was a wish-fulfilment. In the dream, Freud first blames Irma for her own pains. His feeling that the causes may be organic represents both his hidden wish to escape blame for the failure of psychoanalysis, and his fear that he has been confusing psychosomatic and physical problems. He concludes "that I was not responsible for Irma's pains, but that Otto was. Otto had in fact annoyed me by his remarks about Irma's incomplete cure, and the dream gave me my revenge by throwing the reproach back on him". In Freud's wish-fulfilling dream, Irma's "pains" were not caused by his handling of her psyche but by an unclean syringe Otto had used when giving her an injection. Freud's anxiety about his own treatment of Irma was symbolized by the part played by Dr M., to whom Freud had once made an appeal when his own unwitting mistreatment of a patient had led to her fatal illness. The white patch on Irma's throat reminded him of diphtheria and of the distress caused when his own daughter had the disease; the nasal-like bones recalled his worries over his own use of cocaine, which had led to the death of a friend. This account illustrates how complex meanings can be woven together in a dream.

In Freud's view, the id dominates unconscious life, and dreams are the acting out in fantasy form, or the wish-fulfilment, of its desires and energies. Yet dreams do not emerge directly from this mass of anarchic instincts. If they did, they would arouse the dreamer with their disturbing, often antisocial, and potentially psychologically harmful content. Hence, they express themselves only in symbolic form (as will shortly be more fully explained).

In waking life the ego, the rational part of the mind that is grounded in commonsense reality, and adheres to an acquired moral sense, keeps the id's primitive urges at bay. In sleep, however, the ego relaxes its conscious control, and the id comes to the fore, flooding our mind with its mischievous agenda. To protect the sleeping ego from being disturbed by this inundation to the point where the dreamer is actually awakened, a mental device that Freud termed the censor struggles to translate the id's material into a less disruptive form. The purpose of dreaming is therefore to preserve sleep by symbolizing dream content in a way that renders it innocuous to the censor. Dreams thus operate in much the same way as neurotic symptoms, which preserve an equilibrium in the ego by striving to allow potentially overwhelming anxieties and instincts to be expressed in a form which it can handle.

Much recent criticism of Freud's ideas has centred upon the hierarchical aspect of his view of the mind. Freud believed that "secondary" functions such as rationality, morality and the role of the ego are developed only after the "primary" wishes and instincts of the unconscious have been tamed and repressed, as if learning depends on a child's ability to beat his or her way through the dark forest of primary processes in order to reach the open, daylight clearing of the conscious ego. Later research suggests that it is more likely that there is no

such struggle in the mind between primary and secondary processes, and that rather than continually competing with each other they in fact coexist as partners.

For Freud, dreams always have a manifest and a latent content. The manifest content is what the dream appears to be saying, often a jumble of apparent nonsense, while the latent content is what the unconscious is really trying to communicate to consciousness. The manifest content has two major methods of disguising latent content in a way that can evade the censor. The first is condensation: the fusing of two or more dream images to form a single symbol. For example, Freud often interpreted images of older men in his patients' dreams as a condensation of their fathers, on the one hand, and of Freud himself, their analyst, on the other. Working by association rather than by logical connections, the manifest content amalgamates

The Wolf Man's Dream

In 1910 a rich, depressed Russian aristocrat, Sergei Pankeyev, was referred to Freud for treatment. The analysis continued for many years and helped Freud to develop his theories. Freud postulated that Pankeyev's obsessional, masochistic tendencies stemmed from an early sexual trauma. The experience revealed itself in therapy when Pankeyev described a childhood dream, which haunted him for the rest of his life.

The dream: It was winter. His cot was near a window, which swung open and he saw several white wolves sitting on the branches of an old walnut tree. They had long tails like foxes and their ears pricked up like those of dogs. Terrified of being eaten, he woke up screaming and his nurse rushed to comfort him. But the image was so lifelike that it was ages before he could accept it was only a dream. Later he said that what struck him most was the stillness of the wolves and the intensity of their gaze.

The interpretation: Freud's analysis was that in his infancy Pankeyev had seen his parents having sex and that he had been traumatized by what appeared to be the violence of the act and his mother's lack of male sexual organs. The opening window symbolized the young Pankeyev's opening eyes; the wolves, his father; and their stillness was a deflection of the violent motion of intercourse.

the two images to reflect a similarity in our attitudes toward them both.

The second major device used by the dreaming mind is displacement. Like condensation, displacement works by association, translating one dream image into another, rather in the way that metaphor works in language. When one of Freud's patients dreamed of a ship in full sail, its bowsprit jutting out before it, Freud had no difficulty in interpreting this as a displacement image, the ship standing for his patient's mother, the sails representing her breasts and the bowsprit symbolizing the penis that his patient always imagined his forceful mother to have.

Free association was the method developed by Freud to bypass the condensations and displacements of manifest content in order to arrive at an interpretation of dreams. By following the chains of free association that start from an individual dream image, either we continue wherever our train of thought leads us, or we suddenly stop when we meet resistance, a sudden blockage in the mind that usually reveals the nature of the unconscious problem. Whatever the outcome, the process enables us to join the "royal road" that leads to the instincts and desires buried in the id, which Freud thought were the sources of our dreams.

Another important idea in Freud's interpretative method is secondary revision. This term describes the way in which we alter the events and images of our dreams either when recounting them to someone else or when trying to remember them ourselves. A Freudian analyst would look for clues in the way in which a patient might "revise" his or her dreams, lending them greater internal consistency and coherence than they in fact possess.

Freud's theory that all dreams originate from the primal chaos of the id was strongly opposed by those who subscribed to the increasingly widespread belief that dreams may be simply a continuation of the mind's daytime thoughts, or reactions to events that recently took place in waking life. Accordingly, in the 1920s, following disagreements with Jung and other psychologists working on the origin and meaning of dreams, Freud modified his views in order to draw a distinction between what he called dreams from "above" and those from "below". Dreams from below arise from the unconscious and "may be regarded as inroads of the repressed into waking life", while those from above result from the day's events, "reinforced [by] repressed material that is debarred from the ego" – that is, material that is unacceptable to the ego, and thus repressed in the id.

Freud believed that much of our conscious behaviour is also prompted by the need to satisfy unconscious urges. As we go about the business of the day, we channel instinctive energy into socially acceptable forms, using such ego defence mechanisms as repression, denial and projection in order to keep painful material out of conscious awareness. The ego continually strives to placate the id, to persuade it that its drives are not going unheard by consciousness as a whole. If the ego should fail in this task of placation, or of maintaining its defences against the id's more disturbing onslaughts, the pent-up instincts and buried traumas of the unconscious can break through into our conscious minds, leading to full-scale mental breakdown.

Even if we escape such a fate, we may waste a great deal of our energy in conflicts between the ego and the id, leading to the obsessions, depressions and anxieties that constitute neurosis and undermine our happiness.

However, with the help of a psychoanalyst who can coax the content of the id skilfully into consciousness, where it can be seen and understood for what it is, we can avoid such conflicts and strip the id of much of its power. Freud saw the interpretation of dreams as essential to this task.

In Freud's view, there are three basic types of dreams. In the most basic, wish-fulfilment dreams, such as those commonly recounted by children, the manifest and latent content coincide. The dream makes no attempt to disguise its underlying significance: a dream of chocolate or a new teddy bear is simply a wish for chocolate or a teddy bear, particularly when they have been forbidden or withheld by a parent. In the second dream type, the content is similarly transparent – but much more surprising, because we are unable at the conscious level to relate the scenario to our daytime wishes. For example, we may have dreamed of parachuting down into a war zone with a select band of marines – something that in real life we have never wanted to do.

Freud's third dream type is the most intriguing. Here, the manifest content is bafflingly surreal and incoherent – for example, people we know performing irrational actions in an unexpected setting. To penetrate the mysteries of such a dream, we have to delve deeply into our own motivations, in territory where we may feel uncomfortable.

Freud alerts us to a repertoire of means by which wishes are disguised, concealed or repressed in dreams so that the sleeper finds it impossible, next morning, to grasp their true significance. For example, emotional yearnings may be translated into a completely different context that softens their dangerous edge. A grown-up's nostalgic craving for the pleasures of childhood and the mother's tender care, prompted by a longing for affection that is missing from their current life, may be revealed, in Freud's view, in a dream of an abundance of cake, packed with calories and sugar.

Those who are sceptical of Freud's approach to the dream world have tended to concentrate their attacks on what many judge to be an excessive emphasis on sex. For example, not many psychologists these days give credence to the "Oedipus complex" – Freud's theory of a son's supposed attraction to his mother and his rivalry and hostility toward his father. The term comes from Greek mythology: Oedipus was separated from his parents at birth; later, before discovering their identities, he unwittingly killed his father and married his mother. The equivalent of this syndrome for a young girl, less

forceful in its impact, is the "Electra complex", which shows itself in a girl's desire for her father.

Freudian analysts still ascribe a major role to sexuality in the unconscious. They also suggest that the discomfort many feel about Freud's approach reflects, unconsciously, their repression of uncomfortable truths.

Oedipus and Ourselves

Oedipus is the most famous sexual transgressor in Greek myth, yet his sins are unconscious ones. Abandoned as a baby after the oracle at Delphi predicted that he would kill his father and sleep with his mother, he was rescued by a shepherd and adopted by the king and queen of Corinth. Years later he slew a stranger who insulted him: this was King Laius, his father. Later, he rescued Thebes from the Sphinx, a hideous beast who killed anyone who could not answer her riddle. As the city's saviour, Oedipus became its king and married the widowed Queen Jocasta, his mother. Thebes prospered under his rule, until it was visited by a plague. Discovering the truth, Oedipus blinded himself; Jocasta hanged herself. The story enacts a dark psychic drama that springs from the unconscious – the source of our dreams.

Perls and Boss on Dreams

Despite their illuminating theories and analyses, neither Freud nor Jung was able to unlock all the secrets of the dream world, and it is probable that no one ever will. But in the twentieth century a great deal of work was done that greatly enhanced our understanding – not least by Fritz Perls and Medard Boss.

The Work of Fritz Perls

The American psychiatrist Fritz Perls (1893–1970) is best known as a founder of gestalt therapy, which emphasizes the way in which the individual organizes the facts, perceptions and behaviour that make up his or her life, rather than the separate nature of each.

No less than Jung and Freud, Perls stressed the symbolic content of dreams, but he also believed that every character and object in our dreams is a projection of our own self, and of the way in which we have been living our lives. For Perls, dreams represent unfinished emotional business, or "emotional holes", in the dreamer's life history, and their symbolic content stems from the dreamer's personal experience rather than from instinctive or collective drives.

Role play, Perls believed, is a more efficient and accurate technique for interpretation than either free or direct association (see pages 27 and 22). His method was to ask the dreamer to dramatize each dream image in turn, giving voice even to inanimate dream objects, and sometimes adopting the physical positions that such objects had in the dream, to best represent the message they were trying to convey.

In a dream of a train running through woods, for example, the dreamer may find that the rails, or the trees left behind as the train rushes past, reveal more about his or her emotional state than does the central image of the train. Act out how

the trees feel as they are left behind, Perls might suggest, and what the rails would say as the train runs over them.

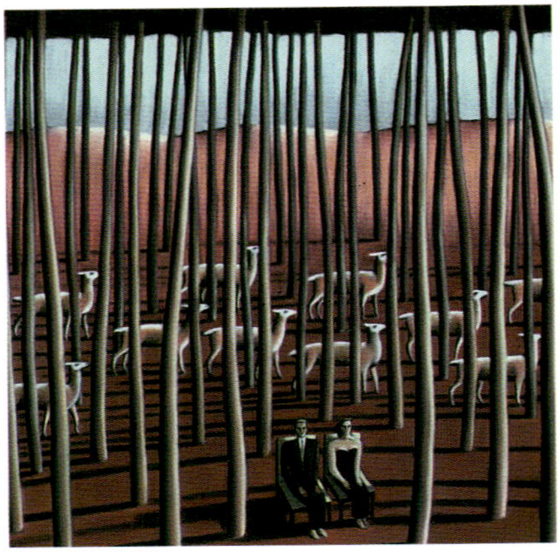

Role play of this kind places interpretation firmly in the dreamer's hands. The therapist may make suggestions, but the dream remains the dreamer's own property: meaning must never be imposed from the outside.

There need be no major contradiction between this approach to dreaming and the approaches of Jung and Freud, despite Perls' insistence to the contrary. Both Jung and Freud emphasized that dream images often symbolize aspects of the dreamer's own self, and that in the interpretation of dreams role-play exercises can be a helpful addition to direct or free association. The problem with the Perls method, however, is that the dreamer risks being seduced by his or her acting skills into losing real contact with the dream. Although Perls was confident that he could recognize this effect when it happened, other practitioners of his technique may lack his expert perception. Moreover, as valuable as Perls' methods are for working with dreams that operate at Level 1 and Level 2 (see pages 65–70), they run the risk of undervaluing the shared meaning of dream symbols, and in particular of ignoring the crucial role of the collective unconscious, as defined by Jung.

The Work of Medard Boss

The Swiss psychiatrist Medard Boss (1903–1990) posited a relationship between dreaming and existentialism. Existential theory argues that each individual chooses consciously or unconsciously what he or she wishes to be. Thus, for Boss, dreams are not a profound symbolic language, but represent straightforward aspects of existential choice.

The use Boss made of dreams in clinical practice showed clearly that dreams can provide psychological help without being interpreted symbolically. By searching always for symbolic meaning, we run a risk of missing what the dream is actually trying to say. Whereas Freud and Jung concentrated on the deeper Level 2 and 3 dreams, Boss's approach directed attention to the real importance of Level 1 dreams.

In place of association, Boss developed an interpretative method that allowed dreams to tell their own story. This depended less upon theories of the unconscious than upon the ability to see "what is in front of one's face".

In one of his experiments, Boss hypnotized five women – three healthy, two neurotic – and suggested that each dream of a naked, sexually aroused man known to be in love with them and advancing on them with sexual intent. While the three healthy women followed the given scenario exactly and enjoyably, the dreams of the two neurotic women were anxious and unaroused. In one the naked man was replaced by a uniformed soldier armed with a gun with which he nearly shot her. Boss pointed out that there was nothing symbolic about the first three dreams: they were open expressions of the dreamers' conscious desires. And even the dream of the soldier had no need of deep symbolic interpretation: it was a simple reflection of the woman's narrow, fear-drenched world in which men were seen as threatening.

It would be a mistake to see this existential approach based on Level 1 dreams as negating the existence and importance of Level 2 and Level 3 dreams. In experiments such as this, the dream scenario is placed in the mind by the experimenter, rather than arising from the dreamer's own unconscious. And Jungians and Freudians would point out that the elements that did arise from the unconscious (lover transformed into soldier, penis into gun) could give insights into the causes of the woman's neuroses. Associations emerging in response to these images might show, for example, that the dream revealed not only repressed sexuality but also a repressed Animus archetype (see page 103), or that the soldier and the gun represented authoritarian and self-destructive tendencies within the dreamer herself.

The Function of Dreams

Are dreams a revelation from some profound creative source within ourselves, or the confused residue of thoughts and images left over from our waking life? Is the dreaming mind a window into the mysteries of the dreamer's deepest self, or a psychic garbage can containing random mental material that we would be wisest to ignore?

Modern research into the physical patterns of dreaming began in 1953 with the work of American physiologist Nathaniel Kleitman and his student Eugene Aserinsky. In their "sleep laboratory" they observed that for short periods the eyes of sleeping infants move about rapidly behind closed eyelids. Subsequent research revealed that adults also manifest this phenomenon, and EEG readings, which record the electrical activity of the brain, showed that these periods of eye movement correspond with particular brain rhythms. The discovery of a link between eye movement and recognizable brain waves was a breakthrough in dream research, and this

REM Sleep

REM (Rapid Eye Movement) sleep is also known as "paradoxical sleep", because while it is happening, brain activity, adrenaline levels, pulse rate and oxygen consumption come closest to those in wakefulness, yet muscle tone relaxes and the sleeper may prove particularly difficult to rouse. It is during REM sleep that most dreaming takes place.

In the 1960s researchers found that REM deprivation appears to lead to daytime irritability, fatigue, memory loss and poor concentration. Volunteers who were systematically deprived of REM sleep by being woken whenever they entered the eye activity phase caught up on subsequent nights by engaging in more REM sleep than usual. If a subject is faced with total sleep deprivation, because of illness or other factors, the REM state has even been known to force its way into waking consciousness. It seems that we may badly need REM sleep, and this could be associated with a psychological need to dream.

Recent research has shown that dreams occurring during REM sleep are more visual in content than those that occur at other stages of sleep. Findings even indicate that the eye movements that take place in REM sleep may be synchronized with dream events, suggesting that the brain does not distinguish between the imagery of dreams and that of waking life. The same may be true of the brain's response to other dream sensations: certainly, stimuli such as a spray of water, a sudden sound (like an alarm clock ringing), a voice, or a flash of light, may all be incorporated into a dream and "rationalized" to fit its content.

Yet however real such sensory experiences appear to be to the brain, something prevents us from performing in full the actions and emotions that fill our dreams. There is a general loss of muscle tone during REM sleep, and the eye muscles appear to be the only ones that are physically involved in acting out dream events. It has been shown that when dreams are at their most vivid, certain inhibitors are produced to prevent muscles from receiving the relevant impulses from the brain, thus ensuring that we do not act on sensory stimuli experienced in the dream.

It is perhaps this effective paralysis that gives rise to the dream sensations of being unable to run, of attempting in vain to scream, or of trying to walk but being stuck in sand, viscous mud or water.

phase of sleep was termed REM (Rapid Eye Movement) sleep.

Further research revealed four distinct levels or stages of sleep, each characterized by particular physiological activities and brain rhythms. During the first fifteen minutes, the sleeper descends progressively through Stages 1 to 3, before spending about one hour in Stage 4, the deepest level, when the body is at its most relaxed and brain rhythms at their slowest. After this, an ascent back up to Stage 1 is often accompanied by a change in sleeping posture, and it is at this point that the first REM period of sleep begins, usually lasting for about ten minutes. Thereafter, the process of descent and ascent is repeated between four and seven times during the night, though sleep rarely again reaches a state as deep as Stage 4. Each REM episode becomes progressively longer, as does the frequency and rapidity of eye movement, and the final REM period can last as long as forty minutes.

There are many theories as to why we sleep. Some scientists point to the evolutionary advantage of sleep as a strategy to conserve energy and reduce food consumption. Another evolutionary argument is that by sleeping during the hours of darkness, when they were more vulnerable to attack from predators, our ancestors increased their chances of survival. A physiological theory suggests that sleep is the body's chance to relax and repair itself, and to use its energies to secrete special hormones: children, for example, produce more abundant supplies of growth hormone at night.

It seems certain that sleep literally gives the brain a rest. Production of serotonin and norepinephrine, chemicals that help to transmit nerve impulses in the brain, is reduced during sleep. Volunteers deprived of one or two nights' sleep show increased irritability, memory failure and poor concentration, and will literally pass out on their feet if deprivation continues. Nevertheless, some people need very little sleep, and certain spiritually advanced men and women pass the night in a state of deep meditation rather than actual sleep. There are rare medical cases of people who, after traumas such as head injuries, have appeared hardly to sleep at all.

Thus much is known, and supposed, about how the dreaming mind operates physiologically. However, when we start to look deeper, into the psychological aspects of dreaming, we enter murkier waters. Although, since the discovery of REM in 1953, scientists have taken dreams into the

laboratory, subjecting them to rigorous tests and analyzing them with some of the aids of modern technology, the question that was posed by Freud and Jung in the first half of the twentieth century remains largely unanswered: do we dream to preserve our sleep, or sleep so that we can dream?

Although scientists tend to agree that there must be a purpose to dreaming, they differ over what this purpose might be. However, the view to which most dream interpreters since the nineteenth century have subscribed is that dreams alert us to important aspects of the state of our unconscious minds.

Freud, as we have seen, believed that dreams are coded messages devised by the unconscious to tell of the repressed desires and instincts that dwell there. Jungians go beyond this, recognizing the collective unconscious, a shared creative sub-level that is vital to our well-being and generates not only the images of our dreams but also those of myth, legend and religious teachings. While this book is built on the twin foundations of these theories, it is worth pausing to test the strength of the "psychic garbage" approach, which asserts that we dream to sort and discard our unwanted mental detritus in sleep, and that although the function of dreaming is important, the content of dreams is definitely not.

Some scientists believe that the brain operates selectively, scrutinizing the mass of detail

Garbage or Gold?

"Garbage" theories of dreaming owed their genesis to the propensity of scientists for separating process from content. Such theories crumble once proper attention is focused upon dream content itself.

No one who maintains a dream diary over a reasonable period of time should have any difficulty in recognizing that dreams have a remarkable coherence as a secret history of the self. Sadly, the belief of "garbage" theorists that dream recall is undesirable precludes them from studying the content of their own dreams, and leads them to disregard the very evidence that would discredit their ideas.

that bombards it during the wakeful hours, categorizing and storing relevant information, and dumping irrelevancies. According to this view, most of this processing takes place during the day, and much of the unwanted material is discarded immediately. The brain, however, also needs a period of consolidation when it can give its full attention to clearing the backlog, and this is what takes place during sleep. Scientists have compared this operation to a mainframe computer that goes "off line" during the night, and searches its files and programs, modifying and updating them to take account of relevant new data and erasing or relegating to limbo any redundant or unwanted items. In dreams, however, fragments of the material being categorized and dumped emerge into sleeping consciousness, hopelessly jumbled together and beset by trains of unwanted associations. According to the "psychic garbage" theory, this mess of random images is what we dream.

There are several compelling objections to this approach. First, it is incorrect to claim that dream content is meaningless. Dreams have been shown to provide vital insights into both psychological and possibly physical health, and they can also be an invaluable aid to problem solving. Although they may appear at first to be confused and random, detailed analysis by an expert can show that they contain a wealth of meanings (sometimes ambivalent, but meanings nevertheless) related to the dreamer's circumstances. Lucid dreaming (see pages 55–64) shows that far from the mind being "off line", full consciousness in dreaming is possible at times (and potentially at all times). There is no evidence that people who recall and work with their dreams are any less healthy psychologically than those who do not – in

fact, the reverse seems to be true. Finally, although most dreams are indeed elusive in their signficance, some of them prove so memorable that years later they are as fresh in the mind as the major events of waking life.

Yet if dreams do contain important messages from the unconscious to the conscious levels of the mind, why is it that we forget much of what we experience in sleep? There are several theories about this, one of which has to do with the manner of our waking. We no longer wake up suddenly as our primitive ancestors did, alert to the dangers of living in the open: instead, we emerge gradually from sleep in the safety of our beds, and it is possibly this that consigns most of our dreams to oblivion between sleeping and waking. Another theory is that we simply sleep too much, and the hours that we spend in dreamless sleep may smother the memories of our dreams. In dream workshops, people often report that their dream recall is greater than usual when away from home and in fresh surroundings (perhaps they are sleeping fitfully in such circumstances) or when sleeping on a harder bed.

It may be that the cluttered, distracted and undisciplined nature of our minds also inhibits dream recall. Adepts of the Hindu and Buddhist esoteric orders, and certain followers of the Western mystery tradition, are said to enjoy unbroken consciousness during their sleep, largely because of their intensive training in techniques of concentration and meditation.

The classic theory of dream amnesia, however, is that advanced by Sigmund Freud, who believed that the main reason that we forget our dreams is that they are often too painful to remember. According to Freud, dream amnesia has nothing to do with incidental aspects of the dreamer's lifestyle, but is directly caused by what he called the censor, a repressive ego defence mechanism that protects the conscious mind from the mass of disturbing images, instincts and desires that inhabit the depths of

the unconscious. For our own mental protection, our dreams are coded into acceptable language.

Introduction to Symbols

When we turn to look more closely at the experience of dreaming and what it can mean for us, it is helpful to look first of all at the principal semantic unit of our dreams: the symbol.

The messages contained in dreams are typically conveyed as symbols, which represent an idea, concept or emotion that is difficult to put into words. The presence of symbols is one reason why dreams appear to be so mysterious and even nonsensical to the waking mind, but once we begin to unlock this symbolic language, we find that dreams are often profoundly meaningful, engaging our feelings in a way matched in waking life only by arts such as poetry, painting and music.

Dreams spring from the unconscious, and use symbols – a primal part of the language of the unconscious that preceded the development of speech. As explained later in this book, many of the symbols used by dreams are personal to the dreamer, having been built up through experience. Others, however, appear to be more universal, arising from shared levels of the unconscious mind. Such universal symbols are often linked to animals or natural forces – for example, birds in many cultures represent freedom, fire represents destruction and purification, while water stands for life itself.

By working with dreams, we come into contact with this symbolic language, which shows us a way to delve deeper and deeper into the unconscious, enabling us to embark on a thrilling (and sometimes disturbing) voyage of self-discovery. We could be given any message on the way, and its special meaning will depend on our wishes, fears and other inner concerns.

Many of the messages we receive in dreams are connected with the hopes, concerns and anxieties of everyday life. Research has shown that women's dreams tend to focus on domestic events, while men's dreams are more often set outside the home. Many dreams, however, arise from deeper levels of the mind. Before attempting the methods of interpretation explained later in this book, ask yourself what message each remembered dream might be attempting to convey. For example, you may have had dreams of meeting a stranger, entering a store, or chopping down a tree. What could such dreams be trying to say?

In a broad sense, dreams often relate to what might be, rather than what actually is. A dream could thus suggest that you might wish to enlarge your horizons, or to explore new avenues and opportunities. Sometimes dreams seem to warn us of dangers, or to caution us to think more carefully about a particular course of action. The one clear message is that dreams are far too important to be ignored.

Quality Sleep

Although some people claim to dream more reliably when their sleep is disturbed, it is generally acknowledged that better sleeping patterns lead to a better quality of dream life. Follow these simple steps to ensure that your nights are peaceful and undisturbed and your dreams enriched accordingly.

- Avoid alcohol and sleeping tablets: both repress REM sleep. Avoid coffee and tea as a bedtime drink: try hot milk and honey instead.
- Before bedtime, clear your mind of all thoughts of the day. Do not allow anger or resentment to disturb your mind.
- If you read before you go to sleep, ensure that the content of your reading is calm and contemplative: avoid a racy thriller, for example.
- Make your bedroom an oasis of peace, free of clutter, with restful lighting.
- Go to bed early and get up early.
- Relax your body, consciously, tensing and then releasing all your muscles, before you retire.

States of Transition

If we think of dreams as wispy, fragmentary experiences, that is probably because we are remembering the typically evanescent dreams from which we often wake in the mornings. Framing the vivid intensity of REM dreaming, our sleep begins and ends with more fleeting dream images on the boundaries between sleep and wakefulness.

Frederick Myers (1843–1941), one of the pioneering British explorers of the unconscious, gave the term "hypnagogic" to the dreams that precede sleep and "hypnopompic" to the dreams that come just as we are waking. These two transitional states are fragmentary and elusive – like a memory slipping from our grasp the moment it is recalled. Both tend to be marked by a series of fleeting, mysterious, sometimes beautiful images.

As the dreamer falls asleep, the brain produces the steady alpha rhythms that characterize a state of deep relaxation; the pulse and breath rates slow down and the body temperature drops. Then the alpha rhythms begin to break up, and the sleeper enters fully into Stage 1 sleep where his or her mind is briefly filled with the weird, hallucinatory dreams of the hypnagogic state. Perhaps visions is a better word for them than dreams, for they lack both the narrative complexity and the emotional resonance of dreams encountered in deeper

Hypnagogic Quick-fix

Try taking a nap sitting bolt upright instead of lying down. As you nod off, your head will jerk forward and wake you up. This is a good way to skirt the borders of sleep, where hypnagogic visions can be found.

stages of sleep. When the Russian philosopher P.D. Ouspensky writes of "golden sparks and tiny stars ... [which transform themselves] into rows of brass helmets belonging to Roman soldiers marching along the streets below", he is describing the magical, visionary quality of hypnagogic dreams.

Recent research on hypnagogia has centred on its visionary quality. Typically, hypnagogic images include formless shapes such as waves of pure colour, designs and patterns often of remarkable symmetry or regularity, and writing not only in the dreamer's mother tongue but sometimes in foreign or even entirely imaginary languages. As if zooming in to scrutinize the dreamer, archetypal faces may swim in and out of view; mysterious characters may appear and disappear, and images are sometimes presented upside down, or reversed as if in a mirror.

Hypnopompic experiences, formed in the process of awakening, share many of the characteristics of their hypnagogic counterparts. Many actually persist briefly into wakefulness. René Descartes, the great French thinker hailed as the founder of modern philosophy, reported frequently seeing "sparks scattered around the room" as he emerged from sleep, while other writers describe waking from hypnopompic dreams to see figures dancing around the bed or to find an alien, surreal landscape stretching from their bedroom window.

Many have also spoken of auditory rather than visual hallucinations in both hypnagogic and hypnopompic states. Voices warning of impending disaster and mysterious snatches of dialogue are heard as clearly as if they come from within the room. Tactile and olfactory sensations are also common, and sometimes there is a complexity of awareness, as if the dreamer is simultaneously seeing a vision, listening in to a quite unconnected conversation, and smelling the sweet perfume of an invisible garden. It is hardly surprising that in ancient and medieval times many people believed that such experiences were visits from the gods.

Observing Hypnopompia

In the late 1990s dream researcher George Gillespie, based in New Jersey, made detailed notes on his own hypnopompic experiences. Occasionally, he would see what looked like a two-dimensional lattice pattern immediately on waking up, just before opening his eyes. This would sometimes remain in his field of vision for a second or two once his eyes were opened. If he kept his eyes closed, he could study the details of the patterns for as long as ten minutes. Interestingly, both Gillespie and one of his correspondents found that the lattice pattern was stationary – it could be scanned by moving the eyes from one side to the other. There is still much work to be done in this field.

Much recent research has attempted to explain the hallucinatory and sometimes trance-like nature of the hypnagogic and hypnopompic states by exploring the role that the ego plays as consciousness drifts between waking and sleep. It has been suggested that visionary hypnagogic dreams are a product of the ego's attempt to regain control over thought processes after the rapid change in consciousness caused by the loss of contact with waking reality. Another view is that these experiences are the very anthithesis of ego.

Hindu and Buddhist meditation adepts teach that to reach a state of deep meditation, the practitioner must discard the ego on the way to self-enlightenment. Typically, as the adept passes from one level of consciousness to another, he sees visions, like those of hypnagogia, whose mysterious images and mandala-like designs serve to encourage him in his quest. These images bear no relation to waking memories, suggesting that they arise from a deep level of the creative unconscious. Hypnagogic visions were certainly an important source of inspiration for surrealist artists, such as Salvador Dalí and René Magritte. Dalí even went so far as to induce them by dozing upright holding a spoon and a pan. When he nodded off he would drop the spoon into the pan, waking him up with the strange images of the transition time fresh in his mind.

The American psychologist Andreas Mavromatis suggested that both hypnopompic and hypnagogic experiences act as anxiety reducers, drawing the dreamer away from the trials and tensions of waking life, and thus serving to promote personal growth and development. By avoiding the narrative and emotional complexity of REM dreams and instead loosening the usual restrictions upon thought, they allow the dreamer to survey the contents of his or her unconscious, like leafing through the pages of an illustrated book. Thus, the dreamer experiences at the level of awareness the creative mental processes that usually stir in the depths of the unconscious. By sorting the wealth of material stored in the mind, these processes engender creative insights which flash as if from nowhere into consciousness.

Exploring Hypnagogic Dreams

The very nature of hypnagogic images means that they are fleeting and elusive, yet it is not difficult to train the mind to conjure them up almost at will.

A good initial exercise, to acclimatize yourself to this fascinating dream state, is to sit comfortably on a sofa with the TV or radio on. Allow your thoughts to drift and give the programme only half your attention, letting the rest of your mind wander randomly. If you find yourself nodding off, focus more fully on the television or radio, using the stimulus to keep yourself just within the boundaries of wakefulness. You will notice how the roving mind moves between levels of consciousness, recapturing snatches of rambling stories, producing vivid images of strange landscapes or mulling over memories so old you had almost forgotten them. This is an effective introduction to the world of hypnagogia.

To explore the hypnagogic state further, it is useful to develop a relaxed watchfulness; When you go to bed, focus on an inner space behind the eyes. Just let your attention rest on this point, gently returning to it when the mind wanders. Allow the images to arise in their own time.

If you find it difficult not to fall asleep while engaged in this practice, you could use a Tibetan meditation technique to remain more alert. Simply visualize a spinning disk of light in the space behind your eyelids or perhaps at your heart, and allow the images to flash through it.

Another approach is to conjure up the images yourself, rather than simply allowing yourself to be open to them. As you drift off to sleep, picture the things that you would like to see. Or visualize the letters of the alphabet in sequence. Often these willed images will transform into related geometric shapes; or they will spontaneously spin off into seemingly random, unrelated visions.

By experimenting with hypnagogia, you are not going to learn about your unacknowledged anxieties and desires – that is the realm of REM sleep. What you will do, however, is familiarize yourself with the workings of the brain – and at the same time have potentially enjoyable, hallucinatory experiences, rather like someone enjoying the Northern Lights.

Lucid Dreaming

The sleeping mind accepts the bizarre without questioning its reality, and so we imagine that what we are experiencing exists in the real world. Hence the power of nightmares. During so-called "lucid" dreams, however, we are aware, or become aware, that we are dreaming, without this causing us to awaken.

Many people have, at one time or another, experienced lucid dreams. Imagine you are dreaming about finding an ancient book in the cellar of someone's house. You know you shouldn't be there, yet when you come across the book, you can't resist the temptation to open it and see what it has to say to you. Perhaps it contains answers to some of your questions about life. Somehow you know that you are dreaming this, yet the realization does not end the dream. You decide – and it's a conscious decision – to open the book. You read a sentence and are amazed at its profound insight. You decide to remember these words and write them down immediately after you have woken up. You are aware that this is an extraordinary and important dream – perhaps a life-changing one. You feel a sense of power, you can make wakeful decisions within the dream. Eventually, of course, you do wake up. And, looking back, you know that you have been conscious all the time you have been dreaming. But you can't recall that enlightening sentence. It was just a dream after all.

So exciting are lucid dreams that we think of them as experiences to be encouraged. And in fact we can, to some degree, train our consciousness to enter the dream state and take control of our dreams. However, it is a discipline requiring preparation and practice.

The British dream researcher Celia Green has pinpointed several key differences between lucid and non-lucid dreaming. Lucid dreams appear to be free from the irrationality and narrative disjointedness of the more usual non-lucid state, and are sometimes seen and remembered with remarkable precision – we may not be able to remember the words in the book we picked up but we can recall exactly what the cellar was like and we can remember the binding on the book in meticulous detail. During lucid dreams the dreamer may have access to all the memories and thought functions of waking life, and may feel no real difference between sleeping and waking. But above all, as we have seen, the dreamer is aware that he or she is dreaming.

Usually this awareness dawns abruptly. Something inaccurate or illogical in the scenery or events of a conventional dream can suddenly

alert the dreamer to the fact of dreaming. The accompanying excitement and an uncanny sensation of what might be termed "mind expansion" make the experience unmistakable. Colours assume a vivid brightness, and objects stand out with illuminated clarity. Perhaps most remarkable is the dreamer's ensuing ability to control dream events, deciding where to go and what to do, and able now to experiment with the dreaming environment.

Yet intriguingly, however much power the dreamer may appear to have, he or she can never totally control the passage of a lucid dream. The decision, for example, to visit a tropical island in a dream may be the dreamer's own, but the island on arrival will prove every bit as novel and surprising as any seen for the first time in waking life. The Dutch physician William Van Eeden, a prolific lucid dreamer who coined the phrase "lucid dreaming" in 1913, described the dream world as a "fake world, cleverly imitated but with small failures", and cited as an example a lucid dream in which he tried to break a claret glass that resisted all his efforts, but appeared broken when he saw it a few moments later, "like an actor missing his cue".

Some of the world's great religions have seen lucid dreaming in a mystical light. Within the Hindu and Buddhist traditions, it is often asserted that advanced adepts in the meditative arts retain consciousness throughout dreaming and dreamless sleep, and thus experience all their dreams as lucid. Tibetan Buddhists teach that lucid dreams give us invaluable practice at exercising control in the afterlife – an environment comparable in many ways to the dream world. By applying ourselves to such techniques, we can eventually free ourselves from the illusory cycle of life and death. Indeed, Tibetan Buddhists maintain that the prime purpose of dreaming is to give us a nightly opportunity to gain this control.

OBEs

Training ourselves in lucid dreaming is sometimes seen as a major step toward enabling our consciousness to leave the body in an "out-of-body experience" (OBE). In lucid dreams, consciousness wanders in the "astral realms" – worlds created by thought and imagination. In OBEs, by contrast, our mind often remains on the earthly plane and is aware of physical reality, often including the presence of its owner's body in the room. The line between an OBE and a lucid dream, however, is often blurred.

Israel Ragardie, a leading exponent of the Western mystery and alchemical traditions, wrote that an advanced practitioner "no longer passes the night in deep oblivion", but instead maintains a consistent level of consciousness so that "all is one continuous, free-flowing stream of awareness". Some esoteric teachings even suggest that seizing the initiative in dreams allows one to perform seemingly inexplicable acts in the waking world. Some Hindu mystics have claimed that adepts can appear at will in a number of places at the same time by practising dream control, then using this control first to visualize a place and then to visit it in a "dream body", visible and substantial to others.

In all cultures, and among initiates as well as adepts, the ability to control the events of a dream arises from a high degree of mental control in waking life. Instead of the unconscious working its Freudian mischief below the level of consciousness, or whispering its wisdom unheeded, in lucid dreaming the conscious and unconscious minds seem to establish effective communication and cooperation with each other. The lucid dream is their joint creation, and by increasingly bringing it under conscious control, the dreamer reaches deeper levels of self-knowledge.

By being aware of, and even dictating, the course of a dream, the dreamer can not only reach further into the unconscious mind, but may consciously decide to face the fears, desires and energies that reside there. Rather than running in panic from a dark and mysterious force or a terrifying monster that inhabits the shadows at the edges of the dream world, lucid dreamers possess the control to summon such demons at will, then turn to confront them, aware that because they are only dreaming there is no real need for fear. Once challenged, such forces usually lose their power, because in dreams, as in waking life, the greatest fear is often fear itself. By confronting these demons in the unconscious, the dreamer not only lessens the terror that they are able to induce, but may also harness the energy of which he or she was previously afraid.

False Awakenings

Allied to lucid dreaming, and perhaps a half-way house to it, is the sometimes disquieting dream experience known as false awakening. False awakening dreams are imbued with a vivid clarity similar to that of lucid dreams, yet the dreamer is not aware of dreaming, but believes that he or she is awake, and may dream in great detail of getting up, washing, having breakfast and setting off to work – only to wake up properly a little while later and realize that none of these actions was in fact carried out. They then have to repeat the whole process for real.

Although lucid dreaming may seem to the uninitiated to be an instance of the irritating tricks our minds play on us, in fact it can be pleasurable and therapeutic, and can even offer a way to increase our self-understanding. At an advanced level we can use lucid dreaming for the purposes of radical self-examination. For example, we might consciously create a door in our dream, behind which we anticipate finding the reasons for a certain action or predicament in our waking lives, or at least a relevant clue or symbol. Controlling the dream, we can unlock the door to find the answers that escape us in our waking hours. Another approach is to imagine a wise counsellor whom we can approach in our lucid dreams to ask for timely advice about our problems or dilemmas. Such a creation might be a personalization of our own unconscious wisdom, but he or she may bring to light information charged with a truth and profundity unavailable to the conscious mind.

In sustained lucidity we also have the power of choice and the ability to question: Which path shall I take? Could I persuade this person to relinquish his weapon? How would it feel to fly high above the rooftops? Or, in a surreal lucid dream, Which of these fishes should I dance with? It can be powerfully

therapeutic to explore in this way the curiosities of our own imaginations, test our responses to events, and slip in and out of control.

People with a high degree of mental discipline are more likely to experience lucid dreams. The best way to encourage them is to hone your mental powers. Techniques such as meditation and creative visualization provide background training for the mind, and can only be beneficial. In addition, a number of more specific techniques can be tried. You might adopt the shaman's approach of studying a significant object closely just before sleep. If the object then appears in a dream, it will jolt you into awareness. Or else you might visualize, as often as possible throughout the day, a simple action, such as a walk in the park or making a cup of coffee. If you then see this action in your dream, it is possible that its appearance will make you conscious that you are dreaming.

The simplest technique of all is that known as "auto-suggestion". Simply affirm to yourself repeatedly throughout the day this simple assurance: that as you sleep, you will become aware that you are dreaming. This in itself may be enough to put your dreaming mind on alert.

Faith and self-belief are powerful mental tools, but patience is the most powerful tool of

How to Be a Lucid Dreamer

For many, lucid dreams are the Holy Grail, or Philosopher's Stone, of a fulfilling dream life. Here is a checklist of some strategies you might like to try in your attempts to master the art.

Meditate regularly

The self-awareness developed in meditation can spill over into your dream life, making you aware that you are dreaming, usually by alerting you to dream anomalies – for example, people who can fly, animals that can talk, or other disjunctions of waking logic. Creative visualization, which involves vividly visualizing your goals as a way to make them psychologically more attainable, can also be helpful in this respect.

Commit to observation

During the day, keep telling yourself that you will watch for any anomalies that may later occur in your dreams. To reinforce this approach, do reality checks while awake – asking yourself, for example, how you know that you are not dreaming at that particular moment (for example, because your cellphone has just rung and you have had a detailed, realistic conversation with your brother).

Use your hands as a cue

This is a shaman's technique. During the day, tell yourself that you will look at your hands in the next dream you have, and that this will be your cue to understand that you are dreaming. Assert this intention to yourself with conviction – you must really mean it. With luck your unconscious will pick up on this intention and carry it out while you are dreaming, thereby giving you the intended signal to become lucid. If you prefer, you can apply this method to an object – such as your front door or your kitchen table.

Banish stress

Anxiety can interfere with our ability to have lucid dreams, so it can be helpful to set up subdued lighting in the bedroom, and perhaps play some gentle music at low volume, just before you retire for the night. If you use a candle, always be sure to extinguish it before you climb between the sheets.

Adopt a shamanic persona

As you lie there before sleep, think of yourself as a shaman who has a mission to accomplish for the sake of the community.

all. It is important that you don't force the pace, nor become too frustrated when early attempts fail. Just keep trying, in a spirit of hopefulness.

For the purposes of experimental research, scientists have invented various machines to aid dream control. Such machines, strapped to the dreamer's wrist, detect REM sleep, and emit a small electric shock, which should not awaken the dreamer but simply startle them into an awareness of dreaming. These are impracticable for use in the bedroom, but if you can harness your own mind's potential ability to bring about lucid dreaming, you will have created a mental machine of your own, which is unsurpassable by science.

Studying the Time Dimension

Lucid dreaming has helped to resolve the question of whether dream events occupy a normal time span or whether, as is popularly believed, they condense time. Findings by Stephen Laberge at the University of Stanford, California, in which lucid dreamers carried out previously agreed eye movements to signify their progression through a series of pre-arranged dream events, suggest strongly that dream time approximates to real time. The dream may cut out irrelevant intervals, but that is the only way that it manages to beat the clock.

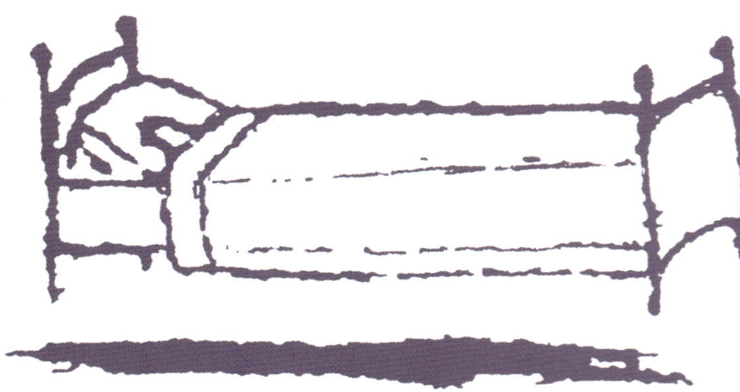

The Three Dream Levels

Freud proposed a threefold hierarchy of the mind, with a fourth level added by Jung: the conscious mind, the preconscious, the personal unconscious, the collective unconscious. In accord with this model there are three main classes of dream.

To understand the nature of dream experiences, the first thing we must do is recognize that they stem from different levels of the unconscious.

However, mind levels have no actual, physiological existence: they are simply labels that psychologists have given the different functions of the brain. Freud was the first to categorize thought processes in this way, by separating the unconscious mind into two distinct tiers: the preconscious and the personal unconscious. Later, Jung added a third, deeper level, which he termed the collective unconscious. Dreams offer us new insights from each of these levels and increase our awareness of them, often providing a vital route toward self-understanding.

Other Classifications

The classification of dreams into three levels is not the only way of approaching the subject. It can be an interesting exercise, when studying your own dream diary, to group your dreams in the following sets of categories, or even make up your own.

- *Past / present / future*
- *Desires / fears / intentions*
- *Self as dreamer / self as dream character*
- *Strangers as the world / strangers as known individuals / strangers as emotions*
- *Action dreams / mood dreams*
- *Mostly surreal / partly surreal / realistic*
- *Mild / strong / neutral*

The preconscious is the most superficial of the three layers of the unconscious mind. Trivial anxieties, factual knowledge, ideas, memories and fully acknowledged motivations and ambitions reside here, and they can be readily accessed by our consciousness and our dreams alike. Dreams that reflect the concerns of the preconscious mind are termed Level 1 dreams. They reflect waking preoccupations and events, and their interpretation tends to be fairly straightforward. Our minds are always looking backwards at events that have recently

Perspectives on the Mind

Like an iceberg with most of its bulk well below the surface, the unconscious mind is difficult to study. Below is a brief attempt to place it in a historical perspective, followed by a summary of the influential three-part division of the mind proposed by Freud.

Nowadays we tend to think of the unconscious as the discovery of Freud and Jung, but in fact the concept predates them. There are references to a deeply stratified mind in the ancient Hindu texts known as the *Vedas*, which date from between 2500 and 600 BC. In Europe the sixteenth-century physician Paracelsus comes even closer to our modern understanding of the mind. In a passage on psychosomatic symptoms he describes how a disease can be caused by an idea, "assumed by imagination, affecting those who believe in such a thing".

Freud broke away from his predecessors in identifying the dark side of the psyche, with all its uncomfortable urges and phobias. He named the principal parts of the mind the id, the ego and the superego. His ideas caused outrage at the time and were seen as besmirching childhood. However, they have since come to form the backbone of modern psychiatry.

The id: When we are newborn babies, the id (which literally means the "it") enables us to get our needs met by crying when we are hungry, cold or craving attention. With no thought beyond the satisfaction of our own desires, the id is based on the pleasure principle. It is primitive, chaotic, and unaware of time or space.

The ego: Born out of the id, the ego (or the "I") usually develops during the first three years of an individual's life. It is based on the rationality principle and takes into consideration the needs of others and the fact that selfishness, impulsiveness and instant gratification may damage our interests in the long run. The ego is our consciousness and confronts reality in a rational way. The ego of infants is weak and unformed and can only let go of bad memories completely, not repress them.

The superego: The superego usually develops by the age of five. It is the moral part of the psyche that develops in response to the values of our caregivers. The superego is essential for the well-being of society as a whole. However, too harsh a moral code will result in guilt and the repression of the id's instincts.

happened, and Level 1 dreams appear to be an extension of this retrospective tendency. However, because Level 1 dreams focus on the routine, unremarkable events of the day, they can mislead us into believing that they are invariably without significance. In truth, everything that we dream is meaningful, and if the dreaming mind has selected commonplace subject matter, instead of deeper concerns, perhaps there is a reason for this. The dream may, in fact, be using low-key events as an indirect means of addressing Level 2 or 3 material that is more difficult to access directly. For example, if you recently dialled a wrong telephone number and that incident occurs in a dream, it might perhaps suggest deep, unconscious anxiety about your failure to communicate your true self to others in general or in the context of a specific relationship. In this way, seemingly inconsequential Level 1 material can serve to release some challenging Level 2 messages if you approach your dream interpretation with sufficient thoughtfulness and imagination.

The second level, the personal unconscious, is again unique to each of us, but cannot

readily be accessed by the waking memory. Freud called this level the id – that is, the primitive, animalistic aspect of self which, when we are awake, is held in check by the ego of consciousness. The id accommodates desires, emotions and motivations that have been repressed, as well as half-forgotten traumas and other experiences locked in deep, unreachable parts of our memory.

Long-forgotten memories and deep personal issues are the stock-in-trade of Level 2 dreams. Often they represent situations and events quite alien to those of waking life. A dreamer may find himself or herself in a strange role or an incongruous situation, interacting with strangers in unexpected ways or behaving entirely out of character. The dream may have an intriguing atmosphere about it, and linger in the memory as if crying out for interpretation.

Each of us has our own distinctive repertoire of symbols stored in the personal unconscious, and these are the symbols that constitute the language of Level 2 dreams. Veiled in metaphor as an acceptable way to address various taboo subjects, these dreams ask us to confront our hidden needs and desires. We might, for example, find our dream selves enacting disturbing scenes of violence or lust in ways that would be unthinkable in waking life. Such

scenarios are important expressions of hidden urges that the ego forces us to control, for our own peace of mind and functional effectiveness, as we go about our daily lives.

The third, deepest level of the mind is what Jung identified as the collective unconscious. Memorably, he described it as the "vast historical storehouse of the human race". Here are stored universal archetypes – the symbolic language of "grand" or Level 3 dreams. Such dreams clothe universal fears and desires in the symbolism of myth – since myths too derive from the collective unconscious. Most of us are unlikely to have grand dreams often, but when we do they will tend to have great impact upon us. They deal with profound themes such as spirituality, life and death, love, sacrifice, transformation and heroism. Typically, the symbols operating at this level are universal in their resonance, and usually they can best be understood by studying their appearance in the myths and legends of different cultural traditions around the world – a technique that Jung termed "amplification" (see page 108).

"Grand dreams" tend to appear at the key transitional stages in life – for example, during the pangs of adolescence, or after the birth of a child, or at the onset of menopause or at times of bereavement.

People differ widely in the frequency and ratios with which they experience these three categories of dreaming. Those who take up self-awareness practices such as meditation, or those who begin a period of psychotherapy, tend to report an increase in the number of Level 3 dreams. Variations in your rhythms of waking and sleeping can alter the usual pattern you perceive in your dreamlife, and it is well worth experimenting to see if this happens. For example, you could try setting an alarm clock to wake yourself at various stages during the night, recording the dream memories in a notebook each time you wake up. You might discover, for example, that your most vivid and meaningful dreams take place in the early hours of the morning and are normally lost to the memory.

Prophetic Dreams

The notion that dreams might give us clues about our destiny, as individuals or as a tribe or nation, is deeply rooted in antiquity. The flight patterns of birds and the entrails of animals were also consulted about the future. But dreams have offered a more poetic and evocative kind of signpost.

Can dreams bring us news or information through channels that defy the conventional logic of everyday life? Many people feel intuitively that they can. Telepathic dreaming, to take one example of what might be called a paranormal dream, has even been demonstrated clinically. In a famous experiment at the Maimonides Medical Centre in Brooklyn, New York, some volunteers concentrated on a selection of target pictures while others slept. When awoken during periods of REM sleep, the sleepers reported a statistically significant number of dreams that were clearly influenced by the images.

Another well-known aspect of paranormal dreaming is precognition – clairvoyant knowledge of future events, by which people have dreamed of impending disasters, including the sinking of the *Titanic* in 1912 and the Japanese attack on Pearl Harbor in 1941. Science has no explanation for this apparent ability to see into the future, but there are many well-documented cases based on reliable testimony.

One of the most striking and strangest examples of clairvoyant and precognitive dreaming are those in which people without any knowledge of horse racing successfully predict race winners. A curious proviso seems to be that the money so gained should be used for charitable purposes. Several dreamers have reported the loss of their ability if they spend their winnings on themselves.

Dreams That Foretold Disasters

The case files of premonitory dreams tend to be dominated by clairvoyant impressions of disasters. Not all of the events dreamed about have ended badly, however – unlike the two examples given below. There are many accounts of people whose lives have been saved by an unsettling dream that deterred them from being in the wrong place at the wrong time – for example, commuting to work on the day of a terrorist attack on their route.

Titanic clash

In April 1912 the supposedly unsinkable *Titanic*, the world's largest passenger ship, sank in the North Atlantic after hitting an iceberg, with the loss of more than 1,500 lives. The event was remarkable not least for the sheer number of premonitions about it. A US businessman cancelled his voyage after his wife in Nebraska dreamed of the incident in concrete detail. More than one daughter dreamed of her mother struggling in the waves – one discovered only later that her mother had booked herself on the voyage. Hundreds of such dreams and other forms of premonition were reported, and nineteen were authenticated.

Premonitory dreams are often highly personal: the dreamer is involved in some way in the forecast scenario, so that the dream presents itself as a paranormal intuition that breaks through everyday consciousness with a warning: do not board that ship, do not take that plane. However, there are also dreams that prophesy disasters in which the dreamer is not directly implicated, as if some kind of social conscience were at work. David Booth's dreams of America's worst air disaster are a poignant example of this type.

David Booth's ten dreams

In 1979 a 23-year-old car rental office manager from Cincinnati, Ohio, named David Booth, dreamed on ten separate nights of an air crash, and found the experience so disturbing that he contacted the Federal Aviation Administration, but of course they took no action. The dreams showed an American Airlines plane banking to the right, turning over, and crashing to the ground. Booth's last dream of the crash was on the very day it occurred – an American Airlines DC-10 came down near Chicago, killing all on board as well as some people on the ground – 274 fatalities in all. Booth subsequently became known, controversially, as a psychic.

An electrical engineer and retired English civil servant named Harold Horwood developed the ability to consistently dream winners as an incidental result of intensive meditation practices, numbering among his successes many major events in the British racing calendar. Another successful dreamer of horse race

results was the Irish peer Lord Kilbracken, who over a short period dreamed nine winners and later became the racing correspondent of a London daily newspaper.

Dr Thelma Moss, an American dream researcher, includes among her collection of tipster dreams the remarkable case of a woman who dreamed up to four winners a week over a period of four months, while Montague Ullman, founder of the Dream Laboratory at the Maimonides Medical Center, Brooklyn, New York (see pages 76–78), reported a case of a man who dreamed the winners and runners-up of horse races on three successive nights.

Belief in the predictive power of dreams is as old as written history. In many ancient cultures a dream that warned of impending flood, invasion, pestilence or the end of a ruling dynasty would be treated with the utmost solemnity and respect. Thus forewarned, a dreamer might succeed in averting the catastrophe by rescheduling the battle, arresting the palace spy or, like Noah, building an ark to survive the coming deluge.

The legacy of European scientific rationalism has filled many of us today with a deep scepticism, yet stories of predictive dreaming remain relatively commonplace, especially when they relate to the dreamer's own family or friends. But it was not until the work of John

William Dunne that any consistent attempt to examine whether or not dreams can really provide glimpses into forthcoming events was published. In 1902 Dunne, a British aeronautical engineer, had a dream that successfully foretold the eruption of Mount Pelée in Martinique. In his dream, he became convinced that the volcano was about to explode and hurried to warn the French authorities of the imminent catastrophe, telling them that 4,000 lives would be lost in the explosion. Subsequently, he was amazed to read in a newspaper that the volcano had indeed erupted. The headlines, however, told of 40,000, not 4,000, deaths, and Dunne was later to conclude that it was not a vision of the volcano itself that had alerted him to the disaster, but a precognitive experience of reading the newspaper story and of misreading the headline that told of the number of deaths.

A further series of precognitive dreams convinced Dunne that coincidence was no explanation for the frequency and sometimes detailed accuracy of his premonitions. He kept a dream diary for more than thirty years, recording his own dreams and those of his friends, to gather evidence for his increasingly radical ideas.

Dunne believed that dreams are able to make use of future events with the same freedom with which they select happenings from the past, wandering backward and forward through time, sometimes combining the past and future within the same dream. His book, *An Experiment with Time*, published in 1927, detailed an intricate and elaborate physical theory to account for this apparent flouting of scientific logic.

In 1971 Montague Ullman and Stanley Krippner, working with the Maimonides Dream Laboratory team in New York, for the first time devised a method to investigate precognitive dreaming under laboratory conditions. They worked with Malcolm Bessent, a gifted English sensitive who had a track record of precognitive dreams. Before going to sleep, Bessent was told that he would be exposed to a "multi-sensory special waking experience" on the next morning, chosen at random by the experimenters from a catalogue of possibilities. Researchers woke him up after each REM period to record what he had just dreamed and independent judges matched his dreams to the "special waking experiences" that followed them. Two separate experiments were done. In the first, lasting eight nights, Bessent had accurate precognitive dreams on five of them; in the second, lasting sixteen nights, of which only eight were designated for experiment, again the hit rate was five.

The degree of success that these experiments enjoyed is almost unparallelled in the history of parapsychology. Of the twelve projects that the Maimonides team completed between the years 1966 and 1972, nine yielded positive results, some of these at a very high level of significance.

During the course of the 1970s and 1980s, the Maimonides Dream Laboratory also carried out a number of experiments to test more general forms of ESP in dreams, such as telepathy and clairvoyance, using famous art prints as targets. An "agent", located in a separate room or building from the subject, would concentrate upon one of these randomly chosen images in an attempt to "transmit" it to the dreamer and incorporate it into his or her dream. Again the results were highly impressive: psychologists declared an accuracy rate of 83.5 per cent for a series of twelve of these experiments, a finding against odds of over a quarter of a million to one.

Researchers have collected a number of clairvoyant dreams apparently related to the sinking of the *Titanic* (see page 73). Similarly, a retrospective appeal in the British press for dreams connected with the tragedy at Aberfan, a mining town in Wales where an avalanche of coal waste buried 140 people alive in 1966, produced impressive results that led to the establishment in 1967 of the British Premonitions Bureau and the American Central Premonitions Registry.

Dreams of the death of loved ones, or so-called "farewell dreams", are not uncommon. One of the best-known is that of the explorer Henry Stanley, who after his capture at the battle of Shiloh during the American Civil War

dreamed in detail of the unexpected death of his aunt some 4,000 miles away in Wales. Abraham Lincoln dreamed of his own death in 1865. In his dream, he wandered around a "death-like" White House following the far-off sounds of "pitiful sobbing". Every room was familiar and light, but there was no one there. He finally entered the East Room to see a corpse laid out with its face covered, and wrapped in funeral vestments. When he asked the weeping mourners who was dead, he was told: "the President, he was killed by an assassin". A loud burst of grief from the crowd awoke him from his dream, and it was only a matter of days before the assassin John Wilkes Booth did indeed shoot him dead at the theatre.

Dreaming Sports Results

An enjoyable and entertaining way to test precognitive dreaming is to try to predict the winner of a sports event. Of course, there is no need to place bets in order to follow this exercise. It is based on a system of elimination developed by Harold Horwood (see page 74). The method is ideal for sports involving multiple competitors, such as a horse race or a motor race. You cannot apply the technique to a binary result – that is, a football or baseball game, for example, where there will be one winner and one loser. But even with binary sports you could adapt this technique to see if your dreams will predict for you the champion team of a knockout competition or league, or the top scorer over the course of a season.

1. Make two lists

Pick a race one or two weeks ahead, give each runner a number and divide the runners randomly into two lists, each on a separate piece of paper. Before going to bed, read the lists and think about the names and numbers. Put one list on the left side of the bed, and the other on the right.

2. Scan the first dream

In the morning, try to remember if your dreams suggested or contained a name or a number. Ask, too, whether "left" or "right" were emphasized in any dream, indicating which list might contain a winner. Make a note of your conclusions.

3. Jumble the lists

On the next night, redistribute the runners randomly into two new lists, keeping the same number for each runner. Repeat steps 1 and 2, filing your successive lists together with your notes on the dreams you have had.

4. Repeat the process

Repeat this procedure every night, progressively isolating a runner by identifying which candidate has been suggested most often – by name, number or inclusion on the chosen list.

5. Use your intuition

Look out in your dreams for any kind of clue or sign. If you find that a name or number is strongly suggested in a dream, there is no need to continue with your work on the lists.

THE *Language* OF DREAMS

When we wake in the morning, it is often the bizarre nature of our dream memories that convinces us of their unimportance. What possible relevance can the nonsensical images of the night – the faceless stranger, the monkey that lives inside your neighbour's wardrobe, the car without a steering wheel – have for our conscious life? However, a similar question could be asked of a foreign language. Until we learn their meanings, the unfamiliar images of the dream world will make no sense to us; but once we start to explore this new idiom, a whole new dimension of significance will be opened up.

Symbolism

Dream symbols are visual metaphors representing objects, memories, emotions, ideas, anxieties, hopes, aspirations, frustrations – or even, sometimes, ourselves or other people. They can take almost any form that could be recognized by the senses: an inanimate object, a snatch of music, a landscape, an event. Symbols are the starting-point of dream work.

Symbols are the "words" used by dream language: each one represents an idea, a memory, a mood, an insight, arising from the dreamer's unconscious. However, unlike the words of a foreign language, many dream symbols can change their meaning from one participant to another. Moreover, again in contrast to a foreign language, the dream has no fixed grammar, instead linking its semantic units together according to idiosyncratic principles of logic which must be studied carefully before they can be properly teased out and understood.

In every sense, dreaming represents a personal language between the unconscious and the conscious mind, and although we can learn the typical meanings of many dream symbols, we can never be sure that we have understood them – and the connections between them – until we have worked upon them in the light of our unique life history and our experience. No matter how weird or laughable particular dream symbols may appear to be, the dream has chosen them for their particular ability to convey the intended message. The most apparently trivial symbol may unlock a potent memory or a telling insight into the way we are now or the way we might be in future.

In waking life, symbols usually denote something specific – a cross, for example, may suggest Christianity, a stork may suggest childbirth. But dream symbols are more connotative than denotative (that is to say, their

meanings are suggestive rather than specific), and so to translate them into waking sense requires attention to the context, mood and setting of the dream, and the circumstances of the dreamer. In other words, everybody has a dream-symbol system unique to themselves.

Generally, Level 1 and 2 dreams, which arise respectively from the preconscious and the personal unconscious (see pages 65–70), make most use of symbols that carry particular associations for the dreamer, or that arise from the general currency of everyday life. Many of these have elements of common usage, but others may make sense only to the dreamer. Thus, a tree, for most of us, may represent protection and fertility, but for a dreamer who once fell from a tree's branches as a child it may stand for danger, darkness, and the guilt of a forbidden escapade.

Although making obvious sense at the literal level, a Level 1 or 2 symbol may carry sufficient emotional charge to be of special meaning in

Symbol Safari

Given that symbols play such a part in our dreams, anyone interested in dream interpretation would do well to acquaint themselves with some of the characteristics of symbolism before they start. Below are a few exercises that will attune you to the symbolic idiom.

Everyday metaphor

Listen for the metaphors (compressed similes or likenesses) that you and others use in speech. You might "sail" through an exam or have a "bruising" encounter. You might feel "shattered" after a long hard day. Be aware of the literal meaning of such expressions, and visualize the literal scenario – for example, if you are shattered, think of yourself collapsing into small shards and fragments of the self.

Visual messages

Consider how people communicate messages visually, through their dress, their interior decoration, and so on. For example, a brooch fashioned as a rose suggests beauty, love, romanticism, with perhaps the idea that the most splendid things in life are those that reach a moment of glory and then start to fade. Since a rose is a lover's gift, there might also be a suggestion of admiration here. Similarly, if you have a miniature seated Buddha on your mantelpiece, perhaps this tells the world that you are quietly contemplative, with a deep spiritual side; or perhaps that you appreciate the mysterious atmosphere of the East.

Products and advertising

Be alert to the packaging, labelling and advertising of commercial products – from cars and cameras to perfumes and shampoos. For each product analyze the associations of the name, the imagery of the label and the broader context of the advertising. In your explorations you will come across trees, flowers, animals, castles, streams, sunsets and sunrises, and much else. Consider why those things have been linked with particular products.

Movies

Study the symbolism of movies – the setting, the lighting, the colours. One critic analyzed the whole of *Casablanca* in terms of the symbolism of white and black, light and shade. Since the movies and dreams have much in common, this kind of thinking will help you to acclimatize to the dream world.

the dreams of particular people. For example, rage may be symbolized for one dreamer by an angry farmer, because it was a farmer who once threatened to shoot him for trespassing; while for another dreamer it may take the form of the Chinese puzzle that once drove her to the limits of frustration over a long summer holiday. Level 1 and Level 2 symbols can be taken not only from the dreamer's direct experience, but also from more peripheral aspects of life, such as books, plays or TV programmes (even though these may have had little apparent impact on the conscious mind). The dream plunders images shamelessly from the dreamer's memory-banks, choosing the motifs that most readily serve its immediate purposes. We might think of the dream as a mixed-media collage artist, poring with concentration over a vivid palette, rummaging through boxes of junk and salvaged materials, combining fragments until just the

right creative impression has been achieved.

Symbols in Level 3 dreams, by contrast, usually carry a universal meaning, derived from the collective experience of humankind. Not only are the archetypes common to us all (see pages 96–109) but so are the forms in which they typically arise into awareness. The problem with Level 3 dreams often has less to do with the interpretation of their symbols than with modern reluctance to recognize that dreams can help us to draw upon a reservoir of wisdom beyond the range of our waking minds.

Freud and Jung disagreed fundamentally over what is meant by a symbol, and this was one of the reasons they parted company. In Freud's view, symbolism takes place to translate sexual and other repressed desires into acceptable form, thus protecting the dreamer from being so disturbed that he or she wakes up. He also gave a fixed meaning to dream symbols, so that, for example, guns, daggers, doors and caves all represent sexual organs – clues to our animal instinct, in whatever context they appear. For Jung, however, this was to treat

images as signs, not as symbols. Jung maintained that the substance of a symbol "consists of our unconscious contents that make themselves felt, yet the conscious is unable to grasp their meaning". A sign, on the other hand, represents a fixed interpretation of a dream image, and therefore one restricted to a meaning that is already conscious. Treating a dream image as a sign not only denies us access to its deeper meaning, but further represses that meaning and thus widens rather than narrows the gap between the conscious and the unconscious.

For Freud, a phallic symbol represented a penis; for Jung, it was "the creative mana, the power of healing and fertility". Most psychologists and anthropologists who have made a study of symbols favour the more creative approach of Jung. The American mythologist Joseph Campbell insisted that "consciousness can no more invent, or even predict, an effective symbol than it can foretell or control tonight's dream".

Unlike a sign, a symbol can carry a variety of meanings which, although they are all facets

of the same truth, each benefit from separate inspection. Thus, under analysis the image of a gun may emerge even for the same dreamer as representing thunder and lightning, male procreation, destruction, and the toy the dreamer once used to terrify a childhood friend into parting with his candy. All of these four meanings reflect the central theme of power, but they show respectively that power can be used to destroy, to do good, to do evil, or to reinforce a childish urge to intimidate and exploit others.

Because dream symbols are often bizarre and apparently unconnected, we tend to dismiss them as irrelevant. We might wonder, for example, at the relevance to our lives of a maze, a puppet, a wild beast or even so mundane an image as an unwanted gift. To understand the meanings of symbols, we must patiently and diligently try to determine how these metaphors bear on our own circumstances. Interpret your personal lexicon of dream symbols in the light of your life history and recent experience: fire might symbolize destruction, but it could also represent starting something afresh, such as a new relationship; a castle might represent security, but it could also imply feelings of isolation. Only by examining your own responses honestly will you arrive at a valid interpretation.

Consider, too, the context of the symbol: a flower offered by a lover may signify something quite different from one offered by an enemy. The meaning of a dream symbol can also be modified by its appearance – for example, its colour, texture and size. A pink dog is likely to symbolize something quite different from a black dog; the meaning of an empty vase is likely to be different from that of a vase of flowers. Finally, think about the connections between dream symbols, by looking for complementary meanings: a train, a dagger and a snake may all be phallic in their significance; a circle, a star, water and a temple may all relate to the desire or need for spirituality.

Starting-points for the meanings of some common dream images can be found in the directory of symbols on pages 158–447 of this book. Bear in mind, though, that any such directory can offer only general pointers. Individual dreamers are far more likely to discover the true meanings of dream symbols if they use the directory entries as prompts rather than literal descriptions. Think of yourself as a detective, a decoder, an explorer of dark places – and as an archaeologist of the mind who, working with fragments, has sufficient skill and imagination to reconstruct the whole.

Dream Symbolism at Work: an example

The dream described and analyzed here shows dream symbolism in operation. The dreamer is a male sales executive working for a large conglomerate. He has always wanted to be a novelist, but now spends much of his time writing misleading but highly effective sales publicity material.

The dreamer describes his dream

"I was in a barbershop awaiting my turn. The place was small and dark and I had the impression of brown paintwork and a seedy atmosphere. There were two men ahead of me, sitting on my right, but the barber called me in first. I was rather put out by this, and thought he wanted to ingratiate himself with me.

"When I went to sit in the chair, however, I found that I was in the barbershop on my own. The mirror in front of me was old and the silvering had decayed with the damp so I was unable to see my reflection. Then I was outside, looking in the windows of some stores. I think I was trying to find some scissors to cut my own hair, but was unsuccessful. I heard a hissing sound and said to myself, 'The balloon has burst'."

An analyst decodes the symbols

The dreamer associated hair and his trip to the barber's with a "seedy" and ineffectual vanity, and associated the barber's behaviour with the way that others lavish praise and attention where it is not due – a situation that he clearly associated with his work as a copywriter.

The two silent men should have been called to the barber's chair before him, yet they missed their turn. Could this suggest that there were deep, still latent aspects of the self, such as his gifts as a writer, that should have been prioritized but had not yet been given a chance to shine.

The dreamer felt that the mirror in which he could not see his face was an indication of his lack of self-knowledge. He had allowed his true self to disappear in the falsity and deception surrounding his professional life.

His scrutiny of store windows indicates the dreamer's search outside himself – though he should have been looking within. The hunt for scissors might suggest some recognition of the need to control his vanity. The final image of the burst balloon may connote both shattered illusions and punctured self-esteem.

The Grammar of Dreams

Pioneers of psychology in the twentieth century have taught us that dreams are not merely a jumble of random events and sensations, but follow an inner logic, reflecting the preoccupations of the inner self. How, more precisely, does this logic work?

Before the ground-breaking work of Freud, scientists thought that dreams were entirely haphazard and in no way logical. Freud, however, refused to pay lip service to such conventional expectations. With subtle and imaginative resourcefulness, he traced various ways in which dreams used their own strange logic to convey their profound messages from the unconscious mind to the waking self. He showed how dreams bend the rules of time and space, presenting events in startling sequences, mixing past and present, near at hand and far away; and he demonstrated how the physics of matter and identity are flouted, so that one thing may become another, or suddenly acquire the characteristics of another – which is a slightly different observation.

Connecting with the Surreal

This simple exercise is designed to increase your sensitivity to the surreal – an essential ingredient of the dream world.

1. Think of three unconnected objects that symbolize different parts of your life – perhaps your work, your leisure time and your principal relationship.

2. Try to think of a surreal story that connects all three aspect of your life and incorporates the three objects. Imagine this story as a strange cartoon – one that you are storyboarding in your head, like the producer of a movie.

Until the revolution in dream theory brought about by the work of Freud and Jung, few philosophers disagreed with the nineteenth-century German physicist Theodor Fechner's assertion that in dreams "it is as though psychological activity has been transported from the brain of a reasonable man into that of a fool". His attitude did no more than paraphrase what philosophers had written about dream logic since Roman times, when the statesman and scholar Cicero maintained that "there is no imaginable thing too absurd, too involved, or too abnormal for us to dream about it". One minor German philosopher wrote in 1875 of the "laughable contradictions [that the dreamer] is ready to accept in the laws of nature and society", while four years later one of his colleagues asserted that "it seems impossible to detect any fixed laws in this crazy activity ... dreams melt into a mad whirl of kaleidoscopic confusion".

What disturbed rational philosophers was not only the apparently "nonsensical" content of the dream images themselves, but also the apparent absence of rational thought and higher mental functions in the logic that links dream images together. In 1877, for example, one writer spoke of "an eclipse of all the logical operations of the mind which are based on relations and connections" so that dreams are in no way "affected by reflection or commonsense".

Freud himself likened a dream, with its absence of helpful interconnections between one image and another, to a sentence that lacks conjunctions – the words, such as "and", "if", "because", "when" and "or", that form logical connections between concepts and give language much of its coherence.

However, Freud observed that connections between things can be demonstrated by means other than words – as is the case, for example, with art. He believed that "the madness of dreams may not be without method, and may even be simulated, like that of the Danish prince [Hamlet]". Although dream connections do not follow the rational logic of language and philosophy, it is possible that they adhere to a more oblique rationale in order deliberately to disguise the meaning of the dream.

The often bewildering nature of this logic reflects the dreams' origins outside the tidy confines of the conscious mind. A dream can be a response to events in the outside world, or it can originate within, expressing aspects of the dreamer's deep-seated preoccupations and feelings; it can be a means of fulfilling desires or of highlighting unresolved emotions in the dreamer's everyday life. The contradictions and

conflicts implicit in these complex processes are, not unexpectedly, reflected in the grammar and syntax of dreams. Often enigmatic, halting and fragmentary, the language of dreams can warp time, bringing historical and contemporary figures together. It can mix the familiar with the unknown, and work fantastic transformations by its own brand of psychic "magic". Like certain kinds of movies, the dream world has dissolves in which one scene merges mysteriously into another. Inanimate things move of their own accord, and may talk, and even become intensely threatening.

People or animals may fly, or a person may bark like a dog, or walk naked in a crowded place. The meanings dreams hold have to be teased out from such complex and contrary happenings.

Clinical experience showed Freud that dream images interconnect by means of four main linking devices. The first is simultaneity, when dream images or events are presented together within a single scenario. The second is contiguity, when dream images or events are presented in sequence. Thirdly, there is transformation, when one image dissolves into another. And lastly there is similarity, revealed primarily through indirect or direct association, which Freud considered to be the most frequent and important linking device and one that operates through association – as when one object resembles another in some way, or recalls or invokes feelings about that second object. Many of these associations are forgotten or repressed at a conscious level, making the connections harder to unravel, but they can be revealed through appropriate techniques of dream interpretation. By deciphering them, the psychoanalyst lays bare not only the operation of dream logic but also its profound subtlety.

The complex operation of dream logic may be demonstrated by taking a relatively commonplace example: that of dreaming of finding someone's clothes in your wardrobe. This dream may have a wish-fulfilment aspect, reflecting admiration for the other person's qualities: by acquiring their possessions, we gain some of their characteristics for ourselves. However, there might also be an aspect of resentment at the intrusion of something foreign into a place that is thoroughly private and domestic. This might possibly suggest the envy with which admiration is sometimes tinged. A comparable dream would be the discovery of someone else's clothes on our bed: we might reasonably conclude that this has a similar meaning, except that there is an additional element of inconvenience, in that the clothes are not neatly stowed away but are lying there untidily, requiring us to deal with their presence. Moreover, the bed is an even more intimate place than the wardrobe. Thus, the dream (depending as always on context) might reflect interference by the owner of the clothes in the dreamer's own life.

Dream researchers since Freud have identified internal consistency as playing a key role in the operation of dream logic. Analysis of Level 1 and 2 dreams (those generated by the preconscious and personal unconscious) shows that each dreamer may have his or her own particular way of manifesting this consistency.

The most common form that consistency takes, labelled "relative consistency" by the American dream researchers Calvin Hall and Vernon Nordby, lies in the frequency with which various dream images appear to individual dreamers over a period of time. Thus, furniture, body parts, cars and cats may appear in descending order of frequency for one dreamer, while for another subject, women may appear more often than men and outdoor settings more often than indoor. From one year to the next it has been shown that these frequency patterns remain remarkably constant.

Another important form of internal consistency in dreaming is the symbolic dimension. When using symbols, the dream is unconcerned with how incomprehensible or bizarre they might appear to the conscious mind. It selects them solely on the basis of their associations with the material to be expressed, and is likely to repeat the more successful ones in dream after dream to get its message through.

Archetypes

Archetypes are the universal themes, or in Jung's words "mythological motifs", that emerge from the collective unconscious and reappear in symbolic form again and again in myths, symbol systems and dreams.

James Hillman, the contemporary (American) founder of archetypal psychology, refers to archetypes as "the deepest patterns of psychic functioning": they are "the roots of the soul governing the perspectives we have of ourselves and the world ... the axiomatic, self-evident images to which psychic life and our theories about it ever return".

Without access to the myth-making vitality of the archetypes, we are confined to a few rooms of the splendid mansion that is the mind, and shut out from the creative source of our own psychic life.

In most instances, archetypal dreams leave us feeling that we have received wisdom from a source outside what we commonly recognize as ourselves. Whether we describe this source as a reservoir of spiritual truth or as an untapped dimension of our own minds is of less importance than that we acknowledge its existence.

In our "grand" dreams, archetypes appear as symbols, or take personified form as the particular gods and goddesses, heroes and heroines, fabulous beasts and powers of good and evil that are most familiar to our conscious minds. Jungians stress, however, that we should never identify with individual archetypes, because each is only a fragment of the complete self. By integrating the many archetypes of the collective unconscious, Jungians hope to move toward individuation (see pages 23–24).

Archetypal dreams are most likely to occur at important transitional points in life, such as

early schooldays, puberty, adolescence, early parenthood, middle age, the menopause, and old age. They also occur at times of upheaval and uncertainty, and mark the process toward individuation and spiritual maturity. Jung saw archetypal dreams as having the special function of helping the dreamer to shape his or her future. He advised dreamers to ask why they might have had the dream, and to assess its potential impact. If archetypes are personifications of our psychic energies, then their appearance in dreams may be a signpost to

the direction of our future development.

As we have seen, archetypal energies can take many different forms, appearing in dreams as symbolic events or realistic or mythical beings. Initially, at least, the archetypes that appear in human form are most easily recognized.

Jung found archetypal dreams occurring in all walks of life, experienced as much by "people who are inwardly cut off from humanity and oppressed by the thought that nobody else has their problems" as by those far advanced on the individuation process. Yet in these two extreme cases the dream content is different: the dreams of the alienated personality reflect personal concerns and the dreams of the integrated personality reflect supra-personal themes such as birth and death, immortality, and the meaning of existence.

However, Jung cautions that if archetypal dreams contain potent material that appears greatly to contradict the ideas and beliefs of the dreamer's conscious mind, or that lacks the moral coherence of genuine mythological material, then a deep division, born of resistance and repression, may exist between the collective unconscious and the dreamer's waking life. Such psychic blocks must be dealt with before further progress is possible.

Dream archetypes are vital to the search for our "true selves". By looking out for them in dreams, and learning to recognize them, we can build bridges that stretch over to our unconscious. Each archetype is a link in a chain of mythic associations. By identifying one archetype, we can draw other archetypes into dreaming awareness, and so delve deeper into the creative power of our collective unconscious.

According to the Jungian analysts Edward Whitmont and Sylvia Perera, we know that we have entered the world of archetypes if our dreams confront us with elements that are rationally impossible in everyday life, and that lead us to the "realms of myth and magic". Many dreams reject in various degrees the constraints of waking reality, but the moment that we find ourselves in a shape-shifting world in which we encounter charismatic men and women who seem larger than life, heroes rise unscathed from mortal wounds, tall, dark strangers enter through locked doors, and fugitives turn into trees as they run away, we may justifiably suspect that we are in the presence of archetypal powers.

Archetypal dream images and events often appear to have a predetermined, all-encompassing, dramatic power, described by Whitmont and Perera as a "numinosity which creates a sense of awe in the dreamer". The dream may be set in a historical or cultural environment far removed from that of the dreamer, symbolizing the fact that he or she is travelling outside the boundaries of waking sensory and psychological experience. It has also been found that archetypal dreams convey a sense of great significance to the dreamer, prompting him or her to see in them "some suggestion of enlightenment, warning, or supernatural help". Above all, archetypal dreams have about them what Jung called a "cosmic quality", a sense of temporal or spatial infinity conveyed by dream experiences such as movement at tremendous speed over vast distances, or a comet-like flight through space, an experience of hovering far above the Earth, or a breathtaking expansion of the self until it transcends its narrow individuality and embraces all of creation. Cosmic qualities can also emerge in our dreams as astrological or alchemical symbols, or as experiences of death and rebirth.

Many archetypal dreams involve magical journeys or quests which often, like the quest for the Holy Grail, represent a search for some aspect of ourselves. A common theme in fairy tales is that of the young hero who must journey

to a foreign land to discover his manhood, or true self, before returning to slay a dragon or rescue a suffering maiden. When such themes appear in dreams, they usually symbolize a journey into the unconscious, where the dreamer seeks to find and assimilate fragmented parts of the psyche in order to achieve a psychological confidence and wholeness that can differentiate him or her from their social background.

A common archetypal journey is the night sea passage, in which the hero is swallowed up and nearly destroyed by the monster that he has attempted to slay. As in the biblical tale of Jonah and the whale, the hero still manages to destroy the monster from within, to escape and finally to reach land in a symbolic representation of the

Swimming to the Stars: an example of an archetypal dream

The dreamer is a university professor. She has a formidable academic reputation but risks compromising it by declaring her increasing interest in mysticism and spiritual growth.

The dreamer describes her dream

"I had been swimming in the sea and went to stand under a freshwater shower further up the beach. The water ran over my back but before I could rinse my front, I found myself in a smart drawing room. Still in my bathing suit, I was dripping water on the carpet. There were several well-dressed women there who looked at me disapprovingly. Next moment I floated up onto the roof. It was night, and the stars seemed larger and brighter than in life. I stretched out a hand to touch them, and for a moment held one in my hand. I wanted to put it in a pocket but was still in my bathing suit. A voice said 'Put it under your chest.' I was trying to fathom out how to do this when I suddenly woke up."

The archetypes analyzed

The archetypal nature of this dream is suggested by its most irrational elements: the transformation of the beach into a drawing room, the dreamer's ability to float to the roof and her power to touch the stars.

She has been swimming in the sea, indicating a desire to travel deeper into the unconscious. But she then tries to wash the saltwater from her body in a shower, suggesting that she wishes to "sanitize" whatever insights she has discovered while swimming. In this she is only partially successful: her back, that aspect of herself that holds her upright in public, is "cleaned" but her front, the side visible to her own eyes, remains unsanitized.

The sudden transition to the drawing room, where she drips water onto the carpet, reminds her that she cannot be her true self in an artificial environment, especially under the disapproving gaze of her colleagues, the well-dressed ladies of the dream.

She then floats up through the house, representing herself, to the roof where she can see the stars, archetypes of higher states of consciousness, and can seize one with her hand. She is still thinking conventionally in wanting to put the star in a pocket, and on waking can still not understand how to put it "under her chest", and so integrate her higher self fully into her conscious life dreamer's successful quest to reclaim life-energy from the depths of the unconscious, and thus deprive unconscious impulses of the power to dominate conscious behaviour.

Other archetypal journeys, such as sea voyages toward the rising sun, can represent rebirth and transformation. Dreams may also involve baptism and other forms of ritual initiation, emergence from the primal depths of a cave, or alchemical archetypes such as the phoenix rising from the flames that destroy the past and leave the dreamer free to create his or her future. Such mythical creatures as the phoenix may not embody primary archetypes in themselves, but may be used by the dreaming mind as representatives of the archetypes. For example, sphinxes in dreams may symbolize the occult wisdom of the archetype of the Great Mother, while the Hindu deity Garuda (half man, half eagle) may stand for the fierce, purifying energy of the Wise Old Man. Jung saw the Dragon, however, as a primary symbol, related to the collective or overbearing social aspect of the Great Mother, who must be slain if the hero is to be free.

One archetype with a profoundly numinous quality is the Spirit, the opposite of matter, sometimes manifested in dreams as an impression of infinity, spaciousness, invisibility. The Spirit may also appear as a ghost, or as a visit from the dead, and its presence often indicates a tension between the material and non-material worlds. Other primary archetypes are described on the following pages.

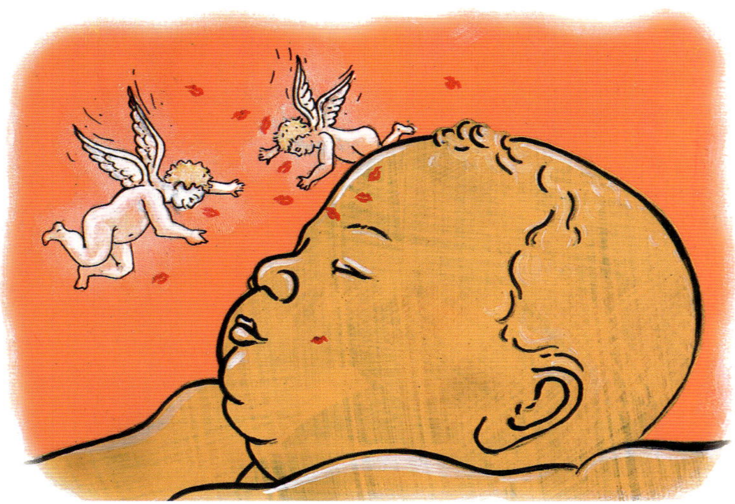

The Persona

The Persona is the way in which we present ourselves to the outside world – the mask that we adopt in order to deal with waking life. Useful and non-pathological in itself, the Persona becomes dangerous if we identify with it too closely, mistaking it for the real self. It can then appear in our dreams as a scarecrow or a tramp, or as a desolate landscape, or as social ostracization. To be naked in dreams often represents loss of the Persona.

The Anima and Animus

Jung's studies and clinical experience convinced him that we each carry within us the whole of human potential, male and female. The Anima represents the "feminine" qualities of moods, reactions and impulses in man, and the Animus the "masculine" qualities of commitments, beliefs and inspirations in woman. More importantly, as the "not-I" within the self, the Anima and Animus serve as *psychopompi*, or soul guides, to the vast areas of our unacknowledged inner potential.

Mythology represents the Anima as maiden goddesses or women of great beauty, such as Athena, Venus and Helen of Troy; while the Animus is symbolized by noble gods or heroes, such as Hermes, Apollo and Herakles. If Anima or Animus appears in our dreams in these exalted forms, or as any other powerful representation of man or woman, it typically means that we need to integrate the male and female within us. If ignored, these archetypes tend to be projected outward into a search for an idealized lover, or are unrealistically ascribed to partners or friends. If we allow them to take possession of our unconscious lives, men can become over-sentimental and over-emotional, while women may show ruthlessness and obstinacy. However, once the process of individuation has begun, these archetypes serve as guides, taking the dreamer deeper and deeper into the realm of inner possibilities.

The Wise Old Man

The Wise Old Man (or Woman) is what Jung called a mana personality, a symbol of a primal source of growth and vitality which can heal or destroy, attract or repel. In dreams this archetype may appear as a magician, doctor, professor, priest, teacher, father, or any other authority figure, who by its presence or teachings conveys the sense that higher states of consciousness are within the dreamer's grasp.

However, like the wizard or the shaman, the mana personality is only quasi-divine, and can lead us away from the higher levels as well as toward them. Jung himself enjoyed a lifelong relationship with a mana personality of his own: he called him Philemon, and frequently passed his days talking and painting with him.

The Trickster

An archetypal antihero, the "ape of God", the Trickster is a psychic amalgam of the animal and the divine. He may appear in dreams, as he does in mythologies around the world, as a monkey, fox, hare or clown.

Jung likened him to the alchemical Mercurius, the shape-shifter, full of sly jokes and malicious pranks. Sometimes seen as an aspect of the Shadow (see opposite), the Trickster will appear mocking himself, but at the same time mocking the pretensions of the ego and its archetypal projection, the Persona.

The Trickster is, in addition, the sinister figure who disrupts our games, exposes our schemes, and spoils our dream pleasure. Like the Shadow, he is a symbol of transformation – indestructible and able to change his shape and disappear and reappear at will. He often turns up when the ego is in a dangerous situation of its own making, through vanity, overarching ambition or misjudgment. He is untamed, amoral and anarchic.

While the Trickster may sabotage our efforts, he may indirectly assist our development by challenging with paradox, and by revealing the absurdity of material possessions.

The Shadow

Jung defines the Shadow as "the thing a person has no wish to be". Everything substantial casts a shadow, and for Jung the human psyche is no exception: "unfortunately there can be no doubt that Man is, on the whole, less good than he wants or imagines himself to be". According to Jung, the more that we repress this side, and isolate it from consciousness, the less chance we have of stopping it from bursting forth "in a moment of awareness".

Concealed under our civilized veneer, the Shadow reveals itself in selfish, violent and often brutal actions. It feeds on greed and fear and can be projected outward as the hate that persecutes and makes scapegoats of minority groups.
In dreams, the Shadow usually appears as a person of the same sex, often in a threatening, nightmarish role. Because the Shadow can never be totally eliminated, it is often represented by dream characters who are impervious to blows and bullets, and who pursue us past every obstacle, and into the blind alleyways and eerie basements of the mind. However, it can also take the form of the brother or sister figure, or the stranger who confronts us with the things we prefer not to see and the words we prefer not to hear.

Because the Shadow is obsessional, autonomous and possessive, it arouses in us strong emotions of fear, anger or moral outrage. Yet Jung insists that it is not evil in itself, merely "somewhat inferior, primitive, unadapted and awkward". Its appearance in dreams indicates a need for more conscious awareness of its existence, and for a more convincing moral effort in coming to terms with its dark energies. We must learn to accept and integrate it because the unpalatable messages it gives us are often indirectly for our own good.

The Divine Child

The Divine Child is the archetype of the regenerative force that leads us toward individuation. It is the symbol of the true self, of the totality of our being, as opposed to the limited and limiting ego which is, in Jung's words, "only a bit of consciousness, and floats upon an ocean of the [hidden] things". In dreams, the Divine Child usually appears as a baby or infant. It is both innocent and vulnerable, yet at the same time inviolate and possessed of transforming power. Contact with the child can strip us of the sense of personal aggrandisement upon which the ego so greedily feeds, and reveal to us how far we have strayed from what once we were and aspired to be.

The Great Mother

The image of the Great Mother plays a vital role in our psychological and spiritual development. Its prevalence in dreams, myths and religion is derived not only from our personal experiences of childhood, but also from the archetype of all that cherishes and fosters growth and fertility on the one hand, and all that dominates, devours, seduces and possesses, on the other.

Not only is the energy of the Great Mother divine, ethereal and virginal, it is also chthonic (generated from the earth) and agricultural: the earth mother was worshipped as bringer of harvests. Always ambivalent, she is an archetype of feminine mystery and power who appears in many forms: at her most exalted as the queen of heaven, at her most consuming as the Sumerian goddess Lilith, the gorgon Medusa, or the witches and harpies of myth and folktale.

For Freud, however, the symbolic dream mother was far more a representation of the dreamer's relationship with his or her own mother than an abstract archetype. Freud observed in fact that most dreams involve three people – the dreamer, a woman and a man – and that the theme that most commonly links the three characters is jealousy. Freud believed that the dream woman and dream man most often represent the dreamer's mother and father, and maintained that they symbolize aspects of the Oedipus and Electra complexes from which men and women respectively suffer. (In Greek myth Oedipus, unaware of his actions, slew his father and married his mother: Freud saw this as symbolizing the early male sexual desire for the mother, and the jealousy of the father. Electra, conversely, desired her father and was jealous of her mother).

The Hero

The Hero is the awakened inner self in both men and women that aspires to inner growth and development, and sets out on a quest for true understanding. The tasks facing the Hero are often symbolized as physical challenges requiring great skill and courage, and often necessitating the help of the Animus (from whom he is at times scarcely distinguishable), the Anima or the Wise Old Man. This archetype may also appear as an antihero – whose mistaken ideals lead him to enter a series of futile adventures from which he emerges with credit, but to no great effect. Whenever a dream involves physical or psychological challenges (fighting adversaries, climbing a sheer rock face, solving a riddle), you can suspect that the Hero is involved.

Working with Archetypes

Archetypes loom large in the collective unconscious and in the realm of dreams. They may go unrecognized by the dreamer, but often their occurrence is indicated by a sense of heightened perception – we may feel a kind of inner resonance when we encounter them.

The universal meaning of any archetype we meet will, of course, interact with subjective associations stemming from our own personal experience. In order to understand an archetypal dream's deeper levels of meaning and specific relevance to the individual, Jung proposed the interpretative method known as "amplification". This involves exploring the myths in which an archetype appears and considering how they might relate to aspects of your own life.

Simply reading mythic stories and reflecting on them in waking life is a good way to prepare yourself. Jung considered Greek myths to be especially suitable for Westerners, although any mythological tradition that appeals to you – Celtic, Egyptian or Hindu myths or European folktales, for example – will be equally appropriate. Some myths may seem intuitively appropriate to your circumstances but all have emerged from the great storehouse of the collective unconscious and will resonate at some level of your experience. The more you familiarize yourself with the mythic repertoire, the easier the process of amplification becomes.

Amplification in practice

Jungian dream amplification typically moves through deepening layers of profundity. For example, if your dream features a knight on horseback, "natural amplification" might lead you to a sense of leadership or combat. Next, you explore "cultural amplification", which might suggest that the knight is a defender of the faith – perhaps your faith in your own abilities. Finally comes archetypal amplification. This might lead you to think of Parsifal, the Arthurian hero who in medieval legend meets the crippled Fisher King and glimpses the Holy Grail. He does not recognize the Grail and fails to ask a question that would have healed the injured king. On learning of his error he undertakes to return to the royal castle and fulfil his quest. He ends up being one of only two knights who accompany Sir Galahad and complete the Grail quest with him. Pondering this tale, you might start to think about how, in life, you failed in a quest, but how in the end you helped someone else to succeed.

Dreaming in Greek

As a preparation for working on your dreams using the Jungian technique of amplification, a helpful first step is to familiarize yourself with the myths of ancient Greece. These form a dramatic body of narrative, with a rich variety of archetypal figures and episodes, often linked together so that the characters – both human and supernatural – drift through each other's stories. Read Robert Graves' masterly source book, *The Greek Myths*, for a detailed overview of the tales.

Two great quests

The voyages of Jason and Odysseus offer a wealth of archetypal meaning. This derives in part from the universal motif of the dangerous journey – whether a homecoming (in Odysseus's case) or the search for a precious object (in Jason's story, the Golden Fleece). But the significance of these quests also draws upon the encounters these heroes have en route – with dragons, giants, seductresses, monstrous one-eyed shepherds, sorcerers, and so on. Jason, for example, wins the Fleece with the help of Medea, a sorceress who falls in love with him: the treasure is guarded by a dragon, but Medea charms the creature with her voice and sprinkles a potion into its eyes.

Hercules' twelve tasks

Another Hero figure is Herakles, or Hercules, famous for his almighty strength. Son of the great god Zeus by a mortal mother, he is given twelve "labours", or tasks, to perform by King Eurystheus of Tiryns, as penance for a terrible murder. The tasks include killing a monstrous lion, vanquishing a nine-headed serpent (the Hydra), and cleaning out the Augean stables piled high with thirty years' worth of dung from 30,000 cattle.

Orpheus in the Underworld

Orpheus was a great musician whose lyre charmed even the animals. He fell in love with a nymph, Eurydice, and married her. Then a serpent bit her on the ankle and she died and was taken to the Underworld. Overcome with grief, Orpheus went to the Underworld, whose king and queen were moved by his pleas. They allowed Eurydice to follow Orpheus back to the land of the living – on condition that he did not look at her before reaching the exit of the Underworld. But Orpheus could not stop himself turning around to see her ... and lost her forever. The story has obvious links with intense love, temptation, loss and human weakness.

Dream Settings

A single dream episode may involve a string of apparently unconnected dream actions, which may take place in a variety of dream locations. These may be realistic or fantastic, or a mixture of the two. Sometimes the dreamer remembers no setting at all – just a featureless space in which the narrative takes place. At other times, the location plays a crucial part in the dream, and may even arouse a strong emotional response: a forest, for example, might be experienced as frightening or threatening, or a house might stimulate feelings of comfort or pride.

Although dream settings may often seem strange or unreal, they are seldom arbitrary: usually, they support or contribute to the overall meaning of the dream, sometimes in unexpected ways. By attending to the setting of a dream, you are more likely to be able to penetrate its meanings.

In fact, dreams are set most often in familiar locations, reflecting the immediate interests and memories of the dreamer. Research has shown the house to be the most common dream location; and, far from implying lack of profundity, we should note that Jung's famous dream of his own house helped to inspire his theory of the collective unconscious, showing how the most apparently mundane scenery can carry a remarkable cargo of symbolic information.

Jung dreamed that he was in a house that was his own yet was unfamiliar. Exploring its many floors, he discovered an ancient cellar, leading down from which was a cave containing pottery,

bones and skulls. He interpreted the cellar as representing the personal unconscious, while the cave he understood to be the collective unconscious – the repository of ageless, archetypal symbols to which all humankind responds.

On the strength of his own experiences, Jung subsequently encouraged his followers to examine the dream scenery that featured in their dreams at progressively deeper levels in order to reveal its symbolic meaning. A tree, for example, that initially represents the cherry tree under which the dreamer played as a child, and which therefore stands for shelter and sweetness, can later in the interpretation serve as a symbol of the mother, later still as the Tree of Life, and finally as the sacrificial tree upon which Christ was crucified. Similarly, a house may be taken progressively to signify the dreamer's body, his mind, his mother's body which once nutured and sheltered him, and even – by a common process of dream punning – his

father's family or "house". Generally, the more creative and imaginative the dreamer, the more likely it is that such progressive levels of meaning will emerge, and that the dream scenery itself will be varied and striking.

Many artists have received their inspiration from the scenery of dreams. Painters such as the Italian Surrealist Giorgio de Chirico (1888–1978) and the Belgian Surrealist Paul Delvaux (1897–1994) are particularly credited with capturing the dream atmosphere, drawing also upon Freudian dream symbolism and setting familiar images in bizarre contexts. It is the juxtaposition of the ordinary and the extraordinary, captured in their paintings, that gives dream scenery its special quality, and that invests nightmares with their chilling power. A house may be the dreamer's own, yet in a nightmare it can appear to be saturated with an eerie emptiness never experienced in waking life.

Frequent shifts of location are characteristic of dreams. The settings may be logically connected, but they may often appear in a disjointed, seemingly random sequence. As with the more obvious foreground elements in a dream, items of dream scenery can also suddenly transform themselves. A sheltered bay may turn into a deep carpet, a distant farm may turn into a slaughterhouse. By means of these reversals, the dream drives its message home, startling

From Scrapyard to Café: a dream setting analyzed

The dreamer is a woman in her late twenties, who holds a responsible and challenging executive position with a firm of realtors (estate agents) in a big city.

The dreamer describes her dream

"This is one of a series of dreams in which I find myself in a scrapyard, surrounded by old and broken objects, or new gadgets that, whatever I do, somehow refuse to work. The scrapyard setting is puzzling, because I have no memory of ever visiting such a place.

"In this dream, I found myself standing at the top of a long flight of steps. They seemed to lead down to a backyard full of rubble and scrap metal, yet the steps themselves were wide and grand, like those in the garden of a château.

"There was a man in the scrapyard working on an old car, and I asked him why it wouldn't go. He said it worked now, he had fixed it, and then we were driving down a freeway, but going so fast that I felt afraid the car would fall to pieces. We stopped outside a café, but there was no one in there to serve us. There were parts of old cars all over the café floor – I tripped over them as I paced the room."

The setting analyzed

Steps downward usually represent a way into the personal unconscious. The dreamer claims to enjoy her dreams, and she has high expectations of what they may reveal to her (the grand stairway), yet in fact the steps lead only to the broken, discarded rubbish of old memories and useless objects.

But things aren't exactly as they seem. There is a man working among the junk in the backyard, perhaps signifying that psychological healing and creative activity continue in the unconscious mind, even though we are usually unaware of them, and that what may seem like psychic rubbish can be of great value, if we approach it in the proper way.

He tells her that he has "fixed" the old car, perhaps symbolic of a disappointed aspiration or ambition. The road on which they speed away together represents escape from the confines of the city (other people). But the car is outside the dreamer's control, and she is afraid. The café might suggest a refuge, but the wreckage of the past is to be found even here. Perhaps working on the problem is preferable to escaping it. The settings of the dream underline this message.

the mind out of conventional habits of thinking so that deep emotions and preoccupations are hauntingly exposed.

Dream landscapes, far from being merely a backdrop to the action, are often deeply experienced in themselves. A landscape may ache with loneliness, or be suffused with a mysterious sense of well-being. If the landscape has gentle contours and evokes strong feelings, one possible interpretation is that it symbolizes the body, especially the mother's body. Freud believed that landscapes in dreams, especially those containing rocky crags (male) or wooded hills (female), often operate as symbols of genitalia. Dream places can also represent the topography of the mind itself: for example, a strange neighbourhood in a remote part of town can be a symbol of the unconscious. Nocturnal scenes, similarly, can suggest the murky depths of the inner self.

It is vital, during interpretation, to remember the details of the dream landscape if the full meaning of the dream is to be revealed. If a scene is set in a garden, is it formal or informal in design? Is it well-kept or overgrown? If there are flowers, how do they smell? If there is a road, does it wind and double back upon itself, or is it long and straight, an easy journey home? Even those parts of the scenery that appear to be mere background can have a significance which may emerge as central when the dream is subjected to thorough analysis.

Ambiguities in the possible meanings of dream settings need to be rigorously explored. For example, if green fields in a dream are bordered by a distant town, does this make the dreamer feel secure to see evidence of civilization nearby, or does it provoke resentment at the man-made intrusion? If the dream shows a cave, could this be a place of shelter if the weather turns bad? Or is it likely that something scary is lurking there?

The circumstances and character of the dreamer will of course be highly relevant to such deliberations. Although unfamiliar surroundings might for one person represent feelings of loss or bewilderment, for another they might signify a desire to travel or to explore. A castle might suggest contented security, or an over-defensive attitude to life. And, of course, it should be borne in mind that the same person is likely to react differently at different times in their life as their circumstances alter.

Dream settings may also be places, insignificant in themselves, where formative or traumatic events occurred, deep in our past. Often our memories of such places will be lost to consciousness, and this may make it difficult for

us to interpret the dream. If puzzled by a dream location, ask yourself whether it is connected with anywhere you once lived or took a vacation. It can help if you describe the setting to another member of your family, who may have clearer memories of your childhood.

Train yourself also to think of landscapes and cityscapes in terms of their underlying symbolism, which works in much the same way as the symbolism of objects. When a dream shows you a mountain, consider the possibility that it might suggest lofty aspiration or an exalted state of being. The forest, like the ocean, can represent the depths of the collective unconscious; but unlike maritime settings, forests also have overtones of refuge – as well as seasonal change if the trees are deciduous. River valleys, which are sometimes read as female sexual symbols, can also suggest fertility and well-being.

People who interpret dreams sometimes neglect the fact that natural features may be subjected to mythic amplification, just like dream characters. Lakes may superficially suggest peace and contemplation, but, the story of Arthur's sword Excalibur lifted from beneath the water by the Lady of the Lake as the king was dying on the lakeside, suggests that they may carry a more melancholy significance.

Children's Dreams

In children's dreams, parents, siblings and teachers tend to loom large, as do friends, who can appear in all their childlike ambivalence – sometimes supportive, sometimes cruelly aggressive. A child's dream world is often characterized by images of insecurity and change, as he or she strives to deal with formidable new experiences.

We are born dreamers. We may even dream in the womb and certainly spend much of our early life in dreams. About sixty per cent of the sleep of newborn babies is passed in the REM (Rapid Eye Movement) state (see page 41) where most dreaming occurs – three times the amount spent by most adults. Since babies sleep for fourteen or more hours a day, this adds up to a great deal of dream time.

Although it is obviously impossible for us to know exactly what small babies dream of, it is probable that much of their dream content is triggered by physical sensations, or consists of dreams about physical sensations. After the first month of their lives, visual and auditory images probably also begin to play a part. Once children are old enough to tell us about their dreams, the content primarily reflects their waking interests and emotions, as we might expect.

Robert Van de Castle and Donna Kramer of the University of Virginia analyzed many hundreds of dreams from children aged between two and twelve, and found that from an early age girls' dreams tended to be longer than those of boys, and contained more people and references to clothes, while boys dreamed more about implements and objects. Animals featured much more prominently in children's dreams than in those of adults, and the ratio of frightening animals such as lions, gorillas, alligators and wolves to non-frightening animals such as sheep, butterflies and birds was far higher. This

frequency of animal images would seem to reflect children's basic interests, but also most probably the way in which animals symbolize their wishes and fears. Van de Castle, however, considers that these themes may also arise from the more primitive, animistic nature of a child's thinking – their closeness to the uncultured self.

Children report around twice as many aggressive acts in their dreams as do adults. Occasionally, children play the role of aggressors, but more usually they are victims, and fear has thus been shown to be their most common dream emotion. Robert Kegan, an American developmental psychologist, has suggested that this high level of aggression represents the difficulty that young children have in integrating their own powerful, spontaneous impulses into the social order and control demanded of them by adults. The wild animals and bogeymen of children's dreams also seem to symbolize children's inner awareness that such impulses lurk just below the conscious surface of their behaviour and may break out and wreak havoc in the conscious mind if self-control is relaxed.

The Exploding Truck: a child's dream

The dreamer is an eight-year-old girl who is having problems with her teacher at school. This dream took place after a school trip to a science museum, which the teacher claims the child did not enjoy.

The dreamer describes her dream

"There was a big truck with a boiler thing behind it outside the school, and my teacher said she thought it was going to explode.

"A man got out of the truck and came toward me, and I was scared and ran away. Then I was in the car with my daddy. We were driving away from this man, and my daddy went through a red stop light and up on the pavement but there was nobody there. Then someone came up to us and said that the thing had exploded, and my daddy said we must go back to the school and see what had happened. But I didn't want to go back there."

The interpretation

Children's dreams tend to be more episodic and fragmented than those of adults. This reflects their more limited experience, but may also be caused by memory failure or a tendency to run several dreams into one. It is a mistake to impose an outside, adult interpretation on children's dreams; instead, children must be helped to find their own associations and draw their own conclusions.

This girl has been having problems with her teacher, which she is unable to communicate to her parents. In the dream, the threatened explosion outside the school is clearly associated with the teacher ("my teacher said ... "), and may represent what appears to the child as the teacher's unpredictable outbursts of anger. The image of a boiler to symbolize anger may emerge from the visit to the science museum, and may also originate from the cliché "to boil over with rage". The threatening man who looms toward her from the truck may symbolize the fear she has of her teacher, and her wish to escape from her.

She relies on her father to make good her escape ("then I was in the car with my daddy"), but knows that he can only do so by breaking the rules of the adult world: jumping a red stop light. But his efforts come to nothing. As soon as he hears of the teacher's anger ("someone said that the thing had exploded"), he decides that they must return to school, the scene of the child's problems. She must learn to accept the adult world that her teacher both embodies and symbolizes.

For Kegan, the common experience in children's dreams of being eaten alive is particularly significant, since it represents a terror of losing an emerging yet fragile sense of self in the face of powerful conflicts between inner impulses and outer demands. In psychoanalytical theory, as well as representing aspects of the dreamer's self, the bogeymen of children's dreams can also symbolize parents and other powerful adults. A young child has serious problems in consciously reconciling the loving, providing aspects of a mother or father with their function as agents of discipline and reprimand. Dream witches and wolves are ways of representing and accepting the punitive role that parents play, while the child's own acts of aggression toward parental symbols in dreams can symbolize rivalry directed toward the same-sex parent, or simply their wish to be free of the dominating force that adults exercise in daily life.

Freud laid particular emphasis upon this last, wish-fulfilling, aspect of children's dreaming, so much so in fact that he considered that children's dreams "raise no problems for solution" and are "quite uninteresting compared to the dreams of adults". He believed that a child's relative lack of sexual desire during the so-called "latency" period (approximately age seven to puberty) simplifies the nature of their wish-fulfilment during this time, leaving the way clear for "the other of the two great vital instincts" to assert itself – desire for food.

Jungian psychology, however, claims a level of interpretation for children's dreams that goes beyond that of wishes and desires, recognizing in the bogeyman, hero and heroine the archetypal images already activated in the child's unconscious, and symbolizing not only aspects of waking life but also the child's mystical sense of his or her own inner nature.

Anthropologists have identified several cultures in which childhood dreaming is allowed by society to play a far stronger role in children's psychological development. While researching among the Temiar people of Indonesia, Richard Noone and Kilton Stewart discovered that children were routinely asked to recount their dreams each morning so that the adults of the group could "train" them to deal with their dream fears and challenges in order to enhance their psychological development during sleep.

Joan Halifax, among several anthropologists interested in tribal attitudes to dreams, has emphasized the crucially important part that dreams play, sometimes from as early as five years old, in the life and training of the shaman, by helping him to deal with the spirit world.

So strong is the belief in the creative power of dreaming among Australian shamanic cultures that children are taught that the world itself was brought into being during the "Dreamtime".

However the images, events and symbols of childhood dreams are understood, there is little doubt that these dreams play a vital role in the psychological development of children, and that they can have a powerful influence upon what happens in the years to come.

As adults we may not dream any more with the intensity that children dream – or not so often. But those early dreams can resurface from time to time, taking us by surprise.

Helping Children with Nightmares

Never say that a nightmare was "only a dream" – it is important not to trivialize dream experiences. Listen to the child's fears, comfort him or her gently and then explain that the monsters we meet in dreams don't really mean to frighten us. Help the child to create a dream helper, who will win unpleasant dream creatures over to their side, or help him or her to confront them.

1. Talk to the child about who they would like to help them in their dreams – it might be a character from a fairy story or a favourite book, a figure who has appeared in their dreams before or, very possibly, an animal.

2. Ask the child to describe their helper – what they look like, what qualities they have and how they might chase off or transform the monsters that appear in their nightmares.

3. Now ask the child to imagine that they are back in the dream and to summon their dream helper there with them. In their imagination they can call on their helper and ask them to assist in chasing the demons away. Talk through the process with them and reassure them that this is exactly what will happen next time they fall asleep.

Helping Children to Learn from their Dreams

As children grow, they pass through a series of developmental stages, each of which helps a different, specialized kind of learning to take place. It is important to grasp these opportunities because it becomes much harder to learn as we get older. The ability to dream is a case in point. If we encourage our children to remember and heed their dreams early in life, while still open-minded, we can save them much effort when they are older.

Children can follow much the same procedures as adults – from keeping a dream diary to using a helper to deal with nightmares (see opposite). Parents, and other adults close to children, can help them by following a few simple guidelines.

- Invite children to tell you their dreams, and find time to listen carefully. Children always learn what is important from the significant adults in their lives.
- Resist the temptation to say to children that their dreams are "silly" – instead, reassure them that their dreams, and their feelings about them, really do matter.
- Confidently suggest to children that they can influence their dreams. This ability depends upon the conviction that it can be done, so try not to sow any doubts in young minds, while at the same time avoiding giving the impression that lucid dreaming is guaranteed.
- Tell children your own dreams – provided that they are not too disturbing. They will love to hear them, and if you follow the habit of exchanging dreams with your kids from time to time, they will no doubt find this an enjoyable and fascinating treat.
- Don't try too hard to interpret children's dreams. Welcome them, rather than worrying that their dreams reveal parts of themselves that they don't understand. You might, however, explain that a dream event can stand for something else. There is no harm in asking, "What do you think this stands for?" or "What do you think this might mean?"
- If the child is really interested in exploring the meaning of dreams, use fairy stories, which have the same archetypal quality as myths and legends, to provide amplification (see page 108). For example, Cinderella is a story of goodness triumphing over evil and of the transforming power of grace. Jack and the Beanstalk demonstrates that a pure heart can bring greater rewards than materialism, and demonstrates the value of courage; it also shows the power of the mind.

Working WITH DREAMS

To obtain the full benefits of a rich and illuminating dream life, there are certain skills we need to obtain – starting with basic techniques to ensure that our dreams do not simply slip away into oblivion, forgotten the next morning. There are a number of methods you can apply to improve your dream recall. It is important to keep a dream diary or notebook, not only to jot down your dreams as soon as possible after they have taken place, but also as a place to record your interpretations. This section covers this and other approaches to dream recall and also offers some practical tips on how you can prompt dreams – even, if you are lucky, dreams on specific subjects of your own choosing.

The Art of Recall

The first stage of working with dreams is the art of remembering them. Many people claim never to recall their dreams, and some deny having dreams at all. However, with practice, and the right technique, it is not unusual for people to remember several dreams each morning.

Start with a positive attitude. Remembering dreams is a habit, and can be cultivated. The best way is to tell yourself during the day that you will remember your dreams of that coming night, and upon awakening next morning lie still for a while, focusing your conscious mind on whatever images, thoughts or emotions have emerged from your sleep. Contemplate these perceptions to see if they prompt dream recall.

Keeping a dream diary makes it possible to build up a detailed, sustained picture of your dream life. Write down (or sketch) everything you can remember – small details as well as main themes – and make a note of any emotions or associations that emerge from the dream's contents. During the day, think back to the dream of the night before, even if its details have faded, and try to relive the emotions associated with it. Reread your notes and be patient: it may take weeks or months before you regularly remember your dreams, but success will come if you persevere. To speed things up, occasionally set an alarm clock for about two hours after you usually fall asleep: you will stand a good chance of awakening immediately after the first, dream-laden period of REM sleep.

Some dream researchers advise subjects to collect at least a hundred dreams before starting analysis, as it may take this length of time before the common themes emerge coherently. It is always worth searching for connections with the

events of the day, but remember: the dream has a reason for choosing these events, and may be using them to symbolize deeper material. Note anything significant about these events and any memories that they spark off. Such memories may lead back to long-forgotten experiences to which the dream is trying, in its own symbolic way, to draw your attention.

Dreams are elusive. Scientific experiments have shown that a dreamer who is awakened as a dream comes to an end will recall roughly eighty per cent of its events. After only eight minutes, recollection falls to around thirty per cent. Over time the dreamer may be left with only five per cent recall or may even lose the dream altogether.

Each of us dreams, but we may not be aware of it. Only by developing our powers of dream recall can we begin to recognize the fullness of our dream life and interact with the dream process to enhance our self-understanding.

A marked difference exists between our recollections of real-life events and those of our dream life. To remember reality, we must exercise memory; to recall our dreams, we must relax the rational operation of memory to allow for the peculiar characteristics of the dream world – incongruities, disconnected narratives, and even subjects that would normally be seen as morally taboo.

The key to dream recall is wanting to remember. A defence mechanism of the conscious mind automatically protects us against memories that may be shocking or distressing. We do not consciously tamper with our dreams, but our process of recollection can in itself act as a censor, so that we unwittingly distort our dream memories to insulate ourselves. As Sigmund Freud noted, dream amnesia may be a repressive defence of the ego. If we can train our minds to develop a more positive attitude toward our dreams, accepting whatever strange encounters come along in a spirit of inner discovery, then we can recapture some of the content that otherwise eludes us.

The possibility that we have been programmed to exclude dreams from our consciousness is another psychological obstacle that may prevent us from remembering them. Repression, the mind's in-built defence mechanism, is designed to cushion us against memories, desires or fears too painful or troubling to be admitted into our consciousness. Material of this kind may be associated with childhood or adolescent traumas or with thoughts or actions that we have been taught make us bad or unlovable. It may relate to socially uncomfortable drives such as sex, or to unrealistic aspirations and hopes that we once entertained but have now had to admit will never be realized.

This is the kind of intimate subject matter that can emerge in dreams, only to be expelled or locked away by the mind at the moment of waking. If we can bring such experiences into consciousness, we may be able to learn much from them. A high proportion of this material is much less damaging and more natural than it might seem (even though it may have been wrongly labelled bad by others before we were old enough to form our own opinion); the rest needs to be recognized and laid to rest.

Catching dreams requires us to be as serene and patient as possible. The best rod fishermen

Memory Training for Dream Recall

Remembering your real life and remembering your dream life are completely different processes. However, your dream recall will certainly benefit from any improvement you can bring to your waking memory. Use the following techniques and exercises to stretch your memory's capacities.

Changing rooms

Closely observe all the contents of the room that you are in, and then go out of it. Ask a friend to make a small change to the room – perhaps by repositioning an ornament or a small piece of furniture, or by introducing something new, like a bowl of fruit or a vase. Now go back into the room and try to spot the change. With practice, you should be able to detect even the tiniest of differences.

The memory house

Train yourself to remember shopping lists, rather than writing them down. There is a way to do this that draws upon time-honoured memory techniques, practised in ancient Greece and Rome. Let's say you have ten items to remember. What you do is identify ten stages or rooms on a walk around your house, starting with the front door. If you don't have enough rooms, use areas of the garden as well if you wish – for example, the shed or gazebo and the compost heap or rockery. Fix these stages in your mind, in a particular, logical order. Then go through your shopping list and allocate each item to each successive stage or room in turn, visualizing each of the items in position there. Use surreal associations to link the item clearly with that part of the house. For example, if you are at the front door and the first thing on your list is toothpaste, imagine cleaning your teeth using the mailbox flap as a mirror. Continue through the house until every item has been placed somewhere. Later, in the store, when the times comes to remember your list, imagine yourself walking through the house in exactly the same way. At each stage ask yourself what you placed there. The memories should come flooding back.

•

Although we cannot use memory exercises and techniques (check out the books of memory champion Dominic O'Brien to find more of them) directly to remember dreams, they do have positive benefits for dream work. Using them keeps your memory supple and strong, and enlarges its capacity – rather as physical exercise increases your bodily abilities.

remain totally calm, but they are observant and quick to cast when they see fish rising. When a dream breaks into consciousness, the fisher of dreams must hook it quickly into memory before it plunges back into the murky depths of the unconscious mind.

You can aid your memory by keeping a dream journal permanently by your bedside. If, one morning, you find that your dreams are especially vivid, try to work out why: are there variables, such as the softness of the pillows, the temperature of the room, or some change in your evening routine, that might be responsible? Experiment to find the ideal conditions for eventful sleep.

Dreams offer a route to self-understanding, so why do we forget them at all? Almost certainly, the stresses and strains of everyday living – the anxieties that rush back into consciousness upon waking – deaden our dream recollections. Those Hindu and Buddhist adepts who are said to enjoy unbroken consciousness (see page 46) while sleeping recollect easily the entirety of their dreams. This clarity would seem to result from their mastery of concentration through meditation techniques. If we can learn, similarly, to clear our minds of unnecessary tensions, we may go some way toward sharpening our own awareness of our rich interior lives.

Other theories suggest that the manner of our waking allows our dream memories to fade during the hypnopompic (drowsy) state. Or that we sleep too much, and so sandwich dreamful sleep between periods of deep oblivion.

Perhaps the predominant reason that we forget our dreams is that we do not regard them as worthy subjects for our attention. In contrast to other cultures and eras, the contemporary Western lifestyle fails to recognize the power of dreams. It would be unthinkable for a Lapp reindeer herder or a Xhosa tribesman to say that he or she never dreamed, or that he tended to forget his dreams. He would have learned of their significance in childhood, especially as a pathway enabling him to get closer to the world of the spirits. Most Westerners, however, are still brought up to believe that dreams serve no real purpose and should not be taken too seriously.

The transfer of material from the unconscious world of sleep to conscious waking life is a

A Vivid Dream, Rooted in Childhood

Dreams from childhood tend to be very memorable, because they are deep-rooted and disturbing. Sometimes such dreams push other, less dramatic dreams out of our minds – until we have exorcised them by accurate interpretation. Here the dreamer is a female athlete, successful and single-minded on the track, but less adept in handling her relationships and wider social life.

The dreamer describes her dream

"It was summer and I was standing on an open road stretching to the horizon. I could feel the hot sun on the back of my neck. Then I saw someone approaching in the distance, and realized that, though they were running, they were moving in terrifying slow-motion. I was rooted to the spot and everything went deathly cold. Then somehow I was sitting on the back of a horse, but it just kept eating the grass, and refused to move. I dug my heels in, but they just sank into its sides and some horrible stuff came out. Then I was suddenly chasing someone, determined to catch them and teach them a lesson for giving me these nightmares. I don't know if it was a man or a woman, but I ran down a long, high-ceilinged corridor, with very high, dusty windows. The creature ran into a room at the end of the corridor, and I thought, 'Now I've got you'; but when I ran into the room the door slammed and locked behind me, and the creature turned a horrible face toward me and screeched in triumph. I woke sweating and shaking."

The interpretation

This is one of the strangely "real" nightmares that have plagued the dreamer since childhood. They typically start with a man or woman running in menacing slow motion. As an athlete, the dreamer can usually "solve" her problems by running faster than her opponents, but in her dream she is unable to escape. She herself interpreted this as her powerlessness when dealing with others. The horse may represent the force of her emotions, which prevent her from forming a stable relationship. Only "horrible stuff" emerges. The horse/corridor is a symbol for her emotional dysfunction: the high windows prevent her from seeing her life in a broader perspective. The final, claustrophobic horror means that "I lead myself into my own difficulties; I am my own worst enemy."

delicate process. It can easily be disrupted by a conscious mind that refuses to acknowledge that the exercise is worthwhile. However, as soon as we start wanting to remember our dreams, we are on the road to succeeding.

A relaxed approach to dream recall, coupled with a hunter's alertness to any signs of dreaming, can not only reverse dream amnesia, but also promote better sleep, calmer dreams and even lucid dreaming (see pages 55–64). Consider what you really feel about dreaming and try to eliminate any negative associations that you have, such as the plague of childhood nightmares. Negative attitudes toward the activity of dreaming can themselves impede recall. There may be deep-seated unconscious reasons why you forget what you have dreamed. Maybe you fear the power of unpleasant dreams. Or you might feel that it is self-indulgent to be interested in dreams, or that paying attention to them may make you less effective in waking life.

Tell yourself that your dreams are helpful, and that you will begin to remember them; make an effort to welcome what your dreams can teach you about yourself, and keep in mind the power of dreams to help you to become a more fulfilled and effective human being. Such affirmations, delivered with confidence, are particularly effective last thing at night. The unconscious is immediately aware of any doubt in our conscious minds, and all too often responds to this uncertainty rather than to the message. Sincerely believe that you can remember your dreams, and you will find that your dream memory becomes far more accurate.

On a physical level, try to sleep on a harder bed or in a different room, or simply change the position of your bed – these alterations may be enough to trigger an alertness that comfort and habit can weaken over time.

Above all, use the power of creative visualization to increase your chances of remembering your dreams. Before you go to bed, spend some time in a chair in your bedroom. Clear your mind of its cluttered thoughts. Then visualize intently the experience of waking up next morning. Imagine the scene in vivid detail: the light through your eyelids, your first view of the room, the feel of the sheets or duvet – whatever is normal to your experience. Weave into this composite image the recollection of your dream. Affirm that you will dream and that you will certainly remember your dream. When morning comes, mentally applaud your unconscious for its efforts. The mind responds surprisingly well to the combination of confident insistence and praise.

Keeping a Dream Diary

The dream diary is an established genre of self-exploration. Many great writers have kept a notebook by the bed to record whatever they could remember of their nighttime adventures of the unconscious. Add drawings and interpretation notes and you will have a fascinating workbook of the inner self.

Whatever methods you use to help you to remember your dreams, a dream diary is essential. Keep a pen and notebook by your pillow, and write in it as soon as you wake each morning. Make as little other physical movement as possible – even turning over in bed can banish dream memories. Don't delay your writing until later: even the most vivid dreams will quickly fade or become distorted in detail.

There are many different ways of keeping a dream diary. Some writers suggest having separate columns for events, characters, colours and emotions, but categorizing memories during recall can be another way of losing them. The best approach is probably to keep the layout simple and open. Use a medium-sized notebook, not a pocket-sized one, because it's good if you can confine all your material to a single double-page – that way you can ponder the whole dream and your first thoughts about it more easily. You might try writing the dreams on the left-hand pages and reserving the right-hand page for interpretations, comments, sketches and any subsequent analysis.

Make sure that each entry is dated, and that as much detail as possible is recorded – sometimes the most apparently insignificant aspects of a dream turn out to be the most revealing. Write in the present tense: try to relive the dream as you record it, and make a careful note of your emotions. On the facing page is a typical entry.

Monday, October 8th

Very vivid, bright colours, woke up with feeling of frustration, even anger

I am in a toy store, surrounded by old-fashioned toys. I buy a box of large wooden soldiers with red coats, but when I take them to the counter to pay, the assistant tells me that they aren't for sale. His face is in shadow, but I notice his black clothes, with triangular wing collar. Instead of the soldiers, he asks me to choose a book from a large bookshelf which I have not previously noticed. Feeling disappointed, I take a book at random, and turn the pages. It is full of pictures, and one of them shows a box of wooden soldiers. I'm annoyed, because the man has tricked me. He didn't even bother to say hello.

Interpretation notes:

Is this about childhood – always wanting more toys than Mom and Dad could afford? Why the old-fashioned setting? – like a Victorian toy museum. Could it be about grandparents? They were keen that I study, and they always gave me a book for birthdays and Christmas – usually an inappropriate one. Related to Sarah [the dreamer's wife] thinking I should read more? Who could the toyseller represent? Work connections?

Your Dream Sketchbook

Even if you would claim no artistic skills for yourself at all, a sketch can often catch the mood of a dream more successfully than a written entry. In any case, making notes immediately after you have roused yourself from sleep requires you to make a mental adjustment that can sometimes interpose itself between you and your dream – it all depends on how natural a writer you are. Some people find they can do a sketch without losing touch with the experience.

- Even hasty doodles in your dream diary will help you to record and remember your dreams. However, for more detailed depictions it's a good idea to keep a separate sketch book.

- Artistic ability is not important in the dream sketch book: what really matters is that you sincerely attempt to convey the emotional feel and atmosphere of the dream. The very process of sketching your dreams may trigger further dream recall.

- Simplify your drawing, even to the point of being diagrammatic. For example, it is best to render human beings as stick people. Often their clothes are more important than their features, and clothes are not too difficult to draw. Animals can be represented in a similar way. Familiar features such as trees and trains are also easy. Do not worry at all about getting the perspective right. However, do take account of scale – one person might be bigger than another because he or she looms larger in your life. If anyone speaks in your dream, write their words in a speech bubble, as if drawing a cartoon.

- The resulting sketch is likely to end up looking like a child's drawing. Do not be embarrassed by this: remember that children are closer to the inner life of the unconscious than we are, because there has been less time for a cultural overlay to be imposed.

- As an alternative to simple pictorial representation, you could try summarizing your dream as a diagram. Place the most significant or unusual feature at the centre of the page, and arrange any subsidiary symbols around it. Use arrows to indicate movement or action. Pondering the diagram as a whole can be a helpful starting-point for interpretation.

How to Encourage Dreams

Each of us has the ability to dream imaginatively and vividly. If our dream life seems barren, we can use numerous techniques to encourage it to blossom. By experimenting with various adjustments in the bedroom, such as moving the furniture around or varying the temperature, as well as by visualization, it is often possible to enrich our dream life to a surprising degree. In time, we can even learn, through auto-suggestion, to guide our unconscious minds into realms of our own choosing.

The circumstances of sleep have a crucial effect on the likelihood of your having a dream. Avoid alcohol and stimulants just before bedtime, but do have a soothing beverage, such as cocoa, if you wish. Ensure that the bedroom is a pleasant, comfortable environment – and perhaps one decorated with objects (ornaments, photographs, mementos and so on) that have personal significance for you. If you find dreams elusive, try varying some aspect of the room, or try sleeping in a different position.

Dreams are essentially visual experiences, so to realize the full potential of dreams for self-enlightenment it is useful to cultivate the art of visualization. For many people, this means rediscovering an ability that has been lost to them since childhood. We may think that we look at the world perceptively, but many of us do not: instead we attend to the world's surfaces with only half our attention, relying on habit and automatism to get by.

As an introductory exercise, try staring, without blinking, at an object or a scene. Close your eyes, but keep the image in your mind, remembering as much detail as you can – watch as it lingers in your imagination. If you find that the image remains rather vague, open your eyes and remind yourself of the details. Then close your eyes and try again. If you find this exercise difficult, choose a simple object such as a lighted candle, building up to more complex visualizations once you have mastered the basic approach. By training our consciousness in this way, and practising visualization exercises before we sleep, we can help our unconscious to dream about particular themes or images. As we sleep, these topics may vividly and memorably play themselves out.

To incubate a particular dream, you need to visualize carefully chosen cues – perhaps the architecture of a house or a significant landscape, or a loved one's face. You could even consider collecting cues in physical form by the bedside. Through these mental devices, we might, for example, incubate a dream of someone who is separated from us by distance – having a photograph of them by your bed, or perhaps a ring or scarf or something you have used together, like a chess set or camera or maybe a book or an old theatre programme, might help to produce results.

Meditation, by cultivating concentration and receptivity and making space for "leakages from the unconscious", can help us to have more fulfilling and revealing dream experiences, as well as paving the way for more vivid dream recall. Furthermore, the meditative state can even encourage lucid dreaming (see pages 55–64).

Deep meditation produces a state of mind akin to that of sleep. The breathing slows, the pulse rate drops, oxygen consumption is reduced and the patterns produced by our brainwaves become more regular. This provides a mental space free from stimulation, a forum for creative imaginings. There may even be fantastical visions, similar to those in hypnagogia (see pages 50–54). In REM sleep the mind is actively dreaming, while the body is still – also a characteristic of meditation. Some people, at advanced levels of spirituality, are able to meditate in place of sleep.

Meditation allows the mind to free itself from immediate concerns. If you have never meditated before, begin with a basic breathing meditation. Sit comfortably in a quiet room. Relax your body by tensing and then releasing its various muscle groups in turn – starting with the toes and moving upward. Fix your attention on your breath, focusing your awareness on your nostrils and experiencing the sensations of breathing in and breathing out. If your attention wanders, concentrate again by mentally

counting one as you inhale, two as you exhale. Don't worry if your thoughts keep wandering: daily practice will make it increasingly easy to control your attention.

Various other techniques can help you to concentrate and attain a meditative state. You can repeatedly and rhythmically speak a word or phrase (mantra) that has no connotations for you. Or you can recite a verse of poetry or a prayer, or visualize an image – perhaps a geometric form such as the mandala used in Eastern meditation, symbolizing wholeness. Authentic mandalas tend to be too esoteric in their symbolism to be of use to any but the committed meditator. However, that is no reason for you not to try meditating on abstract geometrical shapes, even quite complex ones. Do not worry about the symbolism: simply take the image into your mind and let it rest there with your eyes open. Subtly, this process will help to open out your mind and make it more receptive to experiences such as dreams.

More specifically, by meditating on an image that has already emerged in your dream life, you may be able to encourage dreams that develop the idea embodied by this image.

As we have seen in connection with the art of dream recall (see pages 126–133), an invaluable technique for dream-life enhancement is "creative visualization", which is based on the idea that by giving imaginary visual form to our hopes and desires, we may help them to be realized. During a breathing meditation you might visualize your conscious self peeling itself away from your body and crossing over the room to sit in a chair opposite you. Then you might imagine this conscious self moving into the space of the unconscious mind and unlocking the doors leading into your dreams, which it is then seemingly free to explore. All the time, you are controlling the action of your phantom consciousness as it makes its discoveries. It is entirely possible that this control will be absorbed subliminally into your dream life, so that you will be able to make a conscious choice to have a dream that night – with reasonable confidence that such a dream will take place.

The Gates of Ivory and Horn

The ancient Greeks believed that the gods sent true dreams to us through gates of horn, while less meaningful dreams emerged through gates of ivory. Before sleeping, the dreamer would ask his or her chosen god for favourable dreams. You can perform a similar exercise, using the Greek gods to represent your psychic energies. Conjure in your mind an image of the gates of horn, and choose one of the gods – perhaps Apollo, god of the arts, or Aphrodite, goddess of love. Imagine the deity sending you dreams of creative wisdom, inner harmony and well-being.

Contacting the Unconscious

As you progress with your dream work, delving into dream symbols and archetypes and making discoveries about your inner self, the unconscious becomes, in a sense, your companion. It acts as both object and ally of your researches. Your aim is to coax it into giving you the benefits of its insights through dreams that are rich and revealing.

While doing this, however, you must bear in mind that it has its own way of operating, which is very different from that of the conscious mind. The latter is generally rational, logical and linear; it seeks out patterns and relationships, thrives on consistency and predictability, thinks principally in terms of words, and can readily test itself on what it has learned. The unconscious, on the other hand, is much more unruly in its operations. It tends to be stubborn and wilful, and to behave in a manner that is inconsistent and unpredictable. Sometimes it obstinately refuses to cooperate: we are all familiar with the way our minds can lay an anxiety to rest, while our emotions, prompted by the unconscious, continue to worry away.

It would be unrealistic to expect the unconscious to respond to us with an attitude of reasonable compliance. Even after a long period

of determined work on our part, it may apparently fail to yield any insights, or indeed any dreams at all – only to reward us when we least expect it with the result that we have been seeking. It is important to be patient, and not to waver in your belief that the unconscious will perform for you.

The unconscious does, however, resemble the conscious mind in that it responds well to praise. You must befriend it, letting it know how much you value it. Reward it verbally and with warm feelings for the dreams it gives you, and make sure that you thank it for any improvement you see in your dream life. Ask what further help you can give to it, and wait in silence for the answers it provides.

Never regard actions of this kind as fanciful. Eventually, they can become an effective aid to your self-integration, producing a range of psychological benefits as well as improvements in dreaming.

The best way to approach the unconscious is through simplicity and repetition. Give it instructions that are clear and unambiguous, such as "I am going to remember my dreams", or "I am going to dream about my change of career", or even "I am going to fly in my dreams." Repeat such affirmations frequently during the day.

In the evening, listen to music which you feel echoes or represents the dream mood you wish to experience; read romantic or mystical poetry, visualizing its symbols and pondering the deep metaphors involved. Watch and listen as your

Inducing Creative Dreams

Many writers, painters and musicians use their dream life as a source of inspiration. There is probably something self-fulfilling about this process. The excitement generated by a dream that "wants" to turn itself into art alerts the unconscious to a rich and rewarding seam of the self. It is as if the unconscious has been given a new playground – inevitably it will choose to return there.

Shamanic Dream Practice

Shamans induce dreams in order to gain important insights from the spirit world – insights they can use to heal the sick, guide hunters to their prey and learn the destiny of their tribe. In their tents or huts, or just outside, they perform special rituals to ease the transformation to another realm. Devising your own neo-shamanic dream ritual is a good way to deepen your relationship with your unconscious.

- Incense is a safe, pleasant and practical way to provide smoke for a harmless ritual to arouse the creative imagination. Light an incense stick and hold it successively toward each of the four points of the compass, representing the four elements: in your mind, link East with air, South with fire, West with water, and North with earth. Hold the stick high toward the sky (in shamanic traditions, representing the father) and then toward the earth (representing the mother).
- Devise your own visualization and form of words to accompany each of these movements, asking for dreams to be sent from the four directions, and from the sky above and the earth beneath.

mind learns to absorb impressions. Resist the temptation to reduce these impressions to the level of rational, linear thought by expressing them as words.

Contemplating archetypal themes in literature, such as the story of desire and enthralment recounted by Keats in his poem "La Belle Dame Sans Merci", can bring benefits to our dream lives.

It may be helpful to think of the unconscious as the source of your psychological life, and to see the conscious mind as a kind of overlay that filters the unconscious through learning and experience. The more rigid and inflexible the conscious mind becomes, the more thoroughly it prevents the energy of the unconscious from emerging into awareness.

We can also encourage the different aspects of the mind to work in unison by employing a simple visual metaphor. Visualize the conscious mind as a staid, puritanical doorkeeper holding shut the door through which the unconscious is vainly trying to enter. Now imagine the conscious mind opening the door and greeting the unconscious as a long-lost brother or sister, and watch as the two aspects of the mind agree that they both have much to learn from each other. Feel certain that from now on, they will work together in harmony.

Inspiration from dreams can help us to carry out an essential task of creativity: playing with our ideas, trying them for size and rearranging them until they make a coherent whole.

Dreams in View: a parable

Imagine going to the theatre to watch a play, but being shown to a bad seat, far from the stage and behind a pillar. You have a limited view, and are able to take in only fragments of the action. You find that you can make little sense of the play. The next week you pay another visit to the theatre. The play is different this time, but your seat is the same. You try on one more occasion – perhaps you have just been unlucky. But again your evening is disappointing. You are tempted to give up, vowing never to visit the theatre again.

However, theatre-goers who have been to the same plays but have had a better view of what was going on insist that their experiences have been worthwhile, telling you of the beauty and interest of what they have seen.

If you have followed the advice of this chapter, you will have gained for yourself a prime seat in the nightly theatre of sleep. You are now ready to make some significant discoveries about yourself.

Dissolving the Mental Wall

During sleep, our dream selves travel freely through our inner world of the unconscious. The visualization below, based on time-honoured techniques employed in both Eastern and Western traditions, is designed to open up our waking selves to the unhindered creativity of the dream world.

1. Imagine yourself looking out of a window in a stone tower. You see two different types of terrain, with a high stone wall between them. One landscape is the familiar realm of everyday reality. The other is the landscape of the dream world, where the laws of nature and logic are suspended.

2. Imagine the power of your own thought making a breach in the wall – as if a storm had battered it. Through this hole the atoms and molecules of the dream landscape start to flow into the everyday landscape. It is like an invasion of the energies of dreaming.

3. Now imagine the wall between the two landscapes dissolving altogether. What you see is one parish, full of wonders and surprises. You live in your tower, but you can appreciate the landscape beyond.

Dream Sharing

A dream is a very personal experience, and it takes a certain amount of boldness to discuss its symbolism honestly with someone else. The effort, however, is worthwhile. A co-worker in your interpretation can, by their mere presence, prompt you to surprising insights. And if they are skilled, they can help to coax significant revelations into the open.

Most of us, at one time or another, have related a dream to another person. The motivations behind such dream reports are many and various: we may describe our dreams simply to shock or to entertain; or perhaps we seek fresh perspectives on a dream experience that we think might be meaningful; or ultimately we may be seeking confirmation of our own interpretation. However, there is another, more basic function served by dream talk, and that is to help us arrive at a truer understanding of what has actually taken place: by setting ourselves the task of description, we are encouraged to relive the dream as accurately as possible.

Sharing a dream with a friend or partner can also open up a whole world of insights into our inner lives, as we listen to ourselves translating the dream into a narrative. Our own ideas about its meaning, combined with those of our friend, can take us in unforeseen directions as the dialogue develops. It is good to have such conversations as soon as possible after the dream experience, to retain vivid sensations and deeply felt moods. Try to get into the habit of thinking that your dream is recent news, hot off the press of the imagination – akin to what you did last night, only much more personal.

When listening to a friend's dream account, remember that profound sensitivities may be exposed. Even if the dream is being told in a spirit of playfulness, the true motive may be to open up an intimate dialogue, or to elicit your advice on a troubling subject. Conversely, if you are the narrator, do not be tempted to disguise the dialogue as a joke if what you are really looking for is a thoughtful, sensitive reaction.

Your dreams are a deeply personal part of your life, and it follows that you should think twice before using them to entertain mere acquaintances. After observing the ways in which his patients would revise their dreams when recounting them during psychoanalysis, Sigmund Freud identified a process that he termed "secondary revision". This refers to the dreamer's tendency to distort dreams as he or she recollects them, to make them more coherent and consistent and to impose a spurious order upon the outpourings of the unconscious.

Prepare for dream talk by mutually undertaking a vow of honesty. Make it clear that you will present the dream in all its untidiness, rounding off no rough corners. Avoid the temptation of trying to bridge any gaps in logic through the exercise of waking imagination.

Start by recounting the dream, trying to recall as much as you can. Next, give your emotional reactions to the dream and its setting. Did you behave as your waking self would have done? If the dream was unfinished, how would you have liked it to end? If it was unsatisfactory in some way, what improvements would you have liked? You can then generate direct associations from the most potent images and events of the dream, and perhaps lead into a discussion of possible overall interpretations.

When listening to others, the important thing is to help the dreamer to remember his or her dreams as fully as possible. Use open questions – such as "How did you feel about this event or character?" or "How would you like the dream to have ended?" – to help your subject to uncover interpretations. Feel free to suggest some ideas of your own, but always express them as questions. For example: "That suggests so-and-so to me; does that make sense?" Never forget that it is the other person's dream, and that in the end, only he or she can interpret it.

Dream Meetings

The idea of arranging to meet a friend in a dream may strike you as extremely fanciful or surreal – indeed, there has been at least one Hollywood science fiction movie that incorporates the notion. However, someone with a high level of self-awareness and mental control should find dream meetings perfectly possible – if they are prepared to put in the effort.

One way to test our ability to control our dreams is to arrange to meet someone in them, and to share the same dream. This may seem wildly improbable, yet people who are emotionally close to each other can have very similar dreams. This might be because they share many of the waking experiences that provide the dreaming mind with its subject matter, but sometimes the shared dream is quite unexpected in content and can be corroborated by comparing specific details.

Some Western mystical fraternities and Eastern spiritual traditions actively encourage their members to share their dreams as part of the process of realizing their true nature. Although the dream body is usually left to wander aimlessly in the dream world, without direction or purpose, this is by no means inevitable. One way to harness the dream body's energies more effectively is to give it specific tasks, such as meeting a friend.

Oliver Fox, an English researcher and writer, agreed with two friends to meet in a dream on a nearby village green. That night Fox dreamed that he met one of his friends there, but not the other. Next day the friend who had been present recounted a similar dream, while the absent friend could not remember dreaming at all.

It is worth persisting with dream sharing, even if you have no success initially. If you do succeed, it is fascinating to discuss the differences and similarities with your sharer.

Guidelines for a Dream Meeting

Work with a partner, close friend or relative who is interested in the attempt, and who is at least open-minded as to its chances of success. People who have a close emotional bond with each other are more likely to be successful in this undertaking than casual acquaintances.

1. Spend some time planning and preparing for your dream meeting. It is good to start the planning at least a week before the night in question, to allow your unconscious to acclimatize to the idea – and hopefully take the plan for granted.

2. Decide together on a meeting place that has pleasant, but not over-intense, emotional associations for you both. Spend time "tuning in" to each other, talking about the chosen place, discussing your shared memories and enjoying feelings of mutual harmony. It is helpful to engage in such conversations over a series of meetings or telephone calls.

3. When the mood feels right, visualize with your dream sharing partner the place that you want to visit. Describe the scene to each other; as you listen, enter the scene in your imagination, filling in the details and telling each other what you see. This stage of the operation is best performed with relaxed personal contact rather than over the phone.

4. After several of these preparatory sessions, decide to meet at the appointed place on a particular night at a set time, and feel confident that you will do so. Make your arrangements very detailed and rehearse them inwardly as frequently as possible, especially just before sleep. If your companion is a sleeping partner, it is good to snuggle up close to them and say "See you shortly" as well as "Goodnight". Otherwise, convey the same message of au revoir over the telephone late that night.

5. In the morning, make a point of telling each other your dreams as soon as you can. Compare your dreams carefully, and look for correspondences.

6. Be patient, and be prepared to try the experiment many times. Defeatism and scepticism are major obstacles to success.

The Art of Interpretation

The symbol directory in this book (pages 158–447) is intended as a wide-ranging tool for dream interpretation. Before you use it, read this section on some of the basic principles of the practice. There are no inflexible rules, but there are approaches that many have found work for them.

"When read correctly, [dream] images tell us who we are instead of who we think we are. They speak to us about our actual impact on others, not about what we would like that impact to be."

Montague Ullman

Dreams are a conversation between the unconscious and the conscious levels of the mind – levels that speak subtly different languages. Although the conscious mind may think that it understands what the unconscious is saying in dreams, it can, like a naive and inexperienced translator, make a nonsense of the true meaning.

Although the language of dreams is in some respects consistent for us all, we have personal idiosyncrasies that limit the usefulness of dogmatic dream dictionaries, which ascribe specific meanings to dream experiences without any exploration of alternatives. Dreams that arise from the personal unconscious (Level 2 dreams) are especially inclined to use images and associations from the dreamer's own life history and subjective inner world.

Successful dream interpretation depends on learning a few simple techniques and making a special study of your own dreams to unravel their very personal messages. Other people can make suggestions as to the meaning of your dreams, but only you can experience your inner world, and you are the final authority in interpreting the information that your unconscious is seeking to convey.

The best way to analyze dreams is through

the recurring themes that emerge from a dream diary. Whether analysis concentrates on these themes or on powerful individual dreams, a good way to start is to separate the dream material into discrete categories: for example, scenery, objects, characters, events, colours, emotions. You should not be too rigorous about this process: these categories may well overlap, and the memories themselves may be vague or confused. But try not to ignore apparently unimportant details, because these may be the very aspects that carry the most meaning.

Start by selecting something from whichever of the categories appears most relevant, and subject it to the process of Jungian direct association. Write down the object (or whatever) in the centre of a sheet of paper, or a page in your notebook, hold this in the mind, and note down all associated images and ideas that come to you. Keep returning

to the original stimulus. Try to ensure that each association is specific: if the dream contained a red car, it may be its colour, rather than the fact that it is a car, that is of most symbolic significance. When no more associations come to mind, put the paper aside and go on to the next dream symbol with which you want to deal, and so on, until all the desired categories have been covered.

Jung suggested that direct association becomes easier if the dreamer imagines that he or she is describing each element to someone who has never encountered such a thing before. He also advocated elaborating upon direct associations, linking them to any personal reactions or responses that may arise for the dreamer in response to the original dream image.

If few associations arise from a dream's main elements, the dream may be operating at Level 1, carrying little or no symbolic meaning, and simply serving as a literal

Some Dream Interpretation Tips

The guidelines below are not exhaustive but are aimed at providing a set of watchpoints or tips that can be trusted to increase the likelihood of a successful dream interpretation. Use these points to get started as a beginner, or to free the imaginative blockages that will inevitably occur, even to the experienced analyst.

Resemblances

If the meaning of a symbol is defeating you, ask yourself what it most resembles. The textbook example, of course, is the Freudian interpretation of a pencil as a penis or a tunnel as a vagina.

Notice how clever the pencil symbolism is – this is typical of the associations made by the unconscious. A pencil has an appropriate shape for the association, but also contains lead – a creative substance that is expended in a meeting of pencil and paper (male and female). The tunnel also has double significance: it has a vaginal shape and admits a forceful visitor, the train (penis). Bear in mind that dream resemblances need not be sexual. A globe of the world resembles a beach ball; a ribbon, a road; a child's kite, a bird.

Wordplay

Most of our inner mental activity is conducted in language, so it is hardly surprising that language can feature in dreams, even if its role may be disguised. For example, if a dream shows a pine tree, it is possible that the reference is to "pining" in the sense of melancholy emotion – especially if you remember someone using that word in a way that concerned you. When a name appears in a dream, consider the meaning of the word or its individual syllables. "Ray" is a name, for example, but also a beam of sunlight. "Mulholland Drive" includes "Holland", a flat country that may suggest openness or lack of excitement; and "Drive", which might suggest "car" – confinement, or a wish to take to the road. The dreaming mind likes occasional puns.

Function/operation

When an object appears in a dream, consider its function and its mode of operation in all the ways you can think of. For example, a pair of scissors has a hinge and you never find one blade separate from the other. Perhaps in some way the implement suggests balance or inseparability?

reminder of the significance carried by certain events in the dreamer's life. At best, it might be providing clues about the solution to problems that have been worrying the dreamer at a conscious level.

If the dream has a deeper resonance for the dreamer, however, it might be operating at Level 2, using symbolism. This is where dream interpretation becomes really interesting, as we begin to encounter the unconscious mind communicating its deepest messages.

If Jungian direct association fails to uncover any such significance, Freudian free association may be helpful, allowing the mind freely to follow a whole chain of thoughts and images set off by the individual dream element, with one idea emerging spontaneously from another. Jung complained that such freestyle associations lead the dreamer too far away from the original dream, but Freud's method can reveal significant repressed memories, urges or emotions that direct association may fail to reach.

A dream that seems mysteriously important to the dreamer is well worth scanning for archetypal symbols (see pages 103–107), which if they are present suggest that the dream is operating at Level 3. For these "grand" dreams Jung recommended, as a further way of teasing out their meaning, amplification (see page 108), which requires us to trace connections between the symbols of the dream and related archetypes in myth and folktale.

Jung stressed that the analyst should always avoid imposing a dream interpretation upon the dreamer: the meaning is uncovered only if it provides him or her with a self-generated insight, whether welcome or unwelcome, that rings true. Interpretations should always "act" for the dreamer, setting his or her life "in motion" again.

Problem Solving

We normally think of reason and logic as the obvious tools to use in working out the answer to a conundrum. But then again, experience tells us that a breakthrough in our thinking can sometimes come to us from nowhere, as if out of a clear blue sky. Dreams can provide unexpected solutions to all kinds of questions.

The prescription that we should sleep upon problems is well known. Although the conscious ego is inactive while we sleep, some part of the mind continues to work, processing information, storing memories, sometimes untying even the knottiest intellectual, emotional or moral problems. Unencumbered by the conventions of the conscious mind, the unconscious is free to take an unorthodox approach that can provide the very breakthrough that we have been racking our brains for.

Sometimes answers are actually given in dreams. A famous example is that of the German chemist Friedrich Kekulé who claimed that his ground-breaking discovery of the molecular structure of benzene, in 1961, came to him in a dream. Working hard on the problem, he fell asleep and dreamed of molecules dancing before his eyes, forming into patterns, then joining like a snake catching its tail in a dream representation of the so-called "benzene ring".

We can sometimes obtain a demonstration of the problem-solving power of the dreaming mind if we visualize an unsolved anagram or mathematical puzzle while drifting to sleep. Instructing the mind to work on the puzzle, just before sleep descends, can often stimulate a dream solution.

The answer may come literally, unfiltered by symbolism. The Russian chemist Dimitri Mendeleev, after many fruitless attempts to tabulate the elements according to their atomic

weight, dreamed their respective values and subsequently found all but one to be correct, a discovery that led to the publication of his periodic law in 1869.

When dreams offer symbolic rather than literal solutions, interpretation can be more difficult. The scientist Niels Bohr identified the model of a hydrogen atom in 1913 after a dream in which he stood on the sun and saw the planets attached to its surface by thin filaments as they circled overhead. Numerical solutions, in particular, may be conveyed in symbolic form, perhaps using associations lodged deep in the personal unconscious. For example, the number 3 might be indicated by an old three-legged stool from the dreamer's childhood.

One of the most astonishing of all dream discoveries, involving visitation by a dream ghost, is that of H.V. Hilprecht, Professor of Assyrian at the University of Pennsylvania. In 1893, Hilprecht was trying to decipher inscriptions on drawings of two agate fragments believed to come from finger rings dating from c.1300 BC and excavated from the ruins of a temple at Nippur in modern Iraq. Discouraged by lack of success, Hilprecht retired to bed and dreamed that an ancient Babylonian priest appeared before him to inform him with a wealth of background detail that the fragments were not separate rings at all but part of a cylinder that the priests had cut up to make earrings for a statue. If they were put together, the priest told him, the original inscription could be read with ease. Hilprecht awoke and confirmed the truth of his dream, receiving final proof when he examined the fragments in the museum at Istanbul.

Dreams can help with personal problems as well as intellectual ones. Asking your unconscious for help is a matter of holding the issue in your mind before going to sleep, feeling relaxed and confident in the knowledge that you have no need to worry about the solution during the night: your sleeping mind will do all the work, and may reveal the answer in the morning, either as a fully-formed reply or buried in a dream. When you wake up, you may find that you simply "know" the solution. If not, search for it in your dreams, where it could appear symbolically, or as a visual or verbal pun, which may need further interpretation.

We have seen how working with dreams, and particularly their symbolism, over a period of time can enable us to reach a new level of awareness. Many of the ghosts that haunt us can be eliminated by the spotlight of self-understanding, and this is why a psychoanalyst will spend so much time helping us to delve into our past experiences. By bringing our anxieties to the light of day, we can release ourselves from their power – or at least ensure that the pain they cause is considerably diminished.

The anxieties that can be addressed in this way are the deep-rooted ones – the chronic issues in our lives. Often we spend hardly any time thinking consciously about such problems, which is precisely why they are so dangerous to our peace of mind at the unconscious level. However, there are also many anxieties that are specific, temporary, and fully present to our conscious understanding. Indeed, we may spend hours of time turning them over in our minds. Issues related to our childcare arrangements, our life-work balance, our financial prosperity, even our vacation plans, all fall into this category. Often our worries will revolve around a dilemma: there are arguments on both sides and we cannot work out what to do for the best.

In the same way that dreams can come up with blue-sky answers to intellectual conundrums, similarly they can enlighten us about the best course of action in a specific personal situation. Some guidelines for using dreams in this way, as a wise oracle of advice, are given on the opposite page.

The Blue-sky Dream Oracle: your inner life coach

Submitting your personal problems to the hidden wisdom of the dream world is certainly worth trying. Look for quick answers, by all means. But if you fail to find them, interpret the dream as just one further step in the process of self-exploration that you are conducting through your dream work.

Framing the question

Express your dilemma to yourself as clearly as possible. Write it down and tinker with the words until they seem just right. Then try to convert the dilemma to symbolic language. For example, if you are unsure whether to travel or to stay at home (a very simple example by way of illustration), think up an image for each alternative – perhaps a hearth and a train.

Exploring the associations

At some point during the day, think through the various implications of each possible course of action – ponder on all that the hearth means and all that the train means. Do not go through these probably quite uncomfortable thoughts just prior to sleep, however – they would disturb your night and muddy any possible answer that the unconscious might be preparing for you. In fact, it is better to do this analysis a few days before you submit your issue to your dreams.

Visualizing the question

Before you go to sleep, hold the images in your mind, and ask your unconscious if it will kindly give you an opinion as to your best course of action. Think of your chosen imagery, in a relaxed way, without emotion, before you climb into bed or as you lie waiting for sleep to come. Do not think about your dilemma, only about the visual symbols which you have chosen to embody it.

Next morning

When you wake, record any dream you might have had, in the way you normally do. But before you subject the dream to detailed interpretation in your usual way, just consider whether you have received an answer to your question. Did either of your two symbols appear in the dream? If both, what relation was implied between them? If only one, was your dream telling you to avoid it or embrace it? If neither, did your dream choose its own, different language to answer your question?

Dealing with Nightmares

Bad dreams are a kind of haunting – the ghost of a fear or trauma stalks our sleep and may bring terror, which leaves its residue long after we have woken. Occasional nightmares are of no great concern, but regular ones need serious work, starting with a probing analysis of dream symbols.

Historically, nightmares were thought to be caused by nighttime visitations from demons: the "mare" was a monstrous being that descended upon sleeping souls to satisfy its lust. In modern times, however, the most widely held view is that bad dreams force us to confront and deal with the events, actions or reactions that we may feel particularly angry or emotional about in waking life.

During a nightmare, the traumas that we face tend to feel terrifyingly real. We might be locked in combat with a murderous animal or person; be unable to save a loved one from peril; or even be the perpetrator of a violent act. These scenarios cause our dream selves to experience the emotions that we have been grappling with

or suppressing in real life. They permit us to vent fears and frustrations directly, in ways that, because of social pressures, may be difficult or impossible within the confines of daily life.

As a nightmare unfolds, the pulse and respiratory rate of the dreamer can double. In the face of acute danger, the dreamer tends to awaken, using consciousness as a means of escape. But often the dream lingers in the mind, and the dreamer feels unsettled in its aftermath. Nightmares can even "stalk" us – recurring night after night until we may be afraid to go to sleep, or at least we remain in a state of hypnagogia, hovering on the margins of sleep.

Nightmare Quick-fix

Worry about nightmares can be self-fulfilling: if we actively fear meeting the monster or dentist again, we are investing energy in visualization – the same visualization which in a positive context is a highly effective dream cue. The answer to this problem lies in not trying to counteract this syndrome (for example, by imagining a tranquil landscape before sleep); rather, we must accept that the nightmare image may manifest itself and find a way to make the image less threatening if it does so.

Transforming the monster through visualization, just prior to sleep, is one key to success. Picture the creature of your dreams as vividly as possible, and imagine it, with equal vividness, tamed by the superior power of wisdom or enlightenment. It can be useful to imagine wisdom in humanized form, as a dream helper – a figure that you consciously introduce into your dreams. For example, you might visualize Perseus, the Greek hero who rescued the maiden Andromeda from a malevolent sea serpent.

In some nightmares there is no clear enemy, but you can still make progress by visualizing a dream helper to point out to you that the threat in the dream is not real.

KEY TO *Dream* SYMBOLS

Dreams are a conversation we have with ourselves, in a symbolic language that sends messages between the unconscious and conscious levels of our minds. We are the authors and actors of our dreams, and ultimately the best judges of their meanings. Remember that no interpretation offered either by this directory or by any other outsider is likely to be correct unless you, the dreamer, recognize it as authentic.

Themes

Each of our dreams has relevance to ourselves and to our relationships. Just as we have individual personalities in waking life, so we have our own characteristics in dream life, and these aspects of the self must be recognized in any dream interpretation. However, by collecting and comparing the experiences of different dreamers, we can broadly identify the types of dreams that are most commonly reported, and the actions and events that most often take place in them. These predominant dream themes seem to arise out of our common preoccupations, the universal currency of the dream world.

Identity and Destiny

If we are afraid of losing direction in our lives, this may give rise to dreams in which we are trapped in clinging fog or mist, or wandering in a setting shorn of all the landmarks by which we normally orientate ourselves. If our dream journey is fraught with anxieties, we may not be ready to leave the secure confines of the conscious mind, and should take stock before approaching the "true self". Struggling to find the way, we may become increasingly disorientated – an example of a dream using an obvious metaphor to express itself. But if the route in the dream becomes increasingly clear, and the goal is excitedly anticipated, it may be time to tread a new path.

Provided that we can read it, a chart or map is the symbol *par excellence* of a sure and predictable direction; if it proves incomprehensible, however, our loss of bearings may be followed by frustration and panic. In dreams a map can represent self-knowledge, and a failure to read its signs warns us that we are in danger of becoming unknown territory to ourselves.

Fears about loss of identity may give rise to dreams in which the dreamer is unable to recall his or her name when challenged, or is suddenly unable to produce vital identification documents when they are demanded. One of Freud's patients, suffering from an acute identity crisis, dreamed that she was stopped by a policeman as she was walking down a street. The policeman asked her to produce her identity card. When she showed it to him, she was horrified to discover that the card bore her picture, but where her name should have been printed she saw the word "Hysteria" written instead.

Getting lost

A maze in a dream usually relates to the dreamer's descent into the unconscious. It may represent the complex defences put up by the conscious ego to prevent unconscious wishes and desires from emerging into the light. Lost among towering trees or tall reeds, we may feel our progress to be impeded by insurmountable obstacles. As in the tale of Hansel and Gretel which many of us will recall from childhood, this feeling might evoke a profound longing for the comfort of a mother.

Losing control

Anxiety about a loss of direction in life may cause dreams of hurtling out of control in a car or train. Similarly, fears of loss of personal identity can prompt dream experiences in which the dreamer hunts desperately for the correct road or street in a strange town.

Masks and disguises

These represent the way that we present ourselves to the outside world and even to ourselves. If the dreamer is unable to

remove a mask, or is forced by others to wear one, this suggests that the real self is becoming increasingly obscured. Wearing a veil over the head indicates the dreamer's wish to become invisible – an introverted desire to withdraw from the outside world.

Distortions

Looking into a dream mirror and seeing someone else's face reflected there is the classic dream of an identity crisis – the sudden sense of not knowing who we are. The face in the mirror may give clues as to the nature of the identity problem. Closed eyes often indicate an unwillingness to face reality.

Drifting

A rudderless, drifting raft can be a cause of alarm, raising fears of directionlessness and lack of control over our lives. On the other hand, as Rabbi Nachman of Bratslav (1772–1810) said, not knowing where we are going can sometimes be the best way of discovering the real self.

A raft can also be a wholly positive image, representing a means of survival and a realization that we are capable of riding our sea of troubles rather than becoming overwhelmed.

Change and Transition

Our conscious minds are often unaware of the psychological and emotional upheavals that follow major changes in our lives. However, the unconscious mind tends to know better, and some psychologists these days believe that in the two years or so following even propitious events such as marriage or promotion we are more prone not only to psychological disturbance but also to physical ailments that may appear as symptoms of unrest.

If in our unconscious minds we are nervous and insecure in the face of change, our dreams may be filled with comforting images of our former ways of life and our old familiar surroundings. Alternatively, the dreaming mind may show our underlying anxiety about a particular transition by an exaggerated sense of strangeness, perhaps accompanied by feelings of dread. The dream might focus on the worst kind of scenario that we imagine the change ahead is likely to bring to us. Such a troubling dream may be converted to a positive purpose if we can accurately read its significance: acknowledging the fears indicated in the dream is the first step toward finding ways to deal with them.

Sometimes the dream will use coded ways to highlight the need for change, or perhaps its inevitability. These themes may appear in dreams as an attempt to exchange old or faulty goods in a store, or as the act of redecorating our homes, changing our clothes, or buying new books or CDs to replace the ones that we had bought before. Dreams of crossing a road, river or bridge may indicate the risks that change can carry, or symbolize its irrevocable and unavoidable nature.

The Jungian technique of amplification may reveal associations with mythical images of transition, such as the Greek hero Herakles crossing the River Styx: on one side lies the land of the living; on the other side, death, the entrance to the Underworld and the terrors that the hero must face in order to complete his quest. Jonah's voyage, shipwreck and journey inside the whale across stormy seas carries similarly archetypal imagery, suggesting the dangerous crossing of a threshold, the past left behind and the future stretching mysteriously ahead.

Destruction and ruin

Images of destruction can relate to life-changes that dramatically break with the past. A house standing in ruins may convey the broken family that will be left by a divorce; fallen trees can symbolize a move to a new locality or perhaps even a family uprooted by emigration.

Bridge

A bridge marks the frontier between the comfortable present and the unpredictable future. Crossing the bridge indicates our ability to move forward – our underlying strength to cope with life's journey, especially in the face of difficult events such as moving home, leaving a partner or losing a job.

Object coming to life

If an inanimate object comes to life in a dream, it may be that a previously unacknowledged inner potential is now ripe for development. If the metamorphosis is frightening, such inner energies may need acknowledging and channelling into more acceptable forms.

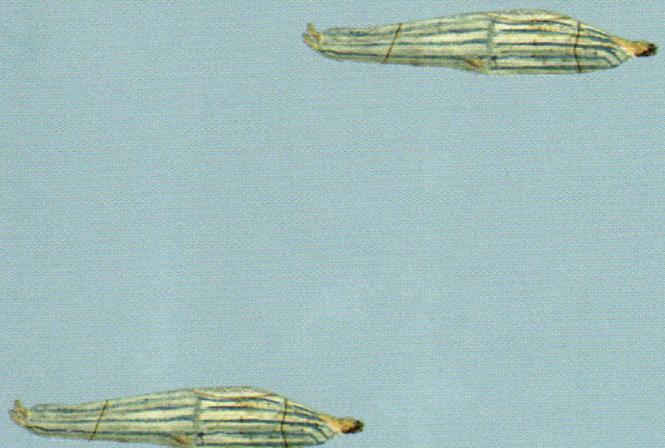

Transformation

Dreams in which the seasons change or where the dreamer metamorphoses – for example, from an infant into an old man – indicate deep inner transformations. A dream can use a transformation to move from one symbol to another, but sometimes it is the change itself that seems to carry significance. A dream in which the protagonist changes sex, for example, may represent acceptance of the masculine or feminine aspect within the self. The werewolf has lodged itself in the popular consciousness through movies and folk legend, and it is not uncommon for such monstrous shape-shifting to appear in our dreams, reflecting deep-seated anxieties of various kinds.

Unfamiliar surroundings

If unfamiliar surroundings make the dreamer feel lost, apprehensive, or full of regret, the dreaming mind may be trying to say that he or she is not yet ready to leave an old way of life behind: it is too soon to master a new set of circumstances. On the other hand, feelings of excitement accompanying the dream suggest that the dreamer is ready for change, and should seize whatever opportunity has arisen. To dream of finding ourselves in an unfamiliar household or workplace often represents an anxiety about being placed in a new and unaccustomed role.

Success and Failure

How we react to success and failure does much to dictate the future course of our lives. These two sides of the same coin are among the most common preoccupations of our dreams, as of our waking lives. We can enjoy success and suffer failure in our jobs or in business as well as in more subtle transactions such as arguments, or in relationships. An upcoming job interview, for example, is a common stimulus for dreams about success and failure. Whatever our anxieties, we often believe in our hearts that failure can be overcome, although more certain still is the knowledge that success is usually short-lived.

When warring against the Greeks, the Persian prince Xerxes dreamed of a crown of olives whose branches spread out over the world but then suddenly vanished, an accurate omen that his conquests would soon be lost. Many other monarchs, generals and statesmen have had prophetic dreams of success or failure. King Richard III of England dreamed of evil spirits before his defeat at the Battle of Bosworth. On the night before Waterloo, Napoleon dreamed of a procession of figures bearing symbols of his triumphs, which were ominously followed by a figure in chains and fetters. Otto von Bismarck, prime minister of

Prussia, dreamed of his country's rise to power before it grew to become the lynchpin of a new unified Germany. However, most dreams of success or failure are linked less to actual events than to the dreamer's state of mind.

Dreams of failure often contain situations such as ringing a doorbell or knocking on a door without reply, or finding oneself without money to pay for a taxi or settle a debt, or losing a contest or an argument.

Success in dreams may be indicated by a favourable outcome to a transaction, often accompanied by feelings of fulfilment or even elation. A fence or hurdle commonly stands for a particular challenge confronting the dreamer in waking life, and jumping over the obstacle may represent not only the possibility of success but also the confidence upon which that success may depend, and which the dreamer must strive to acquire.

Level 3 dreams (see pages 65–70) sometimes reflect success at a deep level of personal growth and transformation. Amplification of Level 3 dreams may reveal associations with classical themes, such as the story of the Greek warrior Bellerophon who captured the winged horse Pegasus and soared toward Mount Olympus to claim a place among the gods. Pegasus threw him; and having fallen back to earth, he passed the rest of his days as an outcast on the Plain of Wandering. Such archetypes remind us of the dangers of overstretching our natural limits.

Prizes

Trophies carry a value far beyond their material worth – just as a cup's value is not intrinsic, but depends upon what it can hold. In dreams, even if the nature of the prize remains obscure, the sense of triumph is normally unmistakable.

Breakdown in communication

Failure to make oneself heard, or otherwise to give a good account of oneself, suggests feelings of inadequacy. By drawing these feelings to the attention of the dreamer, the dream indicates the need to confront them in waking life. Failure to make oneself understood on the telephone can suggest weaknesses in the dreamer's ideas.

Fame

Dreams of sudden glory amid the applause of friends, family or strangers may suggest that the dreamer is starved of attention or lacking in confidence and self-esteem.

Winning a race

This indicates a recognition of any kind of significant potential within ourselves. The unconscious mind may be prompting us to act courageously or with confidence. To come second or third in a race may suggest that the dreamer has underestimated the difficulties of performing at the highest level.

Fear and Anxiety

Anxiety is probably the most common emotional state expressed in our dreams. In waking life, the mind is often able to distract itself from troublesome issues, but in sleep all the doubts, worries and fears that we banish to the backs of our minds march across the stage of our dreams, demanding to be recognized and filling our mind with unsettling, highly charged symbols, and with dark, troubled moods. Such dreams not only indicate how deeply rooted our anxieties can be, but also they remind us of the need to tackle the source of these worries, either by confronting a specific external challenge or by learning to be less fearful of life's predicaments.

The anxieties that we face in our dreams are not necessarily major. Even trivial anxieties will surface: Did I put the cork back in the wine bottle? Will I miss that TV programme? However, we should be aware that a seemingly superficial theme or image can be symbolic of more deep-rooted worries.

Anxiety dreams are recognizable by the emotional charge that they carry. Typically, the dreamer has the sensation of trying to cope with several duties simultaneously, or of trying to complete a never-ending task. Other anxiety dreams include walking through clinging mud, moving in agonizingly slow motion, and crawling through a narrow tunnel (a symbol often believed to represent birth anxiety), being choked by smoke, watching helplessly as cherished possessions are destroyed, and trying in a high wind to hold together the broken fragments of something the dreamer holds dear. If anxiety stems from social inadequacy, the dream may involve public embarrassment such as spilling a drink, grotesque incompetence on a crowded dance floor, or forgetting the names of important guests while trying to introduce them. On the other hand, it is worth examining such dreams closely to see if such seeming ineptitude in fact contains an element of defiance – expressing our feelings of frustration with the oppressive bonds of social convention. One classic dream features an exam paper that appears unanswerable

– the traumas of our schooldays can plague us well into adulthood, providing an image for feelings of inferiority. If we dream of being naked or wrongly dressed for a certain occasion, this can stem from recent social embarrassment, general social unease, or some other vulnerability in waking life. A dream of falling may also be a reflection of insecurity.

The dreaming mind is not always shy of melodrama – a walk to the scaffold, falling into the hands of evil captors, or being forced into committing some terrible crime, may reflect relatively mundane problems. The point of such extreme forms of terror is to impress upon the subject the need to bring into consciousness (as a prelude to dealing with them) repressed desires and energies of a powerful nature.

Whatever form they take, anxiety dreams are not there to torment the dreamer, but to draw attention to the urgency of identifying and dealing with the sources of anxiety, which may wreak havoc in the unconscious if left to themselves. Anxiety dreams also offer the opportunity to exorcise our fears through dream interpretation and discussion. By analyzing the issues that our dreams highlight, we prevent ourselves being dogged by the free-floating worry that can cloud both our waking and dreaming lives.

Drowning

Dreams of drowning, or struggling in deep water, may represent the dreamer's fear of being engulfed by forces hidden in the deepest reaches of their unconscious minds.

Being chased

Dreams of being chased by an unseen but terrifying presence usually indicate that aspects of the self are clamouring for integration into consciousness. The dreamer's fear usually dissipates if he or she can turn and face the pursuer and gain clues as to what this symbol represents at the conscious level.

Social embarrassment

The key to understanding dreams of failing to perform competently in public is to detect the mood of acute embarrassment. Whether the dreamer is revealed as inappropriately dressed (or undressed), inept at a simple task (such as pouring coffee out of a coffee pot) or unable to perform expected transactions with other people (for example, introducing them by name), the underlying message is one of psychological discomfort.

Trying to run

One of the most common anxiety dreams involves trying to run but finding that one's legs stay rooted to the spot. Similar are dreams of walking through clinging mud, or moving in painfully slow motion. Recent research suggests that such dreams may result from mechanisms in the brain that prevent us from acting out our dreams as we sleep, stopping us from running in our beds or wreaking havoc in the bedroom.

Narrow spaces

The distressing dream scenario of being confined in a small space can sometimes be a constructive inner protest, pointing to the struggle of creative energies to find expression. We may be anxious that something or someone, maybe a tedious job or a tyrannical boss, is keeping a lid on our energies.

Optimism and Well-being

An optimistic or happy dream can occur at any time, even when we are feeling the full weight of life's burdens. Such dreams may leave us exultant and content not only with our everyday lives but also with the world as a whole. They may introduce us to higher beings, or take us flying through the dream world, opening our minds to the infinity of time and space.

Sometimes optimistic dreams contain symbols of good luck or peace – either images that are personal to the dreamer, such as a lucky stone or colour, or cultural symbols of good fortune such as black cats, four-leafed clovers, doves or olive branches. Some people interpret these dreams as prophetic of future success; others believe that they show that the journey toward fulfilment has begun, but without any guarantee that the goal will be reached.

Good luck or well-being dreams often contain configurations of the dreamer's lucky number. If, for example, the dreamer's lucky number is 3, they might dream of choosing between three paths or perhaps being given three gifts. More potent still are dream visions of the rainbow, the archetypal symbol of hope and reconciliation. The dreamer may seem to be watching a rainbow forming in the sky over his or her house (a symbol of the self), or flooding the far-off hills in light (a symbol of achievement). In Level 3 dreams (see pages 65–70) the dreamer may even be bathed in rainbow light, suggesting a baptism into a new phase of personal growth and development.

As in waking life, colours in dreams can represent individual emotional or spiritual states. Blue, for example, is often thought to symbolize melancholia,

but it may also stand for the deep contemplative waters of the unconscious mind; while red represents not only anger, but also (depending on the context) the passion and drive of fire.

When worked on through the technique of amplification, dreams that indicate well-being and optimism may produce associations with the Elysian fields, the paradise of classical mythology. Christian symbolism is filled with accounts of paradisal Golden Ages, from the Garden of Eden to the New Jerusalem of Revelation, an era of spiritual well-being that will last a thousand years.

Honey and bees

The Israelites believed that the Promised Land flowed with milk and honey; the Greeks and Romans regarded honey as the food of the gods. Bees were endowed with special wisdom, and their appearance in dreams can be regarded as an auspicious symbol, with connotations of peace and prosperity.

Garden of Eden

Like the land of milk and honey, the Garden of Eden is an ancient mythic landscape of bliss and contentment – but as a paradise lost it may also warn us against complacency. Yet even if we imagine ourselves to be driven from the garden, like Adam and Eve, the vast unexplored landscape beyond can present us with an exciting new vista of challenge and opportunity.

Light

For Jung, the appearance of light in dreams "always refers to consciousness". Such dreams confirm that profound insights are illuminating the conscious mind of the dreamer, as if he or she is about to "see the light".

Authority and Responsibility

People in positions of authority and responsibility in waking life often report dreams that reflect their status. Such dreams may involve episodes such as dealing with emergencies, sitting at a desk and receiving requests for decisions from all sides, or carrying symbols of office such as a ceremonial chain.

On occasion, authority and responsibility dreams merge into anxiety dreams. The dreamer may seem to be giving orders that no one obeys, or suffering a sudden rejection at the ballot box or at the hands of superiors. Such images draw attention to the dreamer's feelings of insecurity and indicate the need to become more fully integrated into his or her public role. Authority and responsibility dreams may also reveal frustrations and resentments felt about the over-dependency of other people: such dreams fulfil a dual purpose by allowing these feelings harmless expression and by drawing attention to the over-stretched role that the dreamer is being called upon to play in his or her waking life.

When amplified, authority and responsibility dreams can reveal classical links – for example, associations with the account in the *Aeneid* of the Roman hero Aeneas. While fleeing from the flames of

burning Troy, Aeneas bravely fulfilled his responsibilities to his family by leading his father and son to safety. This was not an easy task since he had to carry his father, the aged Anchises, on his back while leading Ascanius, his young son, by the hand.

Such classical archetypes may remind the dreamer of the psychological importance and intrinsic heroism of facing up to one's personal and professional responsibilities in waking life, and of wielding the power of one's own authority for the good of others.

Stack of paper

To dream of a desk stacked high with an unending pile of papers is a typical anxiety dream for those in authority, suggesting the near-impossibility of handling the growing demands and stress that come with increasing responsibility. The dream may help the dreamer to see that he or she is not dealing effectively enough with incoming work.

Wearing a tall hat

Crowns and tall hats are traditional symbols of authority, raising the wearer above his or her peers and colleagues. To dream of having a crown or tall hat knocked off one's head may symbolize anxieties about the loss or inappropriateness of the dreamer's status.

Royal or presidential figure

A king or queen often relates to parental authority. A Freudian interpretation of dreams of dining or even having sexual relations with royalty is that they represent classic wish-

fulfilment, disclosing a deep-seated desire for intimacy that substitutes royalty for the mother or father. If a head of state or government such as a president or prime minister appears as a friend seeking advice, the dream might be expressing a yearning for a closer, more confiding relationship with a parent or other important authority figure, or a desire to be entrusted with a position of responsibility.

Parliament buildings

Seats of government, such as the Houses of Parliament in London or the United States Capitol in Washington, may represent a desire to wield power over people we know. Unruly or chaotic scenes in the debating chamber may indicate a crisis in our personal authority at work, or inner turmoil about which of several options to follow when faced with difficult choices between possible courses of action.

Taking control

When we dream of taking control in the midst of catastrophe when everyone around is panicking, we may be expressing an aspiration to exercise more responsibility, perhaps in the workplace or possibly in our personal life. We could also be feeling that our leadership qualities are not appreciated as much as they should be.

Judge

If we are the judge in a dream, this suggests an appreciation of our powers of judgment – perhaps we should follow our "gut feelings" in some matter that preoccupies us. If, on the contrary, we are standing before the judge as a defendant in court, not knowing why we are there, we may be feeling persecuted by the forces of moral or civic authority.

Relationships

When analyzing dream relationships, it is particularly important to remember that the dreaming mind's intention is not to duplicate reality but, rather, to comment on reality. The unconscious thus frequently uses characters in a dream as symbols, rather than as attempts to depict actual people with whom the dreamer is involved in waking life.

As revealed by direct association, a complete stranger in a dream may represent characteristics of a wife or husband, while a partner may stand for some aspect of the dreamer. The dream is more concerned with its message than with portraying people as they really are. The dreamer is already familiar with waking appearances, and the task of the dreaming mind is to draw attention to those things that are less obvious or that have been left unacknowledged, presenting a screen on which our true feelings for others may be revealed.

Thus, in the course of dream analysis, a friend transformed into a stranger may reveal a fundamental ambivalence in the dreamer's general feelings about friendship. Sudden rejection of a loved one may indicate the dreamer's rejection of some part of his or her own nature. Separation from one's children may suggest the loss of cherished ideals or the failure of personal ambitions.

At other times, dream characters do indeed seem to represent themselves, in order to draw attention to unrecognized aspects of our relationships with them. Frequent dreams of family members may show an over-dependence upon the family – perhaps an excessive need for emotional or financial protection or an inability to break free from family ties.

New parents often have anxious dreams – of accidentally rolling upon a baby in the bed, for example, or losing them in a crowd. These dreams don't make them bad parents. Rather, they are an expression of concern and indicate awareness of the great responsibility now resting upon their shoulders.

Even inanimate objects may represent relationships in our dreams. One of Freud's patients once dreamed of borrowing a comb, and this was seen as revealing her anxiety about a mixed marriage.

Failure to make a telephone connection may suggest loss of intimacy in a relationship, while dreams of intense heat or cold may reflect burning passion or cool indifference toward a partner.

During amplification, symbols from a Level 3 dream may provide associations with mythical themes such as the love between the Egyptian deities Isis and Osiris. Isis, the ancient Egyptian symbol of motherhood, is said to have loved her brother and husband Osiris even in the womb. No less strong was the love, in Greek myth, of Orpheus for Eurydice. Orpheus was a minstrel, linked with the gods Dionysos and Apollo; his music tamed wild animals, rivers and storms and even persuaded the rulers of the dead to let him take his lover Eurydice back from the realm of death. Orpheus was told that he could lead his love back to the land of the living so long as he did not look back while leaving the Underworld. He could not resist, however, and lost her for eternity when he turned around. Even after being killed and torn apart by the maenads for refusing any longer to honour Dionysos, his head continued to sing, lamenting the passing of his love.

Another archetype sometimes revealed through amplification is the witch, symbol of the all-consuming, punitive, terrifying role of the Great Mother, and established throughout the world in myths and fairy tales. Russian folklore, for example, tells of an evil old hag called Baba Yaga, who lives in a log cabin that moves around on dancing chicken legs and who kidnaps and imprisons young children, making them her slaves.

From time to time the Great Mother can be a source of guidance – although in folktales seeking out her aid can be dangerous and should not be attempted except by those who are pure of spirit.

Rather as the witch can symbolize the destructive aspect of the Mother, the giant or ogre can symbolize that of the Father. Again, folktales and legends about giants exist all over the world, from the Old Testament Philistine Goliath to the evil Ravana in the Hindu epic the *Ramayana,* and Fionn mac Cumhail, the legendary leader of a band of Irish warriors called the Fianna.

Dreams about malevolent giants may be a subconscious response to a power struggle with an overbearing authority figure, perhaps an employer or a family member. Alternatively, they could indicate a troubled relationship with a partner. We may feel that our needs within a relationship are not being taken seriously enough or that we do not have sufficient influence over important decisions. If this is the case, it may be time to stand up and assert our wishes more explicitly.

Spider's web

The spider, who traps innocent victims in its webs and eventually consumes them, often symbolizes the devouring mother, who devours her children through possessiveness or her power to arouse guilt. The web itself is also a common dream image and may reflect an unconscious fear of commitment and insecurity about intimate relationships in general. Alternatively, we may feel that we are trapped within a specific emotional entanglement and need to extricate ourselves before we are psychologically devoured by our partner.

Mending things

Repairing an appliance such as a radio or refrigerator often indicates the need to work at a relationship to prevent it from deteriorating. An appliance that is broken or has been dismantled may also carry this meaning.

Feathers

Feathers, whether or not they appear in the same dream as birds, often represent a gift, expressing the desire to show warmth or tenderness to someone close to the dreamer. As quills, feathers can have phallic overtones. But feathers fluttering separately through the dream represent warmth and tenderness, perhaps in the form of a peace offering or a gesture of affection.

Hotel

In dreams, hotels often represent impermanence, a point of transition in a relationship, or a shift, or even a loss of personal identity. They may also suggest the price that has to be paid to sustain a relationship – whether financial or emotional. Sometimes they may symbolize the potential for an illicit encounter.

Birds

Birds can take on a meaning associated with the qualities we frequently attribute to them: for example, a bird of prey, a nest-stealing cuckoo or a thieving magpie may represent the threat of adultery, while the soft-voiced cooing of a dove suggests reconciliation or the need to soothe a troubled relationship.

Fire

This is a powerful and ambivalent dream symbol. Fire destroys, but it also cleanses and purifies. In dreams it can signal a new beginning, or represent disruptive emotions – perhaps the flames of passion or envy.

Unsuitable pairing

Concerns about an unsuitable partner, for yourself or for a close relation or friend, can be expressed when the dreaming mind pairs together inappropriate objects. You might, for example, witness a rabbit riding a bicycle or see a man wearing a bird cage for a hat.

Water seeping through cupped hands

Running with two cupped hands full of water to someone dying of thirst can signify a desperate sense of love lost as a close personal relationship draws to an end. A similar meaning may be carried by a dream of gold dust running through your fingers.

Caring action

Helping a person in distress, even if they appear to be a complete stranger, often represents the affection we feel for someone close to us. Conversely, if we dream that we are on the receiving end of the caring action, we might be expressing a need for affection. Some detail of the dream or else the process of direct association can generally be used to identify the person in question.

Family quarrel

An argument with family members or a partner often indicates something unrelated to troubles within that relationship. Children storming out of the house, for example, can represent loss of professional ambition.

Wrong phone number

Repeatedly getting the wrong person on the telephone or being transferred to an answering machine can indicate a breakdown of communication with someone important in your life.

Sexuality

For Freud, unconscious sexuality lay behind much of our conscious behaviour, and he found sexual imagery to be the main driving force of dream symbolism. He believed that many acts of violence, such as those involving knifing and shooting, are associated with rape: the obvious link is the brutal invasion of the body. He interpreted preoccupations with asexual body parts as hidden wishes for abnormal sexual activity. Freudians often associate mutilation with castration; and

beating oneself or others, particularly small children, with masturbation. Riding a horse or bicycle, chopping wood, or taking part in any rhythmical activity connotes sexual intercourse. The same meaning may be attributed to the crashing of waves on the seashore, travelling by train, and the insertion of any one object into another, such as a key into a keyhole. Acts of deflation, such as a collapsing balloon, can refer to impotence; locked doors or windows are seen as representing frigidity.

Jung, however, took a different view of such imagery, proposing that it might relate instead to the archetypal themes of fertility and creativity. Although modern psychologists still agree that sexuality can be a significant part of our dream lives, few now hold with Freud's reductive lexicon of sexual dream symbols. They tend to prefer Jung's approach, which amplifies sexuality into the wider framework of world myth. Jung discovered that erotic scenes on Hindu architecture, far from being pure expressions of animalistic desire, instead celebrate mystic union between earth and sky, mortal and divine, matter and spirit. They represent a wholeness in which man and woman become a single, perfect entity.

The eroticism of sexual dreams may derive simply from the context, mood and colour of our dream landscapes. Where the sexual act occurs explicitly,

Jung believed that it owes as much to the dreamer's longing to live in comfort and peace with a loved one, as with the release of sexual tensions. Many sexual symbols make sense in both Freudian and Jungian terms, and their true meaning may be a fusion of the two. For example, while Freud saw ascending and descending stairs or ladders as a symbol of intercourse, to Jung this was an archetype representing the link between the spiritual and the physical.

Be sure to bear in mind the possibility of an asexual interpretation: climbing stairs might be an expression of ambition or perhaps a recognition of personal growth; falling down stairs, on the other hand, could indicate anxiety about overestimating your abilities.

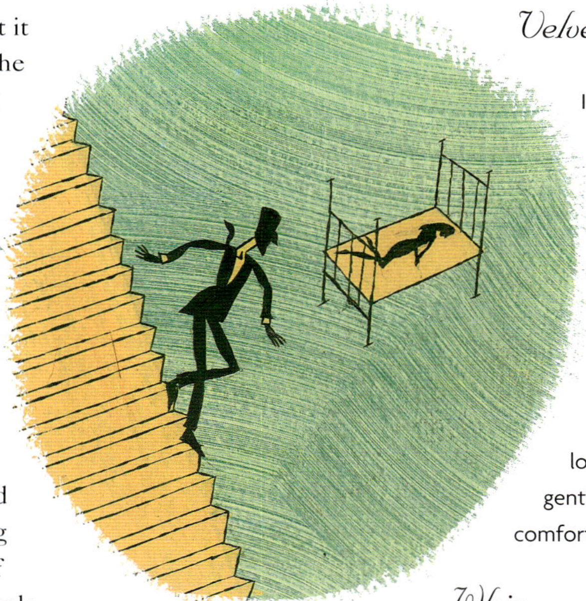

Velvet or moss

In Freudian dream analysis, velvet and moss usually represent pubic hair. Other dream interpreters see in them symbols of a more generalized longing for gentleness or the comforts of nature.

Whip

Whips in dreams can be a negatively charged symbol of sexual submission. They can also however, more generally represent the dreamer's awareness of power, domination and obedience within a relationship.

Quills and candles

Quills and candles often symbolize the penis. They may appear in dreams as general symbols of the Animus (see page 103) and masculinity.

Cup

A classic female sexual symbol, drinking from a cup is interpreted by Freudians as representing oral sex with a woman. Even in the Jungian view, cups are associated with the Holy Grail and therefore the virgin Grail-bearer and femininity.

Purse

The purse is a common female sexual symbol. It can stand both for the female genitalia and for the womb. As a purse can be both opened and closed, it sometimes represents the female power to give or withhold favours.

Cornucopia

The Horn of Plenty is an ambiguous sexual image: if it spills forth its riches and its shape is obvious, it is male; if we plunge into the horn to feast on its gifts, it is female.

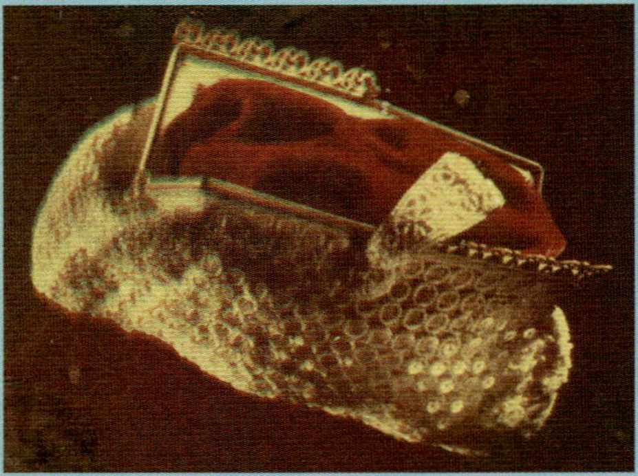

Hats and gloves

Hats, caps, bonnets and gloves are frequently used by the dreaming mind to represent the female genitalia, because they enclose parts of the body.

Shoes

Some dreamers who report seeing shoes in their dreams associate them with sexuality, as they can be entered by other objects, or by parts of the body. Women's shoes can sometimes stand for dominant female sexuality, which may come from the infant's experience of his or her mother's feet. Shoes can also denote authority and domination – recalling times in childhood when our parents "put their foot down".

Explosion

Explosions frequently denote a dream of orgasm. Fireworks can symbolize a sense of sexual well-being and fulfilment, while more destructive explosions may indicate unexpressed sexual urges. The damage caused by a bomb blast or an accidental explosion might relate to the harm we believe might follow – either to ourselves or to our partner – if we were to act upon our pent-up urges.

Domination

Dreams where one partner dominates the other may not overtly be about sex but can have sexual overtones. If in the dream we are the dominator, we may feel insecure within a close personal relationship and resent our lack of control. Alternatively, we may be trying to mask a sense of sexual inadequacy. When a dream does involve explicitly erotic sado-masochistic acts, it might suggest a secret enjoyment of power games or else repressed sexual fantasies that we fear would be unacceptable to our partner. According to Freud, dreams about domination express an incestuous desire for intimate contact with a parent.

Plane crash

Studies have shown that women frequently connect plane crashes with rape, or fear of rape. For men it can be connected to impotence anxiety. Flying, of course, is a common phobia, and the dream may stem from troubled anticipation of a trip.

Church

A dream of a church offers a potent combination of sexual and religious symbolism. A towering steeple is a very masculine, phallic symbol and can represent male sexuality or patriarchial authority. Bear in mind that a dream of a church may also have spiritual connotations.

If we are unable to enter the church, we may have encountered an obstacle on our spiritual path. When we dream of a church with a skyward-pointing spire and an arched portal, the symbolism is both male and female – perhaps reflecting an intimate bond with a partner or an inner conflict between our animal urges and our faith.

Making love

Dreams where we are making love to someone to whom we are sexually attracted are a classic example of Freudian wish-fulfilment, especially if our desire is illicit. For many Jungians and other analysts, dreaming of making love may not be about sex at all, but may simply indicate an

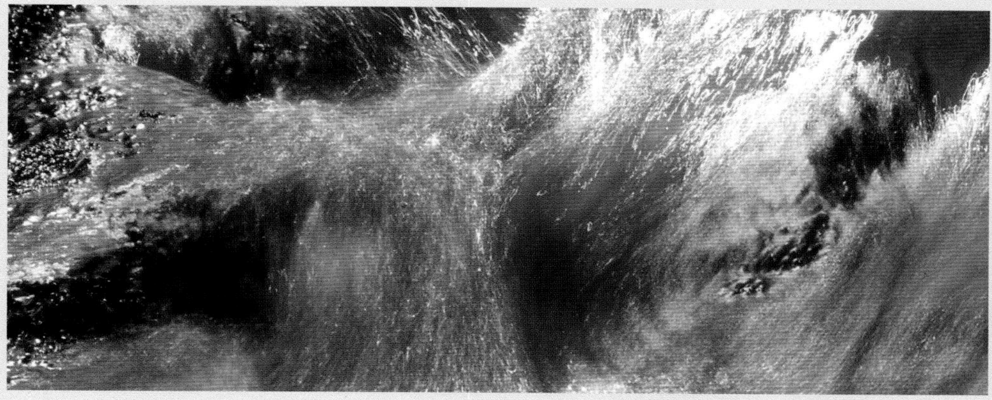

intense yearning for creative expression or the need to integrate contrasting aspects of the self more fully into the personality.

Kissing

The Jungian view is that the image of kissing "derives far more from the act of nutrition than from sexuality". In this interpretation the pleasure of a dream kiss stems from infant memories of our suckling at our mother's breast.

Red rose

Roses are a traditional symbol of romantic love. However, Freud understood red roses to indicate the female genitalia, or the blood of menstruation.

Gushing water

Any object from which water gushes – a flowing tap, for example, or a freshly opened bottle of champagne – is often a symbol of ejaculation. It may also herald a new burst of creativity.

Bed

The bed is often the scene of sexual adventures and can be a loaded symbol when it appears in our dreams. If the bed is unmade, this can indicate that we are being careless in our sexual behaviour. However, if the bedclothes are tucked in tight, we may be feeling inhibited by convention. To dream of searching for a bed can suggest that we are having difficulties accepting our sexuality.

Emotions

Each of our dreams tends to have a distinct mood, which can be more memorable, and no less significant, than the content of the dream itself. Perhaps surprisingly, this mood need not be in keeping with the dream's subject matter: for example, a man dreamed that a woman, for whom he felt unrequited love, begged him to kiss her. This was the fulfilment of his longing, but he found that in his dream, which was filled with a sense of foreboding, he could not bring himself to plant a kiss. The dream's mood had affected its action, just as a movie's musical soundtrack can be a more potent manipulator of the viewers' emotions than even the dramatic events on screen.

Dream moods can sometimes be so pervasive that they tend to linger for some time after we have woken up, even if the events of the dream quickly fade from memory, or cannot be recalled at all. After a disturbing dream we will often awaken with a "dream hangover" – that is, a vague sense of free-floating anxiety. Conversely, a good dream can raise our spirits, allowing us to begin the day bathed in a glow of well-being.

Accurate dream interpretation mostly requires us to recognize the emotions that are stirring within our inner self in waking life, since these emotions are very often pulling us in particular directions that go against the logic of reason or morality. The tension generated

by this conflict can be extreme – though unacknowledged by the conscious mind. Dreams can be helpful in drawing attention to the things that deeply affect us at the emotional level.

We are all familiar with the irrational character of our emotions. If we know that our beloved partner is seeing an attractive work colleague for lunch, this can be enough to trigger intense jealousy. It may preoccupy us until we see our partner again that evening and can reassure ourselves that nothing untoward has happened.

Even such trivial anxieties can erupt into our dreams – perhaps because two kinds of emotion are reinforcing each other: jealousy and fear. Anger, similarly, is often fused with frustration. Some emotions we project onto other people or external situations; other emotions, such as shame and embarrassment, we internalize. Both types can consume us, eating at our happiness and personal well-being.

Anger and frustration

Anger is a powerful emotion that is often denied, repressed or misunderstood by the waking mind: hence its frequent occurrence in dreams. It is not always negative. Anger can represent valued aspects of psychological development such as courage, determination, leadership and self-assertion, and is also associated with the purifying effect of justified indignation. Even its more negative forms can be valuable when they erupt into dreams, because here their absurdity or destructiveness may become more apparent. Moreover, dreams will sometimes indicate areas toward which one's anger should more properly be directed.

Closely linked with anger, frustration is also a commonplace experience in dreams. We may find ourselves missing a train or an appointment, searching in vain for a parking place or for somewhere to leave luggage, or unable to read an important message or to convince someone of the truth of an argument. In all such instances, the dream may be reminding the dreamer of the need to discover the cause of his or her frustration, or to deal more effectively with it if its causes are known.

Amplification of frustration dreams may provide links with archetypes such as the story of Sisyphus, a Greek mortal punished by the gods by being forced to roll a huge rock up a hill for eternity: whenever he reached the top, the rock would roll back down, and he would have to start all over again. Such mythic archetypes may help the dreamer to come to terms with frustration, or to recognize that it is pointless to rebel against the "gods" of the unconscious.

Jealousy and envy

Jealousy and envy are some of the most destructive human emotions and can ruin even the happiest of occasions. Metaphors such as being "eaten up" with jealousy or the "green-eyed monster" abound, and our dreams will often draw on these when we are having trouble assimilating another's good luck or success.

Bottled-up feelings

A dream may draw attention to repressed anger or frustration by images such as a bottled-up gas or volatile substance, and to unbridled anger by flames roaring out of control. Unacknowledged anger toward particular people may emerge in dreams when the dreamer prepares poison for them, or defaces their photograph. Dreaming of decapitating a loved one is common when misunderstanding has compromised a relationship: the dream is not literally portraying the beheading of a partner, but is symbolically removing the source of a current problem.

Thwarted tasks

Several major spiritual traditions deliberately frustrate their initiates, setting them pointless, never-ending tasks to eliminate the proud and tenacious hold that the ego has on consciousness. In dreams, apparently meaningless tasks (such as building a house of cards) may serve a similar purpose or may remind the dreamer that the ability to live with unavoidable frustrations is a sign of maturity.

Dam bursting

Anything that suggests a controlling force giving way before fierce energies from within can be a potent image of anger or frustration contained beyond the point of self-control. A flood blocking a familiar pathway may represent the dreamer's frustration, and may suggest the need to find an alternative and perhaps preferable route. In this way the dreamer is being reminded that there is often more than one way to deal with frustrations.

Loss and Separation

The need to continue with life, valuable as this often is in helping the mind to deal with bereavement, sometimes means there is insufficient time to grieve over the death or departure of a loved one. In such instances, our dreams may do the grieving for us. Images of loss, which often haunt the waking mind for many days after the dream, are part of the healing, however unwelcome they may seem at the time.

Losing a treasured possession can also be distressing, but most dreams of this kind are surrogate dreams about some other form of loss – or fear of loss. This may reflect a similar displacement in life, whereby a missing object causes dismay because it served as a tangible sign of an intangible value. Dreams often use extremes of emotion to highlight disturbances in the psyche, so that a dream in which you grieve over losing an object may in fact be about some other trouble or frustration.

Although death is the most extreme form of loss, we can be separated from people close to us for countless other reasons. When a major intimate relationship ends, either in divorce or separation, the feelings we experience are often in fact very similar to those of bereavement. We can also experience loss when a dear friend or family member relocates to a place far away or if a friendship goes through a difficult patch through some difference of opinion or misunderstanding.

Loss of any kind can be symbolized by the despairing search for a friendly face in a crowd, or by the symbolism of ashes or dust. Dreams may be steeped in nostalgia, providing poignant images of a past way of life or occupation. Some part of the unconscious mind needs to repeat these experiences over and over again as an emotional safety valve until it can finally accept that the loss has really taken place.

Sometimes, bereavement dreams look ahead rather than back into the past. The dreamer may see the loved one in happy circumstances, or be visited and reassured by him or her. Such dreams can leave the waking mind with feelings of well-being, even elation, and in many instances are so realistic that the dreamer feels certain of the reality of life after death.

Amplification (see page 108) may provide links with classical stories such as the loneliness of the nymph Echo, who in response to her lovelorn calls received back only the echo of her own voice. The dreamer may find such archetypal precedents useful as a focus for dealing with loss.

Empty purse

The sudden discovery of an empty purse or pocket may indicate the loss not only of a loved one – through death, divorce or separation – but also of the affection, comfort and security we derived from their presence.

A loved one receding

Distance is often used by the dreaming mind as a symbol of bereavement. A loved one may be seen receding into the distance, or waving goodbye from a far-off hilltop, or going out through a gate or doorway. The feelings of grief that accompany this image are often mixed with resentment – especially if the deceased ignores us when we try to attract their attention.

If, on the other hand, we dream that a loved one is happily waving goodbye to us before fading into the distance, this can indicate that our grief is fading as we become accustomed to our loss.

House without lights

A house in a dream often represents the dreamer or those things that give life its stability and orientation. The mournful image of empty or dark windows suggests the extinction not only of the loved one but also of vital aspects of the dreamer's conscious life.

Ashes or dust

We often associate ashes or dust with the disappearance from our lives of a treasured person, object or experience. Recalling the words spoken at Christian funerals, ashes are a potent symbol of both the crematorium and the grave. Just as funerals take place as much to help the living with their grief as to mourn the passing of the dead, so a dream involving ashes can symbolize laying to rest a painful or difficult experience.

Losing someone in a crowd

The scenario of losing sight of someone we love among a great throng of people is a dream commonly associated with bereavement. We might simply find that they are no longer with us, or we might have the traumatic experience of seeing them get pulled from us by the mass of people. It is not uncommon for a sense of loss to be accompanied by a feeling of resentment and abandonment.

Being locked out

To find yourself standing at a door, unable to find keys or otherwise enter, can represent the seemingly impassable barrier of grief. Simply by making us aware that this obstacle exists, the dream may mark the beginning of the healing process. From this point, we may be able to start envisioning ways to ease open the doorway to a future beyond our grief.

Incongruous emotions

To feel intensely sad, upset or angry at what ought to be a happy event – a birthday party, or a wedding for example – can suggest that we need to take time out from the distractions of everyday life in order to grieve. If we experience inappropriate happiness in a setting which in the waking world would normally be sad, the dream may be pointing out a state of denial – a subconscious refusal to face up to loss. It is very common for people to subconsciously refuse to countenance the reality of death in order to protect themselves from the searing pain of losing a loved one. To feel elation at a dream event such as a funeral can also, however, indicate a very positive state of mind – belief in an existence beyond the grave, perhaps, or an acceptance of death as a necessary – and sometimes welcome – part of life.

Losing an object

A dream of losing a precious or valuable possession may represent the sense of loss we feel when someone important to us is no longer a part of our life. Alternatively, this may be an anxiety dream related to an object that we have actually lost, or it may indicate that some part of the self has changed and moved on.

Faith and the Spirit

Many dreams may be essentially spiritual. With our body's senses numb to external stimuli, the mind enjoys a spiritual freedom, akin to the soul leaving the body in religious ecstasy.

Carl Jung was the first to recognize the ways in which dreams can enact a spiritual quest. He saw the search for spiritual and religious truth, beyond our everyday material lives, as one of the strongest energies of the psyche, welling up directly from the collective unconscious – that vast genetic reservoir of myths and symbols that projects archetypal images into our conscious minds, especially in our dreams.

Religion and spirituality, more than any other themes, express themselves in "grand", Level 3 dreams. The "message" is often imparted through dream revelations that suddenly throw a clear light upon the past or illuminate the dreamer's way ahead. The dreaming mind may encounter archetypal images that communicate profound messages about our spiritual needs and directions. Jung termed one of these archetypes Spirit, the opposite of "matter", which in dreams may appear as a ghost or represented more abstractly as an impression of infinity or spaciousness. The Wise Old Man may also appear in spiritual dreams, as a guide toward spirituality or as a teacher of truths. Other archetypes may take the form of symbols or religious icons. Transcendental experiences may occur, leaving the dreamer with profound feelings of exultation and inner peace.

Level 1 and 2 dreams often depict the spiritual world in more immediate and practical terms. Dreams involving priests and other religious officials may represent the authority of the established Church, while Old Testament prophets, Christian saints, Hindu avatars or Buddhist *bodhisattvas* may symbolize aspects of the our spiritual identity or aspirations or our unconscious reactions to spiritual institutions.

Dreams that we may be tempted to interpret in sexual terms, such as climbing mountains or trees, may actually portray spiritual progress. A church, whose thrusting spire was seen by Freud as a phallic symbol, may represent the purified self or the richness and mystery of spiritual teachings. An eagle's soaring flight may signify spiritual aspiration, while a fall to earth could warn against the dangers of spiritual pride.

Amplification of spiritual dreams could usefully focus on one of the creation or incarnation stories, or perhaps on a quest for enlightenment. The life story of Siddhartha Gautama, who became the Buddha or "awakened one", tells of how he grew up as a prince, sheltered from any suffering, but left that life to seek enlightenment. Another example is the Norse myth of Odin, who gave up his right eye to drink from the Well of Wisdom in order to guide the world through the turmoil of Ragnarok, the battle at the end of time.

Through spiritual dreams, we can regenerate our sense of wonder and regain our awareness of the profound potentiality that lies beneath the surface of things.

The Buddha

The Buddha taught that truth is found within, not without. His appearance in a dream often serves to remind the dreamer of the need to find the stillness at the centre of his or her own being.

Hindu deities

Hinduism is a faith of many deities, with a complex, multilayered symbolism. Brahma is the source of the cosmos, Vishnu is its protector and Shiva (see below) is the destroyer of demons and creator of life. Their appearance expresses disturbing passions but also great love and creativity and liberating energies.

Shiva

Eastern religions have permeated Western culture, and thus may find their way into our dreams. For example, the Hindu deity Shiva Nataraja, Lord of the Dance, may appear as the dual aspect of divinity: he is the

destroyer as well as the creator, paradoxically fearsome yet benign, dancing inside a ring of fire that both purifies and liberates.

Being of light

Central to the Jungian interpretation of dreams, the being of light is an archetypal image embodying a universal spiritual principle relevant to all cultures and all religions. A figure is often shown bathed in light, or surrounded by a brilliant halo – a generalized symbol of divine energy, readily acceptable to the conscious ego.

Virgin Mary

The Virgin Mary embodies the divine feminine principle that appears throughout the religions of the world as a symbol of purity. In dreams, she often represents a supreme and selfless love or compassion, and the power that rules the heavens through grace and sanctity rather than through authority and strength.

Priest

A priest, rabbi, pastor or other holy person may represent the authority of the Church. Such a figure may also stand for a parent dispensing spiritual and moral wisdom to us as children – perhaps we yearn for simple moral certainties.

Jesus Christ

Dreams about Jesus can occur at critical moments of our lives, such as when we are close to death, or at times when personal or spiritual issues are a major preoccupation. One of the most powerful images is that of Jesus on the Cross, a multifaceted symbol of life, death, resurrection, sacrifice and salvation.

Heaven

Heaven may appear as an idealized landscape or it may appear as it does in religious art – skies ablaze with light, and God surrounded by angels and cherubs. Another common depiction of paradise is as a wonderful garden. This may be an intense wish-fulfilment dream or a reassuring message in bereavement.

Angels

In the Christian tradition angels are heavenly messengers bringing the word of God to humans. A dream of the Annunication, when the archangel Gabriel told Mary that she would bear the infant Christ, may occur at a time when we are on the verge of a spiritual transition, while the archangel Michael leading the heavenly hosts against Satan is a symbol of light driving out the forces of darkness, perhaps pointing to a personal "demon" that we need to overcome.

Prophets and saints

Holy figures represent our religious aspirations. In our dreams they can offer guidance or encourage us on our personal quest for enlightenment or spiritual fulfilment.

The Last Judgment

To dream of standing before God may be an image of the Last Judgment. Perhaps some negative aspect of our psyche must be dealt with before we can enter the spiritual plane.

Eagle in flight

A majestic eagle, osprey or condor soaring across the heavens is a common dream symbol of spiritual aspirations, but its sudden fall toward the ground may warn us against the dangers of taking counterproductive pride in our spiritual progress.

ΧϹ

Self and Others

Symbols relating to ourselves and our interactions with others are frequently integrated into our dreams. Bodily symbols, for example, are commonly used in a symbolic capacity by the unconscious to refer to an obvious underlying metaphorical significance. In the case of physical organs, the meaning may relate to their shape (as in the Freudian approach) or to their function – for example, the tongue is necessary for clear articulation of ideas or emotions. Similarly, when a person appears in a dream, it may be their symbolic associations rather than their actual identity that provide the most useful clue for intepretation.

The Body and its Functions

In ancient Egyptian, Greek, Roman and medieval European cultures, the body was used as a metaphor for the spiritual world. This view is reflected in the maxim coined by the philosopher god Hermes Trismegistus, "As above, so below," and in the biblical idea that God created man in his own image. In dreams also, the body may refer to the mind or spirit. The physical condition of the dreamer or of other characters in dreams may reflect traits in the dreamer's psyche, or levels of psychological or spiritual progress.

More straightforwardly, dreams may allude to the body as a warning to attend to health problems, or as a way to express feelings about diet or exercise. For early dream workers, dreams of the body could reveal the future. Artemidorus (AD 170) wrote that for a man to dream that he is clean-shaven can indicate "sudden shame and problems", while Thomas Tryon, a nineteenth-century English dream interpreter, insisted that to dream that one's belly is larger than usual foretells an increase in family or property, while seeing one's back in a dream predicts bad luck or (perhaps more obviously) the coming of old age.

Freud associated dreams of excretion and toileting with the anal phase of psycho-sexual development. The small child experiences erogenous satisfaction from excretion, and this experience, if insensitively handled by adults during toilet training, may leave the individual with permanent feelings of shame, disgust and anxiety over natural functions.

Left and right

For Jungians, an emphasis upon the right side of the body in our dreams often refers to aspects of conscious life, while the left side represents the unconscious. The left is traditionally linked with misfortune or untrustworthiness (*sinister* means "left" in Latin), and dreams that concentrate on the left hand or left side of the body may reflect our reservations, conscious or otherwise, about an individual or a venture. Conversely, the right side is associated with trust (hence the saying "right-hand man") and good luck, and dreams focusing on the right side may have their roots in a sense of optimism.

Bones

Bones can represent the essence of things. Being stripped or cut to the bone may signify a sudden insight, but also sometimes a deep attack on the dreamer's personality. Broken bones may suggest fundamental weaknesses, whereas a skeleton is commonly associated with death.

Eyes

Eyes are symbolic windows into the soul and provide clues about the dreamer's state of spiritual health. Bright eyes suggest a healthy inner life. Dull or closed eyes, on the other hand, may point to feelings of anxiety, emotional blockage or a lack of communication.

Heart

The heart carries archetypal significance as the centre of our emotional life, and in particular as the symbol of love. Blood can connote the pulsing life-force, spilled blood its sacrifice and loss. The heart can reflect our need for unconditional love, nurturing and emotional security. If broken or imperfectly formed, the heart may point to insecurities in our feelings toward someone close to us.

Face

We rarely see our face as others see it: in photographs the colour may not be true and in a mirror the image is reversed. Seeing our own face may therefore alert us to a need to consider who we really are and perhaps discard the face we habitually present to others. A dream image of a face may also be an instance of dream wordplay. Perhaps you need to "face up" to a difficult situation? Or maybe you sense that someone is being "two-faced"?

Head

A head may symbolize an authority figure, such as our father. From the rear, it may signify an emotionally distant father; or, if he has died, a sense of loss. The head can also represent our intellect and capacity for rational thought – perhaps we are not responding to a situation logically?

Mouth

For Freud, a dream about a mouth may represent fixation in an early stage of psycho-sexual development, marked by immature characteristics such as gullibility or verbal aggression. The mouth is also, however, a symbol of communication and self-expression, and its appearance in a dream can represent unexplored creativity or unspoken emotions.

Teeth

Artemidorus interpreted the mouth as the home, with the teeth on the right side its male inhabitants and those on the left side its female. Teeth (falling out, broken, and so on) are the focus of many anxiety dreams – since the mouth is the only part of the head where we can feel sensations in repose, this is unsurprising. To dream of losing teeth can indicate a fear of losing our youth or vitality; and by extension, our sexual energy. But if we dream of losing baby teeth, this can be an optimistic symbol of the transition to a new stage of our lives.

Back

If in a dream a person turns their back on us, we may feel abandoned or let down by someone or something in our lives. If we see the back of a parent, we might feel that they have not given us sufficient support and nurturing. If a group of people have all turned away from us, the dream may be a response to exclusion.

Blood

Fundamentally, blood symbolizes life itself, but it is a complex symbol with many different facets of possible meaning. If the blood suddenly pours away, this may represent violent emotions or the feeling that someone or something is draining the life from us. Perhaps we are exerting a great effort in a relationship or the workplace and not being appreciated for it? Spilt blood can also indicate pain, suffering or injury, either physical or emotional, or if it appears as a stain we may feel some deep-seated guilt. Blood can also be associated with menstruation and therefore with renewal and female sexuality. In male dreamers this may point to a fear of women's physicality or even to fears of sexual aggression.

Nose

For Freudians, a prominent nose is a phallic symbol. The common "Pinocchio" dream of the nose growing longer as a punishment for lies is usually interpreted as revealing guilt over behaviour that is less than honest, especially in sexual matters. Alternatively, a dream in which a nose features significantly may be urging us to "follow our nose" and listen to our instincts.

Ears

When ears appear in our dreams, they may be urging us to pay greater attention to the world around us. Perhaps we are so wrapped up in our inner lives that we have failed to notice the words or behaviour of those around us – they may be trying to tell us something important.

Hair

Hair is a symbol with a multiplicity of meanings. Often indicating vanity, it can also express a woman's sense of femininity or the strength and assertiveness of either sex. In the biblical story of Samson and Delilah, Samson loses his strength when his hair is shorn, and for many people the loss of hair is an obvious sign of vanishing youth. Hair loss can also have positive connotations – to shave one's head can represent new beginnings or the renunciation of worldly ways, and shaven heads are often associated with monks.

Skin

The skin represents the appearance we present to the outside world. Smooth, blemish-free skin may indicate an unrealistic yearning for perfection, while scars and imperfections can express a sense of personal inadequacy. Wounds and scars might also represent painful emotional experiences, our attitude to which may be revealed in the dream – depending on whether we seek to conceal them or wear them with pride.

Hands

Hands represent action, whether good or ill. Washing our hands suggests denying responsibility and evokes the image of Pontius Pilate washing his hands to indicate his innocence of Christ's death. To be unable to wash a stain from our hands might imply a feeling of guilt that has not been absolved.

An open, outstretched hand can symbolize generosity or the hand of friendship, while a hand made into a fist can represent anger, aggression or strength.

Arms

Arms can be either an instrument of punishment or a means of comfort. They can be defensively crossed or open to opportunities. Raised arms might suggest authority or conflict and perhaps arms in the sense of weaponry. If we dream of outstretched arms, we may be craving comfort or physical contact. Arms encircling us might represent a yearning for consolation.

Fingernails

To dream of scratching the face of a friend or colleague does not necessarily mean that we want to hurt them. Rather, we may be expressing a desire to scratch beneath the surface of their persona in order to get to know the true person.

Legs

Legs can represent our foundations, whether we feel that we are strong and well-supported or that we "don't have a leg to stand on". They can also indicate an urge to move forward, perhaps in a relationship or career.

Belly

Since antiquity a round belly has been a symbol of female fertility, for obvious reasons. To women this may symbolize maternal feelings, while to both sexes it can indicate a desire to return to the warm protection of the womb. The abdomen is also said to represent our "gut instincts" and intuition.

Breasts

A woman's bosom can suggest the unconditional love of the mother and may express a desire to be nurtured or to nurture. As the source of all our nourishment and therefore of life itself during our earliest months, breasts are understood by Jungians to represent a desire for spiritual renewal and regeneration. A dream of breasts may also be a sexual wish-fulfilment.

Buttocks

Large buttocks can represent female sexuality or, more simply, frustrated sexual desire.

Bodily functions

Excretion usually represents the dreamer's public anxiety or shame, or his or her urgent wish to express or unburden the self, whether for creative or for cathartic reasons. Menstruation can carry similar connotations, and is often associated with a sudden release of creative energy. To dream of unsuccessfully searching for a toilet may indicate a conflict between the need to express oneself in public and a fear of doing so; while to dream of finding a toilet engaged indicates jealousy of another's position or creativity. Causing a toilet to overflow indicates fear about losing emotional control, or failure to discipline creative energy.

Washing and bathing

Washing can be a potent symbol representing purification and renewal. Many different faiths have rituals of cleansing, from the Christian rite of baptism to the act of washing your feet before entering a temple. Jungians understand dreams of washing as representing an act of purification or rejuvenation that is performed before embarking on a new stage of life or

achieving a higher level of consciousness. More mundanely, a dream that focuses specifically on washing hair may be associated with our desire to rid ourselves of a partner, friend or colleague, while vigorous cleansing of the body may stand for an obsessive need to rid ourselves of responsibilty for an action that we feel was shameful or morally wrong.

Rubbing with a towel

Rubbing the body with a towel can symbolize masturbation, which in turn can be indicative of sexual frustration. Masturbation can also be associated with feelings of guilt or shame if our parents or teachers handled our adolescent sexuality with awkwardness rather than sensitivity.

Lack of privacy

If the dreamer is anxious that a toilet lacks privacy, this may indicate fear of public exposure, or a need for greater self-expression. In Freudian terms, the dreamer may feel frustrated at not finding a suitable opportunity for self-expression. On the other hand, dreamers openly flaunting their toilet functions may reveal a tendency toward exhibitionism. Alternatively, the dream might be an expression of anger at not receiving greater public esteem or financial reward for a creative or professional endeavour.

Birth and Resurrection

The universal human experiences of birth, death and ageing often feature prominently in our dreams. We are all a part of this continual cycle, which not only encompasses the grand progress of our existence and that of the world around us, but also the cycles that occur within our lives: the beginnings and endings of relationships or the passing of the seasons and the phases of the moon. In the Jungian conception of the collective unconscious there is no finality but rather a constant cycle of change. In our dreams, as in our myths, death may figure not as the end, but as part of an overall process of growth and transformation. Just as life is born from death in the natural world (many of the world's religions celebrate the death and rebirth of the year), so our psychological

and spiritual energies constantly recreate themselves. Concerned with existence in all its aspects, the collective unconscious serves as a kind of channel through which new or renewed mental and spiritual energies can stream into the conscious world.

Dreams often enact rebirth and renewal by taking the dreamer back to childhood. A dream of being a child again may thus reflect adult concerns (such as the need for a new start or fresh inspiration), rather than a wish to revisit our formative years. Similarly, if we dream that we are older than we actually are, age may simply be standing in as a symbol for wisdom, or for mental rigidity or physical infirmity. If someone other than ourselves appears in a dream younger or older than they are, it is possible that this reflects envy of their vitality or their breadth of experience.

Resurrection – the return to life of deceased people, animals or trees – is a classic dream archetype, often associated with new life suffusing old ideas. Alternatively, such dreams may warn of the return of problems that have not yet been laid properly to rest.

Egg

In many mythological traditions an egg is described as the source of the cosmos and all existence. Discovering an egg, a baby, a newly hatched bird, or any other form of birth, can indicate the emergence of new possibilities in the dreamer's life, and may also emphasize the need for careful nurturing.

Birth

Birth, whether from the dreamer's own body or otherwise, is frequently associated with new ideas and solutions, sometimes simply as wish-fulfilment, but sometimes as a clear indication of actual possibilities waiting to be explored. Birth can also symbolize a new spiritual awakening within the dreamer, although it is important to remember that as newborns we are vulnerable and dependent on others.

Seed

Dreams involving seeds or bulbs can signify the germination of new ideas or the beginning of a new stage in our life. Great things can grow from small beginnings, so long as they are nurtured in the right environment.

Nudity and Dress

The Western tradition offers two strikingly different interpretations of nudity: on the one hand, childlike innocence; on the other hand, a profane and illicit attachment to fleshly pleasures. After falling from grace in Paradise, Adam and Eve covered their nakedness; shame had entered their consciousness, and the world could never be the same again.

In Level 3 dreams, nudity (like the archetype of the Divine Child; see page 106) can represent the dreamer's spiritual nature, or the authentic self. In Level 1 or Level 2 dreams, it can stand for a range of meanings spanning vulnerability, a desire to shed defences, a freedom from shame and a love of truth. Excessive anxiety about the nudity of oneself or others may suggest a fear of honesty and openness in relationships, or a failure to accept and integrate one's own sexual energies. For Freud, nudity could also represent a longing for the lost innocence of childhood, or an expression of the dreamer's repressed sexual exhibitionism, usually the result of punitive parental attitudes toward the dreamer during the self-display stages of childhood.

Clothing is similarly ambivalent. It can take the form of the brilliant garments of light worn by the saints, gods and angels, or it can stand for earthly vanity, an urge to deceive by appearances or to conceal shame or imperfection.

Although a cover for nakedness, clothes may by their cut, line or function draw attention to what they purport to hide. Dreams about bras or trousers may therefore represent thoughts about breasts or genitals, or about maleness, femaleness or sexuality.

Clothing, particularly in auspicious colours, may represent positive aspects of the dreamer's psychological or spiritual growth, but when over-elaborate may suggest a weakness for worldly display. Because clothes can make the wearer seem taller or thinner, richer or poorer, than he or she really is, they can stand for self-accusations of hypocrisy: a flashy waistcoat, for example, may represent our knowledge that we are deceiving others in some way, creating a false persona.

The female nude

Venus and other classical goddesses were often portrayed naked, or almost so. Such divine nudity was used as a symbol of love and sacred beauty, or in the case of the nine Muses it represented the divine truth of the arts. Nudity in a powerful woman, such as Artemis, the Greek goddess of the hunt, can help to suggest the Animus, the active principle in woman. To Freudians the female nude is usually an expression of sexual desire. For women it may indicate lesbian tendencies or a craving for self-exhibition.

Nakedness

Dreams in which we or other people are naked can have many different meanings and in order to interpret them it is important to look closely at the mood of the dream and the context in which the nudity occurs. In general terms, nakedness often indicates a yearning for lost innocence – a childlike lack of self-awareness that harks back to Adam and Eve in the Garden of Eden. Nudity can also be a sign of openness and honesty, indicating an acceptance of the true self or a willingness to face facts as they are. In an anxiety dream, however, the same sense of openness might translate into a feeling of vulnerability.

Accepting nudity

To be accepting of nudity indicates an appreciation of freedom and naturalness. Although Freudians interpret dreams where we enjoy the nudity of others as wish-fulfilment, they can also indicate an ability to see through the defences of the people around us and to accept them as they are. If we enthusiastically welcome the nakedness of the people we meet in our dreams, we may be frustrated with the affected behaviour and artificial personas of those we meet in waking life.

Nudity in children

Nudity in children often represents innocence, although it is sometimes associated with the archetypal Divine Child (see page 106). If the dreamer attempts to cover up the nudity of the young, this may indicate prudishness, artifice or a general discomfort with self-expression.

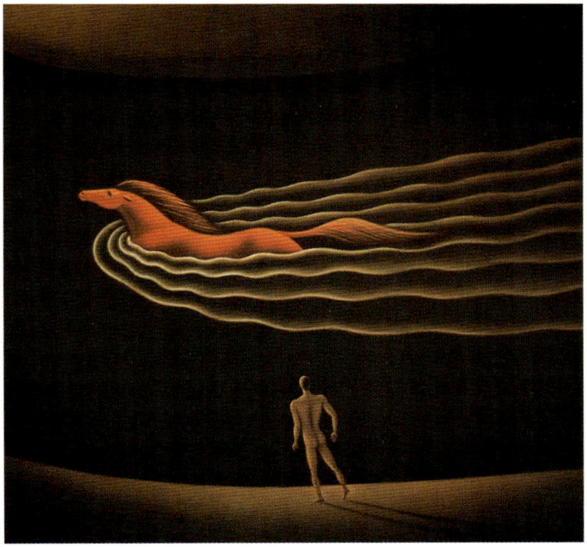

Disgust at another's nudity

To be distressed or disgusted by the nudity of another person suggests anxiety, disappointment or aversion when we discover their true nature behind the pretensions of the persona. Where there is nothing inherently offensive about the body, the dream may show an unwillingness to let other people be themselves. Equally, to respond with revulsion to the nudity of others may indicate that we are over-cautious or unwilling to engage in an emotionally or physically intimate relationship with someone.

Others unconcerned about dreamer's nudity

To dream of being naked in a public place among other people who are unconcerned or oblivious may suggest that we are not worried about what others think of us. Alternatively, it may indicate that we should discard as groundless any fears that we will be rejected if our real self – psychological, spiritual or physical – is revealed. Perhaps we need to learn to be more accepting of ourselves as we are or to open up about past emotional traumas.

Male nude

Dreams involving a male nude are interpreted by Freudians in much the same light as dreams about a female nude, indicating heterosexual or homosexual desire or, if the dreamer is male, unexpressed leanings toward exhibitionism. To Jungians an idealized male nude is associated with classical images of Greek and Roman gods and may express a profound love of culture, beauty and art or an aspiration to higher spiritual goals.

Tight or loose clothes

Over-tight or constrictive clothes (especially formal attire such as a suit or dinner jacket) usually indicate that the dreamer is inhibited or restricted by his or her public or professional role. More rarely, they suggest that the dreamer has ideas above his or her station or that they are aiming at more than can be achieved in present circumstances. The Freudian interpretation fixes on their revealing nature and understands tight clothes to represent a preoccupation with the breasts or buttocks, the shape of which they show. Conversely, wearing loose clothes can indicate a desire to be free of constraints and the inhibitions of morality and social convention. Their shapelessness can also, however, suggest that the dreamer is trying to conceal their true form and, by extension, their nature.

Cloak

A particularly ambivalent dream symbol, the cloak can stand for illicit concealment and secrecy, for mystery and the occult, or for protective warmth and love. Freudian psychology typically associates the cloak with enveloping female sexuality.

Kimono

Kimonos are associated with the East and especially with Japan. We may feel some cultural connection to the Far East or perhaps, if the kimono feels like an incongruous garment, our dream may be pointing to some aspect of our own persona that feels foreign to us.

Sweater unravelling

A dream in which a woolly garment unravels may be drawing our attention to a growing sense of disillusionment, either with an individual or with a cherished scheme or ideal. Jungian direct association can be used to identify what the sweater represents to us.

Hat

Hats hold a number of different meanings: Jung believed that hats symbolize thought and that the type of hat we find ourselves wearing in our dreams is therefore very significant. If we change hats or acquire a new hat, we may be at a stage of personal development where we are open to new ideas and willing to discard previously held beliefs, now outmoded.

Belt

Belts hold up our clothes and may therefore represent social propriety and the need to keep the guise of the persona in place. Anxiety dreams featuring a belt that is malfunctioning often reflect concerns about keeping up our public image and not transgressing the norms of acceptable social behaviour. Belts are also binding and restrictive, and to dream of loosening one may represent a desire to escape our inhibitions or those imposed upon us by the moral code or conventions of the society in which we live.

Turban

To Muslims and Sikhs turbans represent status and membership of a particular community. They carry connotations of dignity and also of dominant male authority. For people who are not a member of a turban-wearing religious or ethnic group, the garment may be associated with the unknown and the exotic. The dreamer may be craving new horizons or experiences.

Boots

We may speak of "giving something the boot" and the boot being "on the other foot": depending on the context, a dream in which boots play a significant role may be drawing our attention to the need to remove a negative influence from our life or it may reflect a change in status or reversal in fortunes. High-heeled leather or lace-up boots can also have overtones of sexual domination, while walking boots, which protect our feet and provide us with stability and grip when walking over difficult terrain, can signify the need to remain grounded during challenging episodes in our lives.

Fur

Wearing fur in dreams may point to delusions of grandeur or to nostalgia for past glories. Used to line the robes of judges and royalty, white ermine is a traditional symbol of moral purity and can represent childlike innocence or an aspiration to a position of moral or social responsibility. For Freudians, fur is a symbol of pubic hair, although a dream in which the dreamer is wrapped in a comforting garment of fur indicates a yearning to return to the warmth and safety of the womb.

Armour

A dream of wearing heavy clothing or armour indicates that we are being over-defensive in our life. The dreaming mind may be indicating that with more self-confidence, openness and social ease, we would not have to take such extreme measures to protect ourselves from the perceived dangers in the outside world.

Underclothes

Underclothes may represent unconscious attitudes and prejudices, feelings that we prefer to keep "under wraps". Their colour and condition can give important clues about the specific qualities concerned. Feelings of shame at being seen in underclothes can indicate an unwillingness to have these attitudes made public.

Dress or skirt

It has become normal for Western women to wear trousers instead of a skirt, so the appearance of a dress or skirt may indicate a need, for both men and women, to integrate and express the feminine aspects of the psyche. Some dresses have particular connotations – a dream in which we are wearing a beautiful ballgown, for example, might be encouraging us to use and display our best personal qualities.

Ring

As a symbol of matrimony, a ring can stand for commitment and fulfilment. It is also an emblem of the continuous cycle of life, with connotations of eternity.

Shorts

Shorts often represent youth and inexperience, so a dream of wearing them might indicate that we do not feel ready for a challenge we face.

People

Over a lifetime, we will probably meet many people in our dreams. Some are straightforward representations of a person we know and are perhaps involved with, in which case the dream is probably about our relationship with this individual; others represent, in a more abstract way, particular qualities, wishes or archetypal themes; others again stand for aspects of the dreamer's own self. Such is the condensed economy of dream symbolism that a single character can at times fulfil all three functions in the passage of a single dream.

Detailed analysis is often required before the exact function of a dream character can be identified; but, as with other areas of dreamwork, certain general tendencies are apparent.

Jung established that a dream companion who appears in various guises in several dreams, but is recognized as the same character, represents aspects of the dreamer's real self. By reflecting in waking life upon the behaviour of this character in the various circumstances of the dream, we are provided with insights not only into the self but also into how the self may appear to others.

Conversely, Jung maintained that the frequent appearance of a dream character who is everything that the dreamer would not wish to be represents the archetype of the Shadow – the hidden, repressed side of the self (see page 105). However, not everything about the Shadow is negative: by recognizing the Shadow, we acknowledge our darker aspects, integrating them into consciousness; if we ignore the Shadow, on the other hand, our darker nature may appear again and again in our dreams, disguising itself in increasingly destructive forms.

When very beautiful or powerful men or women appear in our dreams, they are often representations of the Anima and Animus archetypes (see page 103), the feminine and masculine principles that coexist within all of us at the level of the collective unconscious. Such figures encourage us to cultivate the masculine or feminine aspects of our personality, whichever is weaker at that stage in our lives, and to seek strength in its qualities.

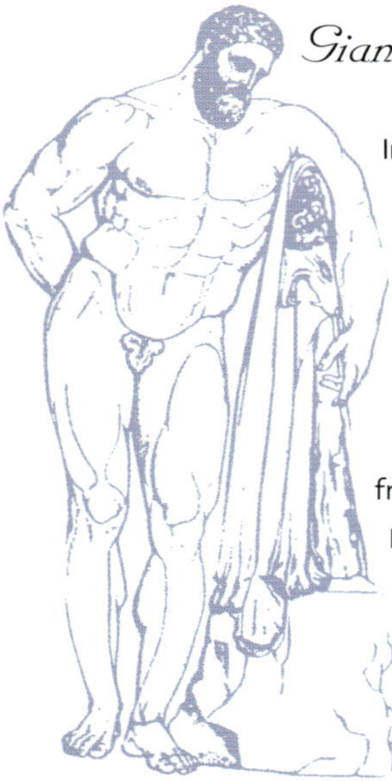

Giant

In adult dreams, giants may represent recollections of childhood, when all adults towered above the dreamer. For children, they may represent present realities, such as the frightening side of the father. But although dream giants are awe-inspiring, not all of them are unfriendly. Some may symbolize the care and protection that the strong can give to the weak. If you see yourself as a Gulliver-like giant, surrounded by tiny people, this can point either to feelings of superiority or to a heightened sense of self-consciousness. Perhaps you are blowing your insecurities out of all proportion?

Old man

An elderly man is often a representation of the Wise Old Man archetype (see pages 103–104). He may provide us with guidance – for example, in identifying the right course of action to take in a difficult situation. If, however, he appears unwell and infirm, he might symbolize fears of ageing or death, or in the case of male dreamers, impotence anxiety.

Hag

The aged crone appears in the mythology and folk legends of cultures across the globe. Closely linked to the Jungian archetype of the devouring Great Mother (see page 106), the hag can be both a helpful figure and a hostile one, but in either case represents our latent inner wisdom. To Freudians, the hag often represents castration anxiety or unresolved issues with our mother.

Beggar

Beggars can appear in our dreams to remind us of the chimerical nature of our material aspirations or perhaps as a symbol for low self-esteem. They are at the very bottom of the social scale and they depend entirely on others for support; however, their lives are not tied to a daily routine of work nor to one place of rest. It is possible that a dream in which the symbol of the beggar, or perhaps a gypsy, occurs may represent a yearning to escape the routine, drudgery or conventions of daily life.

Silent witness

A person who is present in a dream but refuses or is unable to speak often represents an imbalance between emotion and intellect, one overpowering the other to render it speechless or impotent.

Hooligan

Refusing to behave in accordance with the rules of society, the young hooligan can represent the desire to throw off old conventions or inhibitions that may be constricting our personal growth. Conversely, this may be a symbol of our destructive potential, and in Jungian terms may be expressing some part of the urges of the dark side of the persona, the Shadow.

Widow

Freudians see the widow, who has lost her husband and therefore the male energy from her life, as symbolic of castration anxiety for men. More generally, the widow may respresent death, or an experience of great loss.

Child

Dreams in which we picture ourselves as a child often hark back to lost childhood innocence as well as the unconditional love of our parents. A child can also often represent aspects of ourselves – perhaps a sense of vulnerability or a playful side to our nature that we do not often express, or a yearning to start afresh after taking a wrong turning.

Family

When our whole family appears in a dream, we may be yearning for the warmth and togetherness of the home. If we can see our family but are not a part of the group, this may indicate a feeling of estrangement.

Mother

The mother is a complex dream symbol with many layers of meaning. On a universal, archetypal level, Mother Nature is a symbol of rebirth, fertility and continuity. She gives life and nourishes; however, she may also represent

death and the return to earth, which must occur in order to make way for new life. Jungians see the Great Mother archetype (see page 106) as having a profound effect on our psychological growth. In the Freudian interpretation, however, the mother can be either an object of unconscious desire or a figure that represents castration anxiety. Dreams of our own mother may carry aspects of either interpretation, or they may literally be about our relationship with our mother. How we interact with her in our dreams may carry clues as to the nature of our present relationship and to issues that might have resulted from our upbringing.

Father

As with our mother, a dream in which our father plays a significant role may simply be addressing aspects of our relationship with him. The emotions we experience within the dream – anger, resentment or pleasure, for example – are of vital importance when we come to interpret the dream. Freudians, however, view dreams about our father as explicitly sexual – either expressing sexual insecurity or incestuous desire, depending on whether the dreamer is male or female. To Jungians the father is more likely to represent the Wise Old Man archetype.

Twins

Often representing different aspects of the dreamer's personality, happy twins suggest that opposing aspects of the self are integrated and in harmony. If we dream about twins in conflict, however, this may represent inner turmoil.

Brother or sister

Dreams involving our siblings may invoke memories of sibling rivalry and jealousy. Although the intensity of the competition can be startling when it comes to light in our dreams, it may stem entirely from our storehouse of remembered experiences and does not necessarily mean that the rivalry has persisted into adult life.

Uncle or aunt

The dreaming mind often uses uncles and aunts as substitutes for our mother and father when expressing our unconscious feelings toward either or both parents. Jungians might interpret an uncle as representing the Animus of a female dreamer and an aunt as the Anima of a male (see page 103).

Grandparents

Our grandparents can represent the Jungian archetypes of the Wise Old Man and the Great Mother. They may also be used to symbolize the safety and security of familial love and support. Often our relationship with our grandparents is less fraught than that with our parents, and a dream in which they feature may indicate a yearning for a similarly untroubled relationship.

Friends

A dream where our friends fail to recognize us or pretend they do not know us may express a lack of self-confidence. It could also, however, indicate doubts we may be having about a particular relationship. Or it may be the dreaming mind's way of gently reminding us of the ephemeral nature of popularity.

Audience

If we dream that we are greeted with rousing applause at a public meeting, we may have achieved some breakthrough in our waking life. Perhaps we have finally received the recognition we feel we deserve. If, however, we are faced with jeers from an angry crowd, this may reflect feelings of paranoia or low self-esteem.

Party or gathering

A dream where we are the host at a party or gathering might indicate a craving for attention or a desire for the affection of our friends.

It could also express a wish to reconnect with friends or family whom we feel we have neglected. If somebody who is no longer a part of our life, perhaps a former partner or a deceased relative, appears at the gathering, the dreaming mind may be highlighting our sense of loss.

Boss

While a dream about one's boss may reflect anxieties stemming from the workplace, our employer can also represent aspects of our relationship with our parents. If in a dream we find ourselves asking for a pay rise, this might reflect a craving for more attention from our parents or for more overt expressions of love. If, on the other hand, we are made redundant, this may be the dreaming mind expressing the pain of parental rejection. Dreams where we are the boss may stem from a desire for a dominant sexual relationship.

Foreigners

An individual or a group of people speaking an unintelligible foreign language may symbolize aspects of the self that we find difficult to understand or accept. Alternatively, this dream may indicate that we have difficulties with communication, either in general or with one particular issue or individual.

Landlord or landlady

A dream image of a house is often understood to represent the self. To dream that someone else owns our house can therefore indicate that we do not feel in control of our own life. Perhaps a parent or partner is overly dominant, or maybe we feel that our actions are dictated by events rather than by our wishes.

Occupations

Occupations feature prominently in dreams. Whether focusing on one's own trade or profession, or on that of other dream characters, such dreams usually relate to aspects of the dreamer's own personality. The workplace is a rich source of metaphor, embracing both objects and actions, upon which dreams draw freely to express their special purposes.

A visit to the optician, for example, may indicate a short-sighted approach to relationships or to other personal or professional issues. We may find ourselves trying to sell newspapers to unheeding passers-by – a dream experience that may signify an inability to alert others to important information of some kind, and perhaps the need for a fresh approach. A dream of applying for a number of different jobs could indicate a similar need, perhaps emphasizing that the dreamer will become increasingly frustrated and disillusioned unless he or she adopts a clearer sense of direction in life.

Often we find ourselves dreaming of a current role or project, in which case the dream may be highlighting our anxieties about it, or pointing out areas where we are functioning unproductively, or letting opportunities slip by.

Even those dreams that appear simply to replay incidents from the previous working day are usually intent on providing clues about why things went badly or well, or suggesting how matters might be more successfully dealt with in the future.

Bureaucrat

A dream of dealing with bureaucracy often relates to a lack of emotion, either in the dreamer or in those with whom he or she comes into contact. The dream may be urging a more personal and committed approach to relationships. Alternatively, it may be emphasizing the dreamer's helplessness in understanding complex issues, or perhaps signifying that it is necessary to pay greater attention to detail. More generally, bureaucrats may symbolize the impersonal machinery of a world that resists our efforts to succeed, whether in work or in creative projects or even in resolving niggling everyday problems.

Dentist

Perhaps unsurprisingly, a frequent cause of dentist dreams is toothache. When we do not have problems with our teeth, the Freudian interpretation of dreams in which we have a tooth extracted is that they express castration anxiety. Jung, on the other hand, found that when women dream about going to the dentist, this is often associated with giving birth – the dreaming mind renders the symbolic obstetrician as the more familiar figure of the dentist.

Engineer

We may see the engineer as a redeemer, fixing the cogs and wheels of our world in times of trouble. Working in a basement, in the depths of our unconscious, he may prevent destructive urges from disrupting our conscious life. He may be a close friend, beloved relative or trusted advisor.

Builder

Houses are usually understood to represent the self, and as result a person working on a house often represents our father or someone who has been similarly influential in our life. If the house is not yet completed, then the dream may be a reflection on our childhood and the dependent relationship that we then had with our parents.

Conductor

Depending on the mood and context, a dream in which we are the conductor of an orchestra may indicate either a wish to dictate the actions of others or a desire to exercise more control over our own creative impulses. The spiritual associations of music might mean that this dream expresses a yearning for transcendence or for spiritual guidance.

Mechanic

A mechanic surrounded by a multitude of car parts may represent our frustration with the task of keeping our life in order. The seemingly impossible job of reassembling an engine from its constituent components, of finding the right tools and discovering the source of the problem, echoes the challenge posed by the chaotic events of everyday life.

Miner

Anything underground is usually related to your unconscious mind, and so the miner, working deep beneath the surface of the earth, can represent self-discovery. In the same way that ores are transformed into precious metals after they are brought to the surface of the earth, the wisdom that we uncover within our unconscious needs to be subjected to the examination of the conscious mind in order to provide us with true insight.

Sailor

Owing to their connection with the sea and therefore with the unconscious, sailors typically represent the adventurous side of the dreamer, and the desire to explore unknown reaches of the inner self.

Chemist

Jung linked the ancient practice of alchemy to inner transformation. A modern equivalent of the alchemist, a chemist may symbolize the dreamer's quest for spiritual fulfilment.

Doctor

If, in a dream, we are the patient, then the doctor often becomes the subject of what psychoanalysts term "transference" – whereby we redirect toward doctors, for example, the emotions that surround our relationship with our parents, either in the present or in the past.

Admiral

Freudians see ships as a phallic symbol. In a similar vein, a dream in which we are an admiral may indicate a need for more control in a relationship, or perhaps even a desire to dominate our partner sexually.

Plumber

The pipes and valves of a house can represent both our internal organs and the innermost workings of our mind and emotions. A dream in which a plumber features significantly may reveal concerns we have about our health, or else may relate to a process of psychological or emotional exploration and healing.

Nurse

Our interpretation of a dream image of a nurse depends on whether we see ourselves in the role of patient or carer. In the former case, our dream may indicate a desire to be mothered; in the latter, it may be an expression of our maternal instincts.

Mortality

The collective unconscious takes the long-term rather than the short-term view, associating death with change rather than with finality. However, at an individual level, death has always vexed, terrified and fascinated us, and the Level 1 and 2 dreams (see pages 65–70) that lie not far below the surface of our conscious minds may be filled with anxieties about our own death or about the ultimate or actual loss of loved ones or friends.

Fearful dreams about our own mortality may indicate the need for us to come more conclusively to terms, in conscious life, with our inevitable fate. Dreams about the death of others, though, may depict

more generalized fears – for example, a concern about the annihilation of the personality or the self, or a dread of judgment or divine retribution, or of hell, or of the manner of death, and so on.

Death in dreams sometimes carries precognitive warnings about the future. Abraham Lincoln dreamed his own death only days before he was assassinated, seeing his corpse laid out in funeral vestments in a room of the White House. Many dreams of death, however, have no association with mortality at all. Some may relate to aspects of the dreamer's own psychological life, or to a change

in life circumstances. Symbols of death may also draw the dreamer's attention to forthcoming irrevocable events, such as retirement, losing a job, moving house, or ending a close relationship.

Reading the obituary of someone during a dream, or seeing their tombstone, or attending their funeral, may suggest the dismissal of that person from a job, or their relegation from the dreamer's affections, or their fall from grace in some other way.

Dream images relating to the dreamer's own death can carry similar meanings, although *The Golden Dreamer*, a dream handbook published in 1840, saw such images as denoting a speedy marriage and success in all undertakings.

Funeral

The dream image of a funeral often reflects a moment of closure, such as the ending of a relationship, rather than death. Where it is a stranger's funeral, this can be a reminder of the passing of time, of the irrecoverable nature of the past, or of the dangers of entering into too many emotional attachments.

Symbols of death

Medieval churchyards are full of *momenti mori* (reminders of mortality), and scholars of the time often kept skulls on their desks as objects of reflection. The hourglass and the figure of the reaper are also important symbols. Dreams of such deathly paraphernalia may remind the dreamer that life carries a limited span in which to complete projects, or may point to forthcoming finalities such as the end of a marriage.

Burial

Being buried alive can represent feelings of claustrophobia – either physical or metaphorical. More generally, burial may suggest the repression of our instincts – anxieties we choose to ignore or desires we decide not to express. It can also symbolize laying a painful emotional experience to rest.

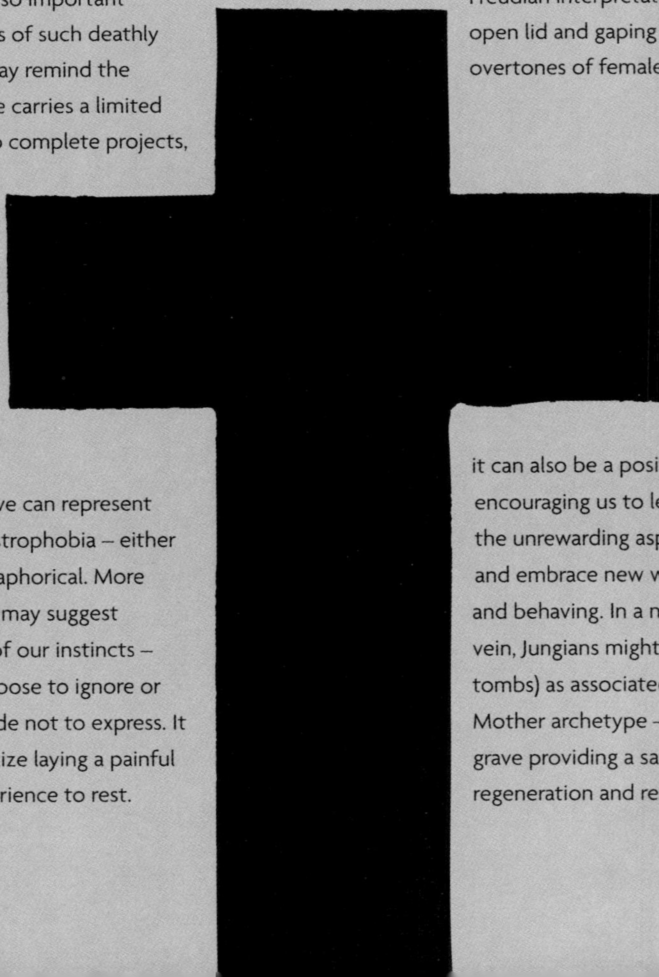

Coffin

While the dream image of a coffin may obviously represent death, or our fear of death, it can also signify the ending of one phase of our life and the beginning of a new one. In the Freudian interpretation, a coffin's open lid and gaping insides gives it overtones of female sexuality.

Grave

An open grave might seem like a morbid reminder of our own mortality. However, it can also be a positive symbol, encouraging us to leave behind the unrewarding aspects of our life and embrace new ways of thinking and behaving. In a not dissimilar vein, Jungians might see graves (or tombs) as associated with the Great Mother archetype – the quiet of the grave providing a safe space for rest, regeneration and rebirth.

Cemetery

A graveyard or cemetery is not only a place in which to mourn and bury our dead, it also provides a focus for remembrance. In our dreams a cemetery may represent family unity, reaffirming the continuity between past and present generations.

Obituary

The experience of reading your own obituary is a fairly common dream. It may point to anxieties about losing your social standing or being fired from your job. If it is the obituary of someone you know, you may harbour some unexpressed resentment against them.

Hanging

Execution by hanging and other means such as beheading by the guillotine was understood by Freud to symbolize male castration anxiety, and therefore fear of impotence and the loss of sexual virility. There might also be a suggestion of feeling guilty about a crime, real or imagined.

Objects

The dream world is furnished with a multiplicity of objects, some familiar to the dreamer, some strange and unrecognizable. All have potential significance, but sometimes it is the more obscure items that provide the richest clues in dream interpretation. However, not all associations are oblique, and some have obvious symbolic links with waking experience. A camera, for example, often represents a wish to preserve and perhaps cling to the past, while hiding things in obscure places may stand for a wish for self-concealment. The object's function is usually its most important aspect, although shape, colour and texture can also be significant.

Tools and Implements

Useful implements often feature in dreams about performance. They may indicate anxiety about our abilities or draw our attention to talents as yet unexplored.

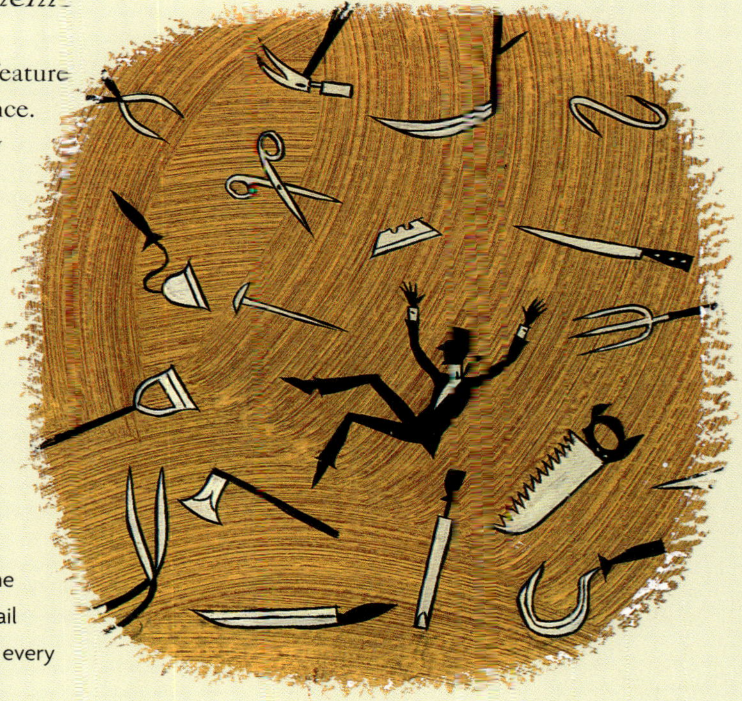

Nails

To Christians, nails may invoke the Crucifixion. They can be symbols of suffering and sacrifice. In some cultures, however, they are believed to have protective qualities – the Romans, for example, drove a nail into the wall of Jupiter's temple every September to ward off disaster.

Hammer

A hammer channels brute force to drive a stake into the ground or a nail into a wall or a piece of wood. It can represent willpower and determination, perhaps in an issue of moral or ethical judgment.

Nuts and bolts

Nuts and bolts can represent the practical aspects of a task, and their appearance in a dream may highlight the need to think beyond the theoretical consideration. Freudians focus on the sexual connotations of their shapes.

Devices

The world as we know it is full of ingenious devices – from hand-wound clocks to the latest in computing technology. Any of these may appear in our dreams, whether we use them on a regular basis or not.

Umbrella

Rain may seem unpleasant when we get wet but it is essential for the fertility of the earth and, indeed, for the functioning of all life on our planet. To shelter under an umbrella in a dream may indicate that the dreamer is denying him- or herself access to sources of physical or spiritual nourishment and growth. The sexual symbolism of an umbrella depends upon whether it is open (female) or closed (male).

Telephone

Telephones more often than not represent communication, or the breakdown of communication. If we fail to make ourselves understood on the telephone, this can suggest weakness in our ability to convey our thoughts, feelings or ideas to others.

Clock or watch

The ticking of a clock equates to the beating of the heart. Hence, a racing clock can symbolize emotions running high; a stopped clock, frozen emotion. Clocks may also evoke the transient nature of life and the relentless passage of time.

Computer

While the Freudian interpretation sees keyboards, disk drives and USB ports as symbols of female sexuality, Jungians prefer to understand computers in the light of humankind's shared wealth of wisdom. A formidable resource, they can also appear in our dreams as representations of work-related anxiety – an overflowing email inbox or impossibly cluttered desktop can indicate concerns about our workload.

Machinery

Competent use of machinery can indicate enhanced personal power. If the dreamer becomes a machine, this may stand for a loss of sensitivity.

Flashlight or torch

Just as we use a flashlight to provide light in the darkness, so in our dreams it can represent the search for truth and integrity in a world which may sometimes seem dominated by the forces of corruption, greed or ignorance. If a torch flickers or goes out, this may symbolize loss of hope or the death of a dearly held ideal.

Television

Dreams in which we appear on television may suggest a need to communicate emotions or ideas that we have difficulty sharing with others in waking life. They can also represent a plea for attention, perhaps from a loved one or maybe from a wider audience. We may even be craving fame or have had a taste of celebrity status and are eager for more.

Radio

The radio is a powerful dream symbol because, more than television or even newspapers, it requires us to use our imagination to provide the visual dimension of the information it broadcasts. A dream-radio may therefore stand for the dreamer's inner voice. Interference or static may suggest that we cannot hear or are not listening to our innermost thoughts.

Camera

Cameras offer us a way to capture memories that might otherwise slip away from us. When things are moving too fast or we are in the middle of radical change we may dream about taking photographs of people or places or events that we feel we might not otherwise remember or that we would, perhaps unconsciously, like to hold firm in our minds.

Household Items

Some objects we handle daily without giving them much thought. These same items also commonly crop up in our dreams. The familiar is a powerful foil to the surreal and the dreaming mind makes good use of it.

Matches

Matches are associated with fire and light, and a dream image of lighting a flame with matches could indicate a desire to ignite any of the qualities linked to these elemental symbols – purification, passion or spiritual enlightenment – for example, a flame that is extinguished or matches that fail to light can signify loss of faith or spiritual doubts.

Books

Books variously represent wisdom, the intellect, or a record of the dreamer's life. Inability to read the words in a book may indicate the dreamer's need to develop greater powers of concentration and awareness in waking life.

Garbage can

A garbage can frequently signifies unwanted memories or duties, or aspects of the self that the dreamer wishes to discard. It can also suggest a desire for new beginnings.

Mirror

Seeing a strange face in the mirror often indicates an identity crisis. If the face is startling, it may stand for the Shadow, the archetype that represents the dreamer's darker side. Somebody walking out of a mirror may hint that new aspects are emerging from the unconscious, while an empty mirror can represent the clean slate of the dreamer's mind before the ego overlays it with wishes and self-images.

Drinking glass

Like the cup, the drinking glass is a classic female sexual symbol. A broken glass can symbolize lost virginity – a wine glass is traditionally broken at Jewish weddings. Jungians see a glass as equivalent to the Holy Grail, and therefore associate it with love and truth.

Basket

Filled with fruit and vegetables, a basket can be a symbol of fertility and abundance. Its shape lends itself to an interpretation of female sexuality. Depending on the state of the basket's contents, the sexuality symbolized may range from youthful exuberance to ripe maturity.

Soap

An obvious sign of purification, soap may represent feelings of guilt you seek to wash away or a desire to cleanse your life of negative influences. The childhood threat of having your mouth washed out with soap may reverberate in your dreams as a warning against casual obscenity or speaking ill of others.

Pins and needles

Pins and needles usually have sexual overtones and dreams that feature actions such as threading needles or sewing can be an expression of sexual desire. We may even prick our finger with a needle and draw blood.

Broom

Just as we would use a broom to sweep dust from a house in the waking world, in our dreams a broom often signifies a process of clearing out old ideas or habits to make way for a fresh approach. A broom can also, however, have overtones of intolerance and authoritarianism – clearing a debate of dissenting voices, for example, or purging an organization of its divisive factions.

Hairpin

The Freudian interpretation emphasizes the arched shape of a hairpin and points to female sexual symbolism. A woman taking a hairpin from an elaborate arrangement and releasing her hair from the confines of a bun or chignon is a classic image of feminine seduction.

Wheelbarrow

A wheelbarrow cannot move unless we push it, and therefore carries connotations of action and energy. We may use a wheelbarrow to clear unwanted growth from our garden or move debris that is blocking a path or obscuring a view. It is a dream symbol associated with change and with clearing aspects of our life or of the self that may be impeding our personal or spiritual development.

Bag

A bag can be a symbol of our hopes for the future. If we feel weighed down and unable to carry it, we may feel burdened by our responsibilities. If the bag is empty, this may signify a sense of purposelessness or, more positively, a desire to seek out fresh goals.

Cushion

A cushion can be associated with an individual who protects us from hard knocks. Sometimes it may be drawing attention to the need to deal with difficulties on our own.

Chair

A chair can be an image of female sexuality. A broken chair, or one that collapses underneath us, may signify the end of a sexual relationship. How comfortable a dream chair is may, for women, represent how comfortable they are with thier sexuality, while for men it may convey how much at ease they are with a sexual partner.

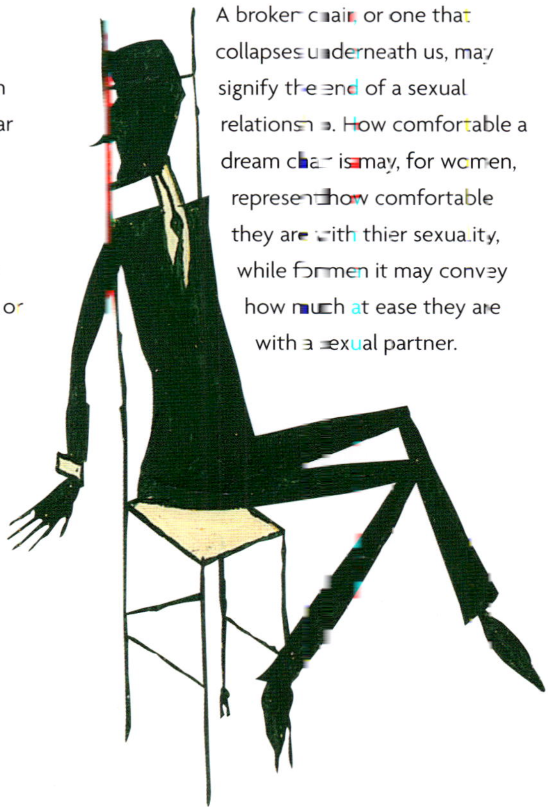

Toys and Games

The most obvious symbolism of toys relates to childhood and perhaps to a nostalgic yearning to return to its comforts. Toys can also, however, have more complex overtones – the world of dolls and mechanical trains is one we can control, and dreams in which these objects appear may occur at times when we are having difficulty controlling the adult world. Individual toys can have specific associations, as can different types of games. In adult dreams games are often microcosmic representations of the dreamer's life. A board game may enact the advances and setbacks of a recent experience.

Toy train

To dream of a toy train may represent our wish to assert control over the direction and power of our own life, even if this means reducing it to something restrictive, predictable and mechanical. A toy train may also suggest the dreamer's urge to return to the small, secure world of childhood where other people take reponsibility for our well-being.

Puppet

If toy dreams focus on asserting control over problems, puppet dreams are about asserting control over people. Glove puppets or marionettes suggest manipulation and a lack of free choice. The dreamer may discover that the puppet stands as a symbol of the wish for power over others, or a lack of control in his or her own life, referring to the cliché that somebody else is pulling the strings.

Spinning top

The hypnotic spinning motion of a top recalls a trance-like state of deep meditation. It is one of the most ancient of toys and may appear in our dreams when we are delving into the unconscious.

Doll

Dolls may represent the Anima or Animus, the qualities of the opposite sex within ourselves. Jung also found that dolls sometimes indicate a lack of communication between the conscious and unconscious levels of the mind.

Soft toy

Dreaming of soft toys often represents comfort, security or uncritical emotional support. The dreamer may be seeking an unqualified emotional acceptance by others, harking back to the relationships of childhood; or alternatively the dream may be registering a refusal to face reality, or the need for more natural or more tactile contact with loved ones.

Swing

Freudians link the rhythmic motion of playing on a swing with sexual intercourse. Other dream interpreters, however, believe that it is more likely to represent the unpredictable – and sometimes – varied, nature of life.

Dice

Dice stand for chance and may express a feeling that random, arbitrary factors, rather than ability, effort or worth, are governing our personal or professional progress.

Board game

Dreams about board games frequently represent the dreamer's progress through life, with all its ups and downs. They may be wish-fulfilments, in which the dreamer competes and wins, or they may reveal a fear of competition. Specific games may have their own symbolism – for example, sin and sexuality in snakes and ladders, or the unconscious and conscious minds battling each other in the "inner" and "outer" tables of backgammon.

Weapons

Weapons are a symbol of both authority and masculinity. Although Freudians do not hesitate to highlight the sexual significance of weapons, there are other possibilities: they can suggest frustration as well as aggression, and they can indicate the strength of our desire for change. They can also represent the power to fight repression and a means of making our opinions heard.

Knives and daggers

The knife is by far the most common male sexual symbol. It can represent the penis in its ability to penetrate, and can stand for masculinity in its associations with violence and aggression. It may also represent the "sword of truth" that cuts through falsity and ignorance, or the will to cut away false desires. As an emblematic item of dress, a Scotsman's dirk or a Sikh's *kirpan* symbolizes traditional male authority and the ability to protect. The dagger is also the weapon associated with furtive assassination and its appearance in our dreams may reveal concealed feelings of animosity.

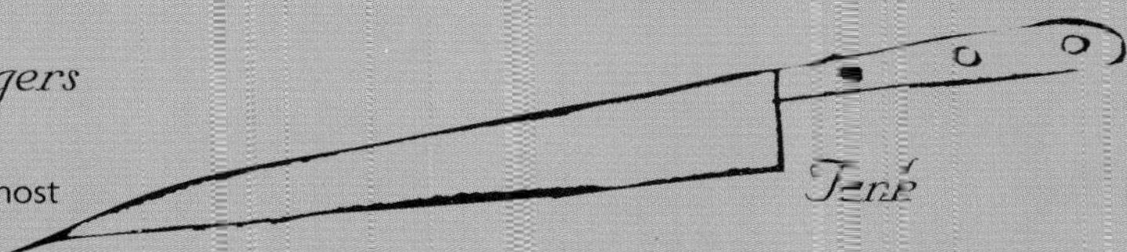

Ineffective weapons

Any weapon that refuses to fire or discharge in defence of the dreamer suggests powerlessness: the dream is indicating to us that we must find better ways of arming ourselves against the challenges of the world. For Freud, a gun or knife that refuses to function suggests sexual impotence or fear thereof, or perhaps the loss of a different form of power.

Tank

A tank indiscriminately flattens everything in its path, and its appearance in our dreams may suggest that we are unwilling to listen to opinions other than our own. The turret and prominent cannon of a tank make it one of the most aggressive of phallic symbols, and our response to it can prove enlightening. An accompanying feeling of panic may suggest underlying sexual anxieties, while a sense of excitement might indicate a craving for a more boisterous, even violent, type of sexual experience.

Torpedo

Phallic in shape, the torpedo is another symbol of male sexuality. Travelling by stealth underwater, it may imply a desire for illicit sexual relations.

Artillery

High-power missiles, cannons and field guns are all obvious phallic symbols. They can also represent the obstacles that seem to be ranged against us. This can be especially true for women in traditionally male occupations. Who are the "big guns" blocking your road to success?

Bow and arrow

The traditional weapon of Cupid, the dream image of a bow and arrow can symbolize the tension of holding the arrow of our socially unacceptable unconscious impulses in check.

Axe

An axe has the potential to be a creative rather than a destructive symbol, clearing away unwanted growth in order to make space for new life. It can symbolize the dreamer's readiness to make a clean break from the past or their determination to find a way through an emotional impasse. Sometimes an axe can represent an executioner's axe – a powerful symbol of judgment: perhaps we have a guilty conscience and need to take steps to assuage it, or perhaps we seek retribution for others.

Mace

The function of a mace is now primarily ceremonial rather than aggressive. The spiked club, often ornamented with precious metals and jewels, has become an emblem of authority, and its appearance in our dreams can denote a desire for status or responsibility.

Ornaments

Objects that are not primarily useful but are valued for their aesthetic qualities or inherent worth make for interesting symbols. Many, such as those embellished with diamonds or rubies, have traditional associations (eternity and passion or power respectively); others, such as shells or vases, may be significant because of their shape or function.

Shell

The shell is a profoundly spiritual symbol which often represents the unconscious – and, through its links with the sea, the imagination. It also stands for the divine female: Venus was born from a shell off the coast of Cyprus.

Jewel

Jewels often suggest a valued aspect of the dreamer. Diamonds (see also page 256) typically represent the incorruptible true self. Rubies denote power or passion, sapphires truth, and emeralds fertility. Jewels may also represent buried treasure, the archetype of divine wisdom hidden in the depths of the collective unconscious. Any lost jewel can suggest bereavement, separation or loss of virginity.

Turquoise

The vibrant blue colour of turquoise associates it with the sky and in our dreams it can represent our higher aspirations. Turquoise is believed to have protective qualities: in Europe and Asia it is traditionally used to ward off the "evil eye".

Pearl

Pearls are associated with water, the moon and shells. They represent the feminine, love and marriage. Freudians understand pearls to symbolize female sexuality, especially if inside an oyster (an image of the vagina) or adorning a woman's neck or ears. Pearls also have overtones of purity and are seen by Jungians as an aspiration to spiritual maturity and transcendence of the material world. In China pearls represent genius in obscurity, hidden as they are inside the coarse oyster shell.

Diamond

Diamond is created when coal is subjected to intense pressure. The appearance of a diamond in a dream may be an unconscious suggestion that a stressful situation may result in the creation of something brilliant. The dreaming mind might use the idea of a diamond in the rugged rock to suggest that we may need to look beyond the rough exterior of an individual to understand their true nature. Diamonds can also symbolize clarity, eternity and pure being.

Jade

In China, jade is traditionally said to be the sperm of the celestial dragon, vitrified as it fell to earth. The substance represents a powerful union of heaven and earth, and symbolizes fertility and the primal cosmic energies.

Plastic flower

Flowers often symbolize sexuality, and fake flowers could suggest that a sexual partner is

perhaps not being completely honest about their emotions or sexual conduct.

Fan

Fans were once imbued with a rich symbolism and could even be used as a means of communication, transmitting furtive messages, usually about love. Today, much of the language of the fan is lost to us but the object has retained its association with flirtation and is still very much an image of female sexuality. A fan that appears to be cooling the dreamer's ardour may in fact be fanning the flames of passion.

Horseshoe

Horseshoes are a well-known good luck charm and their appearance in our dreams suggests the promise of success. Their cup-like shape gives them a sexual symbolism made explicit in the game where they are thrown over iron pegs.

Vase

The hollow form and lithe lines of a vase make it a possible symbol of female sexuality. Its shape means that it may also be a representation of the heart and the emotions.

Food and Drink

Food represents nourishment, whether physical, mental, emotional or spiritual. Different types of food have very different meanings. A shiny red apple, for example, should be interpreted in a very different light from a juicy red steak. Moreover, food can be rich in personal associations. Whether you love or hate a certain type of food, were forced to eat it by your parents or were told that it was exceptionally nourishing will have an impact on its significance when it appears in your dreams.

Ham or bacon

For many people bacon is a fundamental part of a filling cooked breakfast, while a joint of ham conjures up memories of homely family meals. Both are associated with a sense of satiety and fulfilment. For Jews and Muslims, however, these are prohibited foods and their appearance in dreams might represent the constraints of religious morality or a sense of not belonging or of exclusion.

Oyster

To Freudians, oysters, with or without a pearl, are a representation of the female genitals. They also may suggest esoteric knowledge.

Spaghetti

Spaghetti is a highly charged erotic symbol evoking pubic hair and the genitals of both sexes. We may dream that we are swimming in spaghetti or perhaps that our hair is made of pasta. These dreams might suggest a need for sexual fulfilment.

Eel

A phallic symbol, on account of its shape: whether we respond to an eel with excitement or aversion can be indicative of our attitude to sex. The dream image of an eel may also be wordplay on the phrase "as slippery as an eel", suggesting that an acquaintance may not be trustworthy.

Cucumber

Freud, an inveterate smoker, once claimed that "sometimes a cigar is just a cigar" – meaning that not all elongated shapes are phallic. However, he would probably not have said the same of a cucumber – an unapologetically phallic symbol. The size of a cucumber in a dream may provide information about our sex drive.

Grape

Grapes often stand for luxurious sensuality. They are a fruit to be shared and playfully fed to a lover, expressing oral sexuality. Grapes are also associated with the product of their juice: wine. Wine symbolizes intoxication, wild abandon and the ability to transcend the prosaic routines of daily life. But for Christians wine may represent the blood of Christ and therefore have overtones of sacrifice and rebirth.

Fig

Figs can represent a man's testicles if they appear whole, or the female sexual organs if they are cut in half. In either case as befits a sumptuous fruit filled with seeds, figs are a symbol of fertility and sexual desire. Adam and Eve are traditionally depicted wearing fig leaves.

Peach

In traditional Chinese iconography, peaches are a symbol of purity and immortality – peach boughs were laid outside houses in the New Year. In the West, however, peaches more commonly represent lasciviousness.

Chocolate

Chocolate or any other luxury food generally represents self-indulgence and self-reward. It may suggest guilt and, by extension, various experiences or indulgences that the dreamer feels should be resisted or denied.

Oatmeal or porridge

A deeply comforting food, oatmeal or porridge, is associated with our early years when we received unconditional love and care from our parents. Its sticky, glutinous texture could also, however, stand for an emotional impasse or a feeling of sluggishness or stagnation.

Bread

Bread is a powerful symbol of life, of the abundance of nature and of fertility. Whether it represents male or female sexuality depends on the shape of the loaf – a French baguette has obvious phallic connotations, while a round loaf may remind us of the pregnant female form.

Toast

A great comfort food, toast may remind us nostalgically of family life when we were growing up. It can encourage us to enjoy life's simpler pleasures and to relish the daily routines of domesticity. Burnt toast might signify the distress caused when our relationship with a partner or our family is acrimonious.

Jam

The dreaming mind often uses jam to symbolize a sticky situation from which we need to extricate ourselves. Like other red substances, strawberry or raspberry jam can represent blood and therefore anger or violence. Alternatively, it might signify anxiety linked to female sexuality and the issues surrounding it, such as virginity or menstruation.

Cornflakes

Cornflakes have been inextricably linked, through advertising, to an idealized image of family life. When they appear in our dreams, they may express a wish for domestic harmony.

Carrot

As well as being an obviously phallic symbol, carrots are associated with good sight and especially with the ability to see in the dark. A dream image of a carrot might suggest that we need to examine events closely in order to clearly perceive the truth.

Salt

Salt is a powerful preservative and has remarkable purifying properties. Its appearance in our dreams may be a sign that we need to protect ourselves against corruption. Although today we treat salt as a commonplace table condiment, in ancient Rome and ancient China it was considered so valuable that it was used as currency. Perhaps our unconscious mind is drawing our attention to the potential value of someone or something that might otherwise escape our attention.

Mashed potato

If we dream that we are eating buttery, creamy mashed potato, this can be an expression of nostalgia for the comforts of childhood. Lumpy, tasteless mash, on the other hand, might recall unpleasant experiences at school or the neuroses of adolescence.

Wedding cake

A wedding cake can represent new beginnings full of potential. If we find ourselves dwarfed by the cake, staring up at its many tiers, we may feel overwhelmed by a commitment that we have made, marital or otherwise. To see ourselves as one of the tiny figures on top of the cake can be an expression of satisfaction at our achievements so far.

Coffee and tea

A daily part of life for many people, coffee and tea carry overtones of routine and rejuvenation. Both can be social beverages and as such may suggest a desire to spend more time with our friends. Coffee is generally seen to be the more caffeinated of the two and can imply a need for stimulation. Tea enjoys a more domestic image and might suggest that we could do with spending more time at home or cultivating our relationship with our family.

Banana

This is an obvious phallic symbol. A dream about eating or peeling a banana can be highly charged sexually. However, bananas can have non-sexual symbolism too: a banana skin lying in our path might convey misgivings about the potential hazards of pursuing a course of action.

Butter

In the past, butter was used in the preparation of sacrificial meats and can therefore be associated with prayer, renunciation and sacred energy. In another instance of dream wordplay, butter may signify flattery, as in the common phrase "to butter someone up". Perhaps our unconscious is warning us that someone is encouraging our conceit for their own ends.

Apple

The Old Testament story of Adam and Eve imbues apples with a rich and varied symbolism. As the forbidden fruit of the tree of knowledge, they can represent temptation, self-awareness or a paradise lost. There are also significant sexual overtones to the biblical tale, and a dream about stealing apples might suggest a desire for an illicit sexual relationship.

Ice cream

Ice cream is a sweet treat that must be enjoyed immediately. If we try to save it for later, it will melt and we won't be able to enjoy it at all. The dreaming mind may use ice cream as a metaphor for the importance of living in the moment and partaking of life's pleasures and opportunities without dwelling too much on the disappointments of the past or the potential of the future.

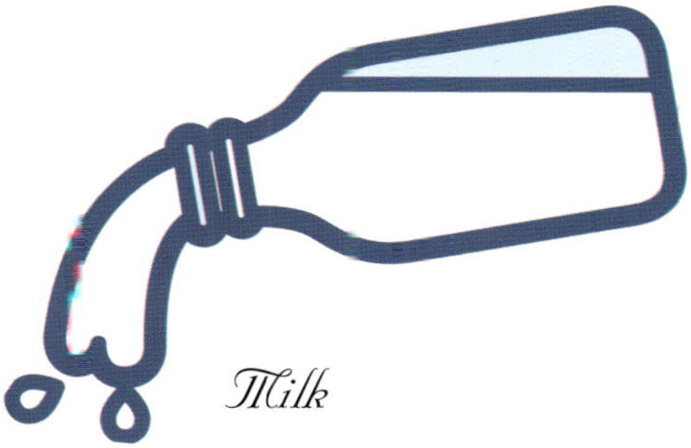

Milk

Milk usually signifies kindness, sustenance and nourishment, often associated with maternal love. Freudians might understand it to represent semen.

Activities and States of Being

We perform many activities in our dreams – some may be routine things we do every day, such as eat and travel to work, while others may seem completely alien. Dreams of flying, for example, might seem impossible and absurd, but they frequently symbolize important aspects of personal or professional life – and they may bring a remarkable sense of exhilaration. Other common dream actions include climbing, falling, travelling and escaping (or trying to escape) capture. All have their own particular connotations and must be interpreted carefully in the light of the mood of the dream and the context of the dreamer's own intuitions and experiences.

Captivity and Freedom

Dreams often focus on the preoccupying conflict between the restrictions that life places upon us and our urge for freedom. Another common theme is our need to dominate others by holding them captive, possessing them, or placing them under some kind of obligation to us. Even a seemingly selfless desire to protect or nurture those closest to us may arise from an unacknowledged self-gratifying tendency, in which service becomes a form of domination. Although it can, of course, symbolize more genuine motives, the urge to save others from danger frequently represents the dreamer's desire to secure their dependency or indebtedness. These motives can be shown more blatantly, as when the dreamer forcibly holds down or smothers another person, or withholds from them a key or some other means of escape.

The dreamer's own need for freedom may be symbolized in similar ways, with the dreamer playing the role of victim and struggling to break free from the restraints imposed by others.

Awaiting execution is the most extreme curtailment of freedom, although in dreams this may relate to apprehensions about potentially auspicious events, such as marriage or the birth of a child. Freedom or captivity may also symbolize aspects of psychological life that are being too tightly controlled by the dreamer, or have been repressed into the unconscious and are clamouring for expression. Potential abilities that the dreamer is refusing to acknowledge may also be represented by captivity dreams, as may ideals that are being denied, or the urge to find spiritual purpose.

Being tied up

A dream of being tied up may indicate the dreamer's need for freedom, but was seen by Freud as a reflection of repressed sexual fantasies – often the desire to indulge in some form of bondage or sado-masochistic sex. Such dreams may date back to early childhood, and can be connected to emotional domination by parents, or the urge to dominate a parent of the opposite sex.

Domination

Bondage, of course, can have overtly erotic overtones in a dream, reflecting sexual urges in the dreamer that are perhaps unacknowledged by the waking mind (see page 189). However, in a non-sexual context it can also suggest repressed aspirations or beliefs.

Setting people or animals free

Dreams of setting someone free may indicate the dreamer's altruistic urge to serve that person by releasing him or her from psychological bondage. Freeing animals from captivity more often relates to releasing the dreamer's own emotions or primal energies.

Confinement

In waking life the things that confine us are more usually practical or psychological than physical. A prison in which the dreaming self finds itself locked up may represent a relationship or job in which we feel trapped or frustrated. It can also signify a set of fixed ideas or beliefs, a moral standpoint which is restricting our personal development and preventing change.

Liberation

Dreams in which we escape from shackles or bonds often represent a desire to be released from a situation or a relationship that no longer makes us feel happy or fulfilled. If you are religious, or come from a religious background, you may be finding the spiritual, moral or physical demands of your faith a burden rather than a source of enrichment.

Breaking out of jail

Escaping from jail, perhaps over a high wall, can represent a desire for unhindered expression, emotional or creative. It can also signify a determination to take control of our destiny and a realization that we need to create our own opportunities in life. Some dream interpreters, however, would suggest that such dreams actually carry a much darker symbolism – a desire for the ultimate release, an escape from life itself. If you have been feeling troubled or depressed, a dream of this type could be a signal to seek outside help and speak to a professional, or at least to a trusted friend.

Leaving jail

A dream in which we are released from jail may be accompanied by feelings of elation. It can represent a positive response to the beginning of a new phase of our life or a sense of the desirability of change. Feelings of anxiety accompanying a dream of liberation are

also, however, not uncommon and can be an expression of concern about the challenges of freedom – when we leave the family home, for example, or when we retire from work.

Lock and key

The dream image of a lock and key has overt sexual overtones and can be a highly charged dream symbol. To see ourselves unlocking a box may convey a sense of sexual liberation; if the box will not open, however, this may be a sign of sexual frustration.

Trap

Animals are often the creative or destructive aspects of the self in their uninhibited form. Dreams in which an animal gets caught in a trap – a mouse in a mousetrap, for example – may suggest that you feel that your creative energies are being stifled.

Being arrested

To dream about being arrested often indicates feelings of guilt, especially if stolen goods or past misdemeanours are subsequently discovered.

Climbing and Falling

Logic suggests that climbing dreams indicate success and falling dreams failure, but other interpretations can reach a deeper level of meaning. For Freudians, climbing dreams represent a longing for sexual fulfilment. They also connote aspirations in other areas of life. Falling can sometimes symbolize unjustifiable pride, as in the fall of Icarus who flew too close to the sun; but it can also represent an abrupt and unsettling descent into the unconscious.

Tripping and falling, an experience that happens particularly during hypnagogic dreaming (see pages 50–54), often emerges as a reminder of the perils of over-intellectualization – living too much in the head and failing to take care of the more emotional aspects of life. Dreamers rarely report distress when hitting the ground: they either wake up just in time, or find the ground to be soft and yielding. Such dreams remind us that apparent disasters may often lead to no long-term harm.

Dreams of falling from a rooftop or from a high window usually indicate insecurity in an area of worldly ambition, such as a profession or social milieu. Falling from a burning building may suggest that the dreamer has been under insupportable emotional pressures as a result of his or her aspirations.

Amplification on climbing and falling symbols may provide links with mythological archetypes such as the biblical figure of Jacob, who saw angels climbing up and down a ladder set between heaven and earth. In the Renaissance, Jacob's ladder became an important Rosicrucian and alchemical symbol, usually shown with seven rungs (seven steps to heaven), representing the link between the physical and the spiritual self.

Ladders

A ladder can symbolize the attainment of higher awareness or the descent into the unconscious, depending on whether the dreamer is ascending or descending. A ladder featuring in our dreams can also be linked to the rise and fall of our fortunes.

Elevators

As with ladders and stairs, elevators (lifts in the UK) can represent the connection between the spiritual and the physical life or they can be a dream reflection on our personal or professional progress. Elevators differ from most other means of ascent or descent in implying that our fate is less the result of our own efforts than a consequence of chance and the actions of others. Sometimes an elevator may suggest the rise of thoughts from the dreamer's unconscious, or a descent there in search of new ideas and inspiration. An elevator and shaft may also have sexual overtones, similar to those of a train and a tunnel.

Climbing a mountain

Mountains are the male aspect, or, on a loftier plane, the higher self. They suggest the determination needed if we are to reach the summit, as well as the dangers and the rarefied nature of the environment. Freudians see mountains and hills as symbolic of breasts, conjuring up a nostalgic yearning for our mother's embrace.

Vertigo

The spinning sensation that can overtake us when we are at a great height tends to be a dream symbol of anxiety. Often it represents the unease that accompanies a heavy burden of responsibility, or sheer volume of work, at home or professionally. The dream may be urging us to talk to our partner or superiors about our concerns.

Tripping or stumbling

To dream of tripping or stumbling may suggest that we are taking too intellectual an approach to life, relying too much on logic rather than intuition to solve problems. A stumble often relates specifically to emotional or psychological problems, in relation to which listening to only our head and ignoring our heart is especially perilous. Tripping can also be a metaphor for social awkwardness.

Steps and stairs

Climbing a flight of stairs is a common dream image representing personal growth or career advancement. To dream that we trip and fall down a set of stairs might suggest that we have taken on more than we can reasonably cope with, or that we are overestimating our abilities. Ascending or descending stairs can also have spiritual or psychological connotations. Jungians understand stairs as having a similar archetypal significance to the ladder in the biblical story of Jacob's ladder (see page 269), representing the link between the spiritual and physical life. Walking down stairs can also represent the descent into the unconscious; how easy we find the journey or what we discover at the bottom of the stairs can be significant indicators of our psychological state.

Freudians take a different view and see going up and down stairs as a symbol of intercourse. Similarly, a gaping stairwell may invoke the female sexual organs and a staircase with its balustrades and banisters could even represent the phallus.

Slippery slopes

The relatively common dream in which we attempt to climb up a descending escalator, a slippery slope or a greasy ladder suggests failure to make progress in a desired area and may serve as a reminder either to abandon the attempt or to seek a more appropriate way up. You may have taken on more responsibility than you can handle and be in danger of jeopardizing the project and your own well-being as a result.

Travel and Motion

Freud was convinced that dream events incorporating travel or motion typically represent disguised wish-fulfilments about sexual intercourse, the specific details of the dream reflecting the dreamer's sexual tastes. However, travel and motion can stand for many other aspects of life, in particular for progress toward personal and professional goals.

The destination of dream journeys may hold mythical or metaphorical associations. To travel westward may indicate a journey toward old age and death, while an eastward journey may signify rejuvenation. Travelling to Rome, where proverbially all roads lead, may indicate thoughts about fate, love or death. Other dreams about dying, symbolized in travel, may concern themselves with holding onto or letting go of luggage.

Jung noted the appearance in grand (Level 3) dreams of the archetypal quest for meaning and fulfilment, and certainly dreams of setting out on a journey are far more frequent than those of arriving at the journey's end. The dreaming mind reveals the need for progress in life, but indicates that decisions on ultimate goals must be taken at the conscious as well as the unconscious level: as these conscious decisions are made, so they are mirrored in the unconscious, and taken further in dreams.

Some dream images connected with travel reveal their meaning without much difficulty. Much is conveyed by the nature of the pathway that stretches ahead. An open road usually suggests new possibilities for progress, while a rocky path may indicate obstacles.

The scenery through which the dreamer is passing on the journey also reveals aspects of his or her inner life. To dream of a journey through a desert, for example, may indicate loneliness, aridity, or lack of creativity. Further insights come from the means of transport: Jung noted that travelling in a public vehicle often means that the dreamer is behaving like everyone else instead of finding his or her own way forward.

Departure

Leaving the familiar behind us to depart on a journey can be symbolic of making a new start or of the beginning of a quest for a higher meaning to our existence. If we dream about leaving our baggage behind us, this suggests that we are ready to move on from ingrained patterns of thought and behaviour or the trappings of our everyday life.

On the move

Closely linked to the dream symbol of departure, travelling involves a sense of progress toward a personal, spiritual or professional goal. Freudians associate dream journeys with the rhythm of motion and therefore a desire for sexual intercourse.

Walking

A walking figure is a classical image of the solitary thinker and when it appears in our dreams it may suggest that it is time for a period of serious reflection. The landscape that provides the background to our walk may be a figurative representation of either our aspirations or our troubles.

Car

Freud considered that the smooth running of a car was a symbol not so much of sexual wish-fulfilment as of progress in psychoanalysis. Alternatively, it may represent free will or voluntary actions performed by the dreamer.

Taxi

Taking a taxi can symbolize a tendency to take a back seat in life and let others do the driving, rather than relying on your own efforts. However, if you see yourself driving the taxi, the image may express a willingness to guide others on their personal journey.

Station

A station suggests a conscious decision. The choices available at a rail or bus station are analagous with those faced in life – whether to stay or to go, to travel far or near, to make a journey cheaply or expensively. Waiting at a station implies feelings of expectation which can result in disappointment or a pleasant surprise, depending upon the context.

Train

A train is a male sexual symbol according to Freud: its rhythmic noise and motion is understood to represent sexual intercourse, particularly in the dream image of a train entering a tunnel. A train journey can also be representative of our journey through life. The fixed route of the rails can suggest that we feel trapped into following a certain path and are no longer in control of our own destiny. Missing a train or discovering that you are on the wrong train can denote missed opportunities, while a broken-down or derailed train may turn out to be a blessing in disguise – what may at first appear to be a disastrous disruption of our plans may in fact be a signal to change course and take our own route away from the tracks.

Sea voyage

Jungians understand a sea voyage to represent our exploration of the unconscious mind. If the sea is calm and our passage is smooth, this may imply that the dreamer is at ease with the deep waters of the unconscious. Being tossed about in a stormy sea connotes strong emotions. Amplification may connect a dream of a sea voyage to the biblical story of Jonah and the whale, highlighting the danger of being deaf to the messages of the unconscious.

Ship

Freudians view the sea as representative of the womb and a ship therefore as a highly charged sexual symbol. They link the size of the ship to the voracity of the libido, a jutting prow to a phallus and the figurehead to breasts. A stormy sea that tosses the ship to and fro can suggest high passion or a tumultuous phase in the dreamer's sexuality. A ship that sinks can signify overwhelming desires or a doomed love.

Ferry

A ferry can symbolize the transition between different states of awareness. A ferryman, suggesting Charon in Greek mythology, must be paid for his services and may be a representation of the archetypal Wise Old Man.

Docks

Docks may appear in dreams of departure and can suggest that familiar ground is being left behind as we start out in a new direction or begin the process of self-discovery. If we dream of arriving into port after a long journey, the dock can represent a place of calm and safety after a turbulent time in our life.

River crossing

Amplification associates river crossings with the five rivers which in Greek mythology were said to link the realm of the living with that of the dead. The dream symbol of a river crossing can have connotations of death or may represent the transition between different states of consciousness and a journey into the deepest depths of our mind.

Row boat or canoe

Freudians emphasize the phallic symbolism of canoes, which makes paddling representative of masturbation. Other interpretations would link a row boat to our journey toward personal development and highlight the effort that exploring the self, like rowing, demands.

Horse-drawn vehicle

A horse-drawn vehicle careering out of control, with the horses wild and uncontrollable, can be a very anxious dream image and one that signifies concern that we are not in control of our own destiny. If we dream that we are travelling in an old-fashioned cart or carriage, this may suggest that our personal development or professional advancement has been hindered by an attachment to an outmoded pattern of thought or action.

Bus

Any type of public transport is usually understood by Jungians to represent a tendency to conform, do what we are told and follow the crowd. A bus dream may therefore be encouraging us to be more independent in our thoughts and in the way we act.

Motorcycle

A motorcycle is a compelling symbol of independent action. In the Jungian interpretation the dreamer who sees him- or herself riding a motorcycle is determined to direct their own destiny. The faster the

motorcycle goes and the more exhilarating the ride, the stronger the desire for independence. Bicycles and motorbikes also represent the need for balance – we must maintain an equilibrium between the forces of the conscious and unconscious minds in order to make progress. Freudians focus on the sexual symbolism of straddling a roaring engine and see this dream image as highlighting a powerful desire for sex.

Wheel

For Buddhists and Hindus, a wheel symbolizes the cycles of life, death and rebirth. It also carries overtones of morality and truth, and the eight-spoked Wheel of Dhamma is used by Buddhists to represent the Buddha's teaching of the path to enlightenment. Jungians associate the wheel with powerful creative energy, seeing it as a symbol of the sun and therefore of the libido as a source of life.

Intersection or crossroads

In dreams, as in waking life, crossroads represent a point of decision. Decisions have both a positive aspect and a negative aspect: the road that we choose to take – for example, with a new partner or a new job – may entail rejection of what went before. Depending on the context and mood, a crossroads can also symbolize a coming together of people or ideas, or a parting of ways.

Congestion

Bustling crowds impeding our progress on foot are one of the irritations of urban living and in our dreams might express the stresses of city life. Alternatively, a dream where we struggle through a large crowd or get stuck in a traffic jam may symbolize our frustration with the slow progress of an important project.

Running

The dream significance of running depends very much upon what we are running toward or away from. Running to escape pursuers is a common anxiety dream (see page 173), while running toward something can suggest impatience to reach a desired goal or conclusion.

Road

When roads appear in our dreams, they frequently symbolize our journey through life. A narrow road can represent the moral or practical constraints that dictate our choices, while the open road represents freedom. If we dream about a motorway or major highway, we may want to fast-track our ambitions or spiritual progress.

Path

Obstacles to our progress toward spiritual enlightenment or fulfilment can be represented in a dream by a steep or rocky pathway. However, in keeping with the biblical imagery of the broad way leading to perdition and the narrow way to salvation, interpretation sometimes reveals that a seemingly difficult pathway is, nonetheless, the one to take.

Towpath

A horse toiling along a towpath dragging a heavy barge can represent a sense of being weighed down by the burden of our responsibilities or, alternatively, of our life's journey being slowed by troublesome memories or difficult emotions.

Swimming

Large bodies of water are usually interpreted as representing the waters of the womb or the depths of the unconscious mind. Swimming may therefore symbolize birth or the desire to return to the womb's safety. Jung understood the dream image of swimming toward land to represent spiritual rebirth. Swimming against the tide can suggest a personal struggle.

Flying

Flying dreams often bring a remarkable sense of exhilaration, and some dreamers speak of a strange recognition, as if flying is a skill that they have always possessed, yet for some reason have forgotten how to use. Rarely are flying dreams experienced as unpleasant or fearful, and the sense of freedom and exultation that they convey often opens the dreamer's imagination to the infinite possibilities of life.

Dreamers do not always fly alone, but may be surrounded by friends or strangers, suggesting that others share their insight into the true nature of things. They may be accompanied by an animal or by an object, perhaps symbolizing important aspects of personal or professional life. Instead of flying under their own power, dreamers may find themselves in a vehicle of some kind, no matter how incongruous, or they may be leaping into the air in giant strides, like the three strides with which the Hindu god Vishnu measured the boundaries of the universe.

It is rare in dreams for flying to become confused with falling. Usually the dreamer floats gently to earth, having enjoyed panoramic views of the world below. On occasions, the descent may be by parachute, sometimes interpreted as indicating the safe resolution of a difficult challenge. Alternatively, flying may involve an exhilarating element of delightful danger (as in hang-gliding), perhaps suggesting the wish to take more risks in some aspect of work or of a relationship. Being taken into the air against one's will, on the other hand, may indicate that the dreamer is being forced into taking risks that they don't feel comfortable with.

Flying a kite

A dream of flying a kite carries similar connotations to other flying dreams, but emphasizes the controlled freedom of some aspect of the dreamer, just as a kite is controlled in the wild natural forces of the wind. Such dreams can also represent exhilarating but ultimately unproductive schemes.

Airplane

Flying in a plane often carries relatively straightforward associations, such as a wish to travel or see the world, but can also suggest a desire for rapid progress, or to achieve spectacular success in a particular enterprise. Freudians see airplanes as phallic symbols, often associated with a new sexual adventure.

Flying in an incongruous vehicle

Often the incongruous vehicle that transports us through the air in our dreams is something that represents comfort and security, such as a bed or an armchair, and the dream suggests a desire for adventure tempered by a strong predilection for ease and safety.

Hot-air balloon

Balloons are associated most frequently with fantasy, the wish to escape and the desire to rise above the conflicts of daily life. They can also represent the need to be more objective and far-sighted in our thinking. The fire heating the hot air is similarly significant – signifying the drive behind a much-loved personal project, it may need to be tended carefully to ensure that it burns evenly and doesn't go out.

Wings

Greek and Roman myth associated wings with fame, in the form of Mercury, swift-footed herald of the gods who spread renown accross the globe. A dream in which we grow wings and fly may represent a yearning for celebrity and success. It might also, however, be a warning against excessive pride, recalling the story of Icarus who made wings from feathers and wax but plunged to his death when he flew too close to the sun.

Parachute

Parachutes provide us with a safe way to fall when an aircraft runs into trouble. A dream about a parachute may express relief at the end of a difficult or dangerous ordeal – an operation perhaps, or a lucky escape from an accident. A parachute may also suggest that we need to "bail out" while we still can: we may be involved in a business venture or an emotional entanglement with which we are not entirely comfortable.

Floating or hovering in the air

Floating in the air, the world spread out beneath your feet, can be an exhilarating and optimistic activity when it appears in a dream. There may also, however, be a warning inherent in this fundamentally impossible scenario: do not lose contact with reality. Perhaps our unconscious mind is urging caution in the face of overweening ambition or a meteoric rise to social or professional prominence. It is important that we do not take on more responsibility than we are capable of fulfilling, or we may find ourselves brought down to earth with a bump.

Cooking and Eating

Eating has always been associated with sexuality. Freud recognized that the mouth is the first erogenous zone discovered by young children, and that throughout the lives of individuals with certain forms of personality fixation, orality may remain inextricably linked with sexual gratification, and may give rise to specific personality traits, such as verbal aggression.

Even before Freud, however, dreams involving eating and food were often interpreted in sexual terms. Certain foods such as peaches and other fruits traditionally stood for lasciviousness, while others such as bread symbolized a more restrained, fertility-orientated sexuality.

However, as staples of life, food and eating demand a wider interpretation than the strictly sexual. Spoilt or bad-tasting food can suggest a sourness at the heart of the dreamer's emotional life; while waiting for a meal that fails to arrive can point to neglect, emotional disappointment or lack of adequate support.

The dreamer's reactions to food can also be significant. Impressions of having overeaten can variously represent greed, lack of discrimination, sensuality, or short-sighted behaviour. Refusal to accept food may suggest a desire to end dependency upon others, while cooking food for other people can indicate the urge to nurture, to give support or to offer emotional involvement.

Frying

There is a constant risk of burning your food when you fry it, and it needs to be tended carefully. In this sense, the dream activity of frying may represent a project that we need to pay special attention to in order to ensure its successful completion.

Alternatively, frying may be significant because of the smoke that it produces: smoke can be a symbol either of sacrifice and death or of cleansing and purification.

Picnics

Eating in the open air usually represents a desire for naturalness and simplicity, and for an escape from convention. You may feel frustrated with conventional formality.

Social meals

Social meals that carry a positive emotional charge often reflect a feeling of intimacy with others, whether they be friends, family or individuals in our local community. Shared interests, harmony, peace and warm social relationships may be involved. Meals experienced as uncomfortable may represent frigidity, a threat to fundamental happiness or social distance, and may suggest that you feel unable to communicate with or cut off from the people around you.

Baking

Whether we are baking bread, biscuits or cake, the dream activity of baking has overtones of fertility and nurturing. Freudians would see the rhythmic process of kneading dough as representative of the act of sexual intercourse, while the way in which yeast causes bread to rise echoes the swelling of a woman's belly during pregnancy. Baking is a fundamentally creative process and may also represent a need to express unexplored artistic urges.

Eating in a restaurant

Eating a meal in a restaurant involves a multitude of transactions. A menu that we are unable to read, or that we have difficulty choosing from, might signify a troubling or overwhelming decision. A bill that we cannot possibly pay could represent worries about money, while an unexpected or ungracious dinner companion might betray a subconscious mistrust of a close friend, lover or business partner.

Fasting and gorging

For Freud, food often represented the two vital life-instincts – self-preservation, or greed, and species preservation, in other words sex. He saw the mouth, through which food enters the body, as the primary erogenous zone, and fasting and gorging as a symbol of sexual desire (denied or indulged). A dream in which we gorge ourselves senseless might suggest feelings of intense sexual desire, perhaps the result of a long period of deprivation. It can also be a violent, self-destructive activity conveying repressed anger, especially if we tear apart our food in a bestial, ferocious way. Fasting may stand for self-punishment or for purification and self-denial.

Fish

Jungians understand fish to be symbolic of the unborn child and therefore of the primal life-force, "because the child before its birth lives in water like a fish". Freud saw fish as a genital symbol, although the exact symbolic significance depends on what we are doing to the fish – eating it, for example, or just watching it swim; and the state it is in (whether it is whole, headless or gutted). A prolific spawning of fish increases its sexual connotations, while a great shoal can represent the abundance of nature.

Innards or offal

Intestines were used in ancient times to divine the future. Their appearance in our dreams might be a subconscious suggestion that we follow our "gut instinct" and listen to our intuition.

Meat

In Nordic and shamanic belief, to eat the meat of an animal or adversary is to absorb its strength and energy. Freudian psychology suggests that for the modern dreamer this absorption is of one's own instinctive energies, which have hitherto been repressed or denied.

Sunday roast

The Christian tradition of roasting a chicken or a joint of meat on a Sunday and eating it as part of a large family meal might conjure up nostalgic images of our childhood. If we have abandoned the weekly rituals of going to church and sitting down at the table with our loved ones, the dream may be expressing a desire to partake more in traditional family or community activities.

Fruits

A great proliferation of fruit is an archetypal image of fertility and its appearance in our dreams might suggest a desire to be pregnant.

We also talk about a project coming "to fruition", in which context fruit can signify the rewards of hard work or creativity and the fulfilment of our expectations or ambitions.

Drinking

Jungians see liquid of any kind as representative of life-force, and dreams of drinking may signify a desire to better understand the nature of the universe. Drinking alcohol to the point of inebriation may imply a need to develop a higher level of consciousness.

Vegetables

A generous spread of vegetables, perhaps as part of a Thanksgiving meal or harvest celebration, can signify a desire to enjoy the generous bounty of nature. This can be a very positive dream image, reflecting satisfaction with a job well done that is now bringing rewards. If, however, we are yearning for an abundance of vegetables, we may be concerned about our financial welfare.

Spices

Spices add flavour and variety to otherwise dull dishes and a dream in which they feature prominently may suggest a craving for more excitement in our lives. The upright jars of a spice rack can have phallic overtones and can indicate a need for more sexual spontaneity.

Work and Relaxation

Most dreams are highly active, and it is rare to find oneself relaxing: a dash to the airport to catch a rescheduled flight is a more likely image than lazing under a palm tree, cocktail in hand. However, dreams that symbolize a *desire* for relaxation, or that involve active preparations for potentially relaxing experiences such as vacations, are commonplace enough.

Dreams are realistic about vacations, and recognize that in many cases they can be highly stressful episodes. Thus, the unconscious mind may use vacation dreams symbolically – perhaps a particular vacation experienced in the past – to represent anxieties in other areas of the dreamer's life.

Sometimes the dream contrasts the dreamer's own agitated state with the relaxed behaviour of people all around, emphasizing the subject's own need for stress-reduction. At times, the dreamer may feel intensely irritated by the inactivity of others, and this suggests a deep-seated resentment at receiving insufficient help in waking life, or anger at his or her own impotence. The dreamer may even find other dream characters reduced to dummies or dolls, and find himself or herself furiously but ineffectually trying to shake them awake.

Work-related dream episodes characteristically take on aspects of anxiety dreams or nightmares. Such themes as loss of control or failure to perform a job successfully recur regularly.

If your situation at work is so bad that you dread being there at all, this might appear as a dream journey to the workplace that takes the form of a punishing race through knee-high mud.

Colleagues may also be symbolically represented, in ways that reveal your emotions or responses toward them. For example, an overbearing boss might be a mugger who attacks you as you work.

Dreams can show us the way forward in our working lives by highlighting problems that our professional pride might otherwise prevent us from acknowledging. By heeding their messages, we can make needed changes to enhance job satisfaction.

Troubles on vacation

Being on vacation yet still beset with trouble and anxiety frequently suggests an inability to escape from the responsibilities of normal life. One disaster after another – troubles with the hotel reservation, bad weather, sudden illness – can signal a fundamental pessimism that may be the result of a habitually stressful life or alternatively it could be a warning against over-idealizing an alternative lifestyle to our own.

Isolated places

A mountain retreat or remote cottage might express an urge to run away from the trials and tribulations of our waking life. We might feel as though there are too many people making demands on our time and be desperately yearning for some peace and solitude. An isolated place might also represent a wish for a more minimalist, less materialistic way of life, or the idea that we could do with some time alone.

Packing for a vacation

Preparations for a vacation generally suggest a need to escape from everyday problems, or to seek new excitements or experiences. A wish to travel light can indicate a recognition of the unnecessary "baggage" that we usually carry with us throughout life. Overpacking may suggest a perverse insistence on clinging to the problems that burden our inner lives. Anxiety about how much baggage to take away may represent a fear of, or preoccupation with, death.

Desert island

Standing alone on a desert island may indicate a sense of abandonment and isolation, perhaps in the wake of a divorce or bereavement. The image of an island, marooned in a boundless sea, could also reflect the relationship between the conscious and unconscious minds. We may be more comfortable on the firm ground of the conscious mind, yet we cannot escape the troubling presence of the deep unknown – the unconscious.

Beach

We often associate beach vacations with long holidays and happy childhood memories. The combination of sun, sea and sand can be purifying and rejuvenating, and a dream visit to a beach may leave us feeling refreshed and revived. Beaches can also, however, have some much more disturbing connotations. Freudians might see the tall towers of a sandcastle as phallic symbols, suggestive of castration anxiety when they are washed away by the sea. Equally, burying our mother or father in the sand could be understood as an expression of a murder wish inspired by an Oedipus or Electra complex.

Rush to the airport

A frantic dash to the airport in a car or taxi, to catch a plane for our vacation, can reflect our fear that life's pleasures will elude us.

Seclusion on vacation

An erotic adventure in a romantic arbour or a small cove screened by high rocks is a commonplace topic of vacation dreams. As well as being simple wish-fulfilment, such dreams can highlight dissatisfaction with aspects of a real-life relationship. We may be craving the freedom, exhilaration and heightened emotions that so often accompany a holiday romance. Or perhaps we are longing for greater spontaneity in our sex life with our regular partner.

Swimming pool

The water in a swimming pool can represent our conscious or unconscious emotions. The appearance of a pool in our dreams may suggest a need to dive in and explore the true nature of our feelings. A swimming pool with no water in it might reflect a feeling of emptiness and an absence of emotion.

Secretary

There is an ambivalence about the dream figure of a secretary. Typically female, she shields an executive from unwelcome calls and organizes his or her timetable. In this sense, secretaries are associated with a nurturing, motherly persona. A dream in which a secretary features in a subservient role, however, might be an expression of unexplored desires for sexual domination.

Falling from an office window

A dream in which we fall from a window in a tall office block might stem from concerns about our abilities to fulfil managerial responsibilities, or perhaps deep-seated anxiety about the possibility of losing our job.

Desk

When, in a dream, we sit down at a desk, our unconscious mind may be urging us to take some time to evaluate our problems and come up with some rational solutions to them. An untidy or cluttered desk might suggest that our personal affairs need attention and that we need to reconsider our priorities.

Filing cabinet

The dream image of a filing cabinet may suggest that we need to keep our facts straight and preserve logical distinctions. An open filing cabinet perhaps denotes a willingness to learn and an openness to new ideas and points of view. If the drawers of a filing cabinet are closed, we may be concealing something – perhaps an incident in our past or an aspect of the self.

Meeting

A dream in which we are late for a meeting might reflect anxieties stemming from our workplace responsibilities. If we arrive only to discover that we have left our notes or equipment at home, we might be worried that we are not sufficiently prepared to face a forthcoming challenge.

Losing a job

A dream in which we are fired can signify a desire to end a relationship or situation that is having a negative impact upon us. It could also reflect a lack of self-esteem. Deep down, we may not be convinced that we are capable of fulfilling the responsibilities that we have been given.

Ceremonies and Rituals

From the dawn of history, the cultures of the world have used festivals and rituals to celebrate important recurrent events, to honour the gods for maintaining life's course and to mark the passage of time. Every society uses ritual to celebrate transitions in our lives, as we pass from one stage to another, from birth through puberty, marriage, parenthood and death. By sacrificing animals or enemies captured in battle, our forebears hoped to imitate nature's cycle of birth and death, offering the life of another so that their own existence could be spared and the gods could bring fertility to the earth.

Ritual is also a form of drama, and in dreams invites the dreamer to escape the confines of the conscious mind, passing into the fabulous world of the imagination. Performers may wear masks or special clothes, sing a particular song or recite ritual incantations to assume their new roles, leaving their everyday identities behind to enter the archetypal world of the unconscious.

Dreams associated with Christmas or other major religious celebrations can represent peace, generosity, goodwill, family and friends or, at a deeper level, a confirmation of spiritual truths. Wedding or other anniversaries can serve as reminders of transience, or, more positively, as indications of the significance of human and family ties, of the vows and undertakings associated with them, or, if the emotional charge is negative, of the restricting commitments involved.

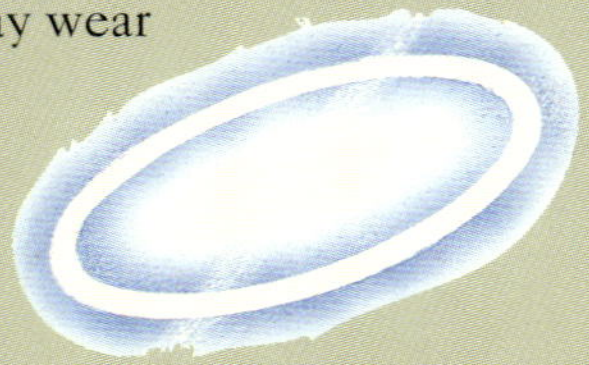

Dreams involving baptisms or christenings frequently represent purification, new beginnings, or the acceptance of new responsibilities. In Level 3 dreams, they can symbolize important initiations into whole new areas of wisdom or spiritual progress.

Fertility rite

Images of fertility rites in dreams often emerge from the collective unconscious. Jung saw them as indications of attempts to abolish the separation between the conscious and unconscious minds, and to forge a union between the dreamer and his or her inherited, instinctive self. Such rituals may involve sacrifice to a corn god or harvest deity, representing the death of the past so that future fertility and prosperity may be ensured. For Freudians, individuals who often dream of symbols associated with fertility are probably preoccupied with pregnancy.

Sacrifice

A dream image of human sacrifice might be a warning from the subconscious mind of the psychological dangers of acting like a martyr. A "martyr complex", where we give excessively of ourselves in the hope of receiving the approbation and gratitude of others, is ultimately unfulfilling and psychologically unhealthy. The sacrifice of a human victim might also recall the death of a loved one. We may need to let go of their memory to be free of our grief. If the deceased passed away after a long illness, the dreaming mind might even be expressing a sense of relief.

Wedding

A wedding often suggests the union of opposite yet complementary parts of the self, and the promise of future productivity. In the case of Level 3 dreams (see pages 65–70), it may be of archetypal significance, symbolizing the union within the dreamer of the fundamental creative forces of life – male and female, rationality and imagination, conscious and unconscious, matter and spirit.

Wedding dreams can also represent a positive affirmation of family ties or important commitments. If we, or a close friend or family member, is getting married in the near future, our unconscious mind might use dreams about weddings to highlight concerns we have about their relationship. If the bride or groom fails to attend or if someone loses the wedding ring, we may have doubts about the commitment of either party. If no guests turn up, then we might be concerned that one or other of the two families does not approve of the union.

Receiving an award

Jungians might associate a dream in which we are presented with an award – a medal for bravery, perhaps, or a trophy at a sporting event – with a desire to identify with the Hero archetype (see page 107). A thirst for recognition could also point to underlying insecurities and lack of self-esteem. It may be that we are worried that other people will not value us unless we can provide them with proof of our worth.

Ritual renunciation

Any ritual that involves taking symbols of vanity from the dreamer such as hair, clothes, or jewelry, may adumbrate the need for a renunciation of worldly power or pride, or of some aspects of the ego. Very often such renunciations are undertaken for religious reasons, and a dream where we take up the habit of a monk might express a desire to concentrate more fully on the spiritual aspects of life.

Coronation

A coronation invests a monarch with both the power and the responsibility of kingship or queenship. A dream in which we are the monarch being crowned could be an affirmation of our readiness to take on a new role. It could also, however, be a sign of excessive vanity or self-centred egotism.

Communion

The Christian sacrament of communion represents the transubstantiation of Christ, or the union of matter and spirit. Its appearance in our dreams might express a powerful desire to connect with higher spiritual powers.

Halloween

Halloween, or All Hallow's Eve, is a festival that derives from an ancient tradition of marking the transition between the light and dark parts of the year. It was believed that on this night the boundaries between this world and the Otherworld became blurred, allowing spirits, both good and bad, to pass through. It is a time of transformation, and when it appears in our dreams it may represent a profound shift in our outlook on life. The celebration as it occurs today is invested with a panoply of symbols, from dressing up as black cats, ghosts or skeletons to carving pumpkins and ducking for apples. Jungians would have little difficulty identifying most or many of these motifs with a wide range of archetypal symbols.

Circumcision

For Freud, the circumcision of young Jewish and Muslim boys represented a ritual substitute for castration. He understood it as a preemptive strike by the father against a possible rival.

Bar Mitzvah

Freud believed that the Jewish rite of passage, the Bar Mitzvah ceremony, was saturated with Oedipal symbolism. He felt that both the declaration, "Today I am a man", and the opening dance between the thirteen-year-old boy and his mother represented the rivalry between a young man and his father.

Diwali

The festival of light celebrated by Hindus, Sikhs and Jains signifies the triumph of good over evil. A dream in which we take part in Diwali celebrations might represent a personal triumph over our baser nature, or an awakening after a long period of depression or mourning.

Art, Music and Dance

In various ancient cultures, such as those of Greece and Hindu India, it was believed that the arts already existed in another dimension, and that the task of the artist was to act as a channel through which these blessings could enter into the physical world. Thus, the arts were always associated with the gods. The Greeks honoured Apollo, deity of music and the sun, and the nine Muses, daughters of Zeus, each of whom was responsible for one of the artistic domains. Hindus worship Sarasvati, the harp-playing goddess of learning. It is noteworthy that the poet Robert Graves attributed his poetry to a muse he called the White Goddess. Similarly, in dreams, the arts represent not only the personal creativity of the dreamer,

but also a way by which we can access higher levels of consciousness.

Sometimes we awaken from our dreams with the dying notes of an exquisite melody in our heads. We may be unable to remember what instruments played, or what sequence of notes they produced, but we wake up uplifted and inspired. Such music usually comes from Level 3 dreams (see pages 65–70), and symbolizes the states of mind associated with higher levels of inner development.

The eighteenth-century Italian composer Giuseppe Tartini dreamed that the Devil appeared to him, and played such a beautiful solo on the composer's violin that even the inferior copy recalled by Tartini upon waking (*The Devil's Trill*) is considered to be his best work. The Greeks would have recognized the archetype that appeared in Tartini's dream not as the Devil but as Pan, the lustful fertility god, half-man and half-goat, who charmed the nymphs of heaven and enchanted mortals with his insidious music.

If we dream of giving an artistic performance, this may be emphasizing our own unrealized potential; while being an observer or listener may evoke the joy of sharing in a creative experience, or it might highlight a need to draw inspiration from others. Certain instruments, such as the harp, have always symbolized especially celestial qualities, while others (such as wind instruments) have often stood for more sensual energies. Similarly, different genres of music have entirely different connotations. While punk music or rock and roll might be associated with rebellion, folk music in our dreams could represent the more down-to-earth side of our personality.

Because dreams draw upon the same sources as the imagination, they can provide artistic inspiration, yielding ideas, or sometimes complete pieces.

Discordant music

The chaos and confusion of discordant music can suggest creative potential that has become distorted. Alternatively, clashing or off-key music in a dream can indicate a sense of disorganization or tension within areas of the dreamer's everyday life. It may be that our circumstances are "out of tune" with our needs or desires. The discomfort suggested may be profound, pointing to a feeling of being badly adjusted to the pressures of daily life – for example, we might be ill at ease in our job or unhappy about the invasiveness of the internet.

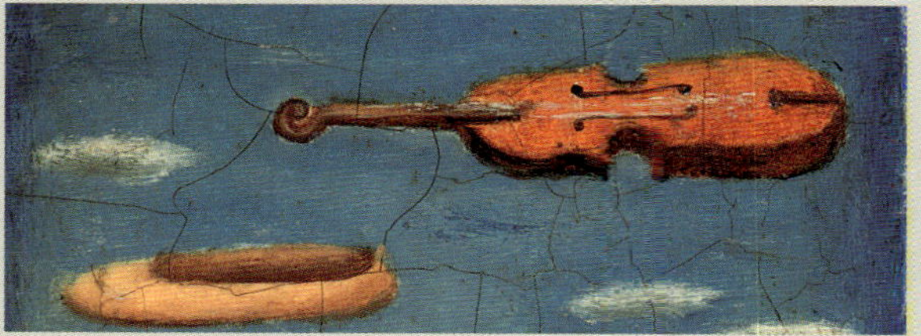

Familiar music

A snatch of a familiar song or melody will often have nostalgic associations and you might consider analyzing the lyrics or even the title of the piece. For example, the jazz standard "Autumn Leaves" might express regrets about the passing of time.

Beautiful music

Beautiful music in dreams can symbolize the infinite potential of creative life, the heavenly "music of the spheres" that the Greco-Roman world believed could be heard by the human ear.

Dancing

For Jungians and Freudians alike, dance in Level 1 and 2 dreams can represent sexual courtship, or stand as a metaphor for sexual intercourse. In Level 3 dreams it often symbolizes awareness of the rhythms of life, the powers of creation and destruction (symbolized in Hindu culture by the dance of Shiva Nataraja), or the wild creative power of the imagination. It usually carries positive connotations. Dancing in a frenzy may be an expression of a powerful desire to achieve unity between the body, mind and spirit, or of an overheated sexual appetite. Group dances such as line dancing or Scottish *ceilidhs* might invoke a sense of community.

CD or MP3 player

These platforms for playing recorded music may be neutral in themselves, the important thing being whether they are working correctly or not. A malfunctioning device might be a generalized indication of some frustration or physical ailment. A scratched CD may suggest that a small imperfection is niggling away at our peace of mind: perhaps we feel guilty about our perfectionist expectations.

Gramophone

A gramophone can indicate nostalgia, or a yearning for times past. A broken gramophone might evoke feelings of disappointment – for example, some event we have been eagerly anticipating may have been cancelled. If we dream about a broken record that endlessly repeats the same few bars of music this may represent a warning from the unconscious about the dangers of constantly talking about our problems. Our friends may have had enough of listening to the same gripes endlessly and perhaps we should consider lending a listening ear to the people who have been so patient with us.

Clarinet

Sometimes the symbolism of musical instruments depends more on their shape or the way they are played than on the sounds they produce. Freud saw clarinets, oboes and other wind instruments that are played vertically as symbolic of oral sex or potential indicators of excessive gullibility or verbal aggression.

String instruments

The shapes of many string instruments – violins, cellos and guitars, for example – evoke the shape of the female body, and playing them can represent the act of sex. A violin might remind us of Nero, the Roman emperor who is said to have played the fiddle while Rome burned.

Singing

The sound of voices raised in song has celestial qualities, evoking hymns and songs of praise as well as angelic choirs. Singing is a profound expression of human emotion, and a dream in which we sing might signify intense feelings, of sorrow or love, or perhaps devotion to a higher being or cause.

Trumpet

Trumpets can herald both great success and great disaster, from the fanfare that greets a king to the bugling notes announcing a cavalry charge. Also, trumpets are supposed to herald the Day of Judgment and may signify a need to make a major and immediate change.

Flute

All kinds of pipes, flutes and reed instruments are linked to Pan, the goat-horned fertility god, giving them strong sexual connotations. The story of the Pied Piper of Hamlyn, who lured the children of the town from their homes, might suggest overtones of seduction or bewitchment. The dream image of a fife (a type of small flute used in military marching bands) might represent repressed feelings of anger or aggression.

Piano

A piano seen playing on its own might represent the death of a good friend or aquaintance. If it is out of tune, then perhaps we need to pay more attention to the urges of our mind or body – we may be out of tune with our own needs.

Drum

Drums which symbolize earth magic and altered states of consciousness, have particular associations with the shamanic cultures of Siberia and elsewhere. Drumming plays a fundamental part in shamanic ceremonies and can have a meditative and even visionary effect on participants. If a drum or a drumbeat is a significant part of a dream, this may suggest a deep-seated need to reconnect with our roots and to explore the spiritual aspects of the self. The drum also has martial associations and might be linked to otherwise unexplored feelings of aggression.

Procession

A dream procession may have all the features of a flamboyant carnival or it might be a formal occasion such as a grand state pageant. An exuberant parade is a dream symbol of celebration and an expression of joy, affirming all that is good in life. It is helpful to consider the significance of the costumes being worn and any floats going past. Also, was there anyone you know in the audience or in the parade? A solemn procession can represent the importance of standing up for a cause we believe in.

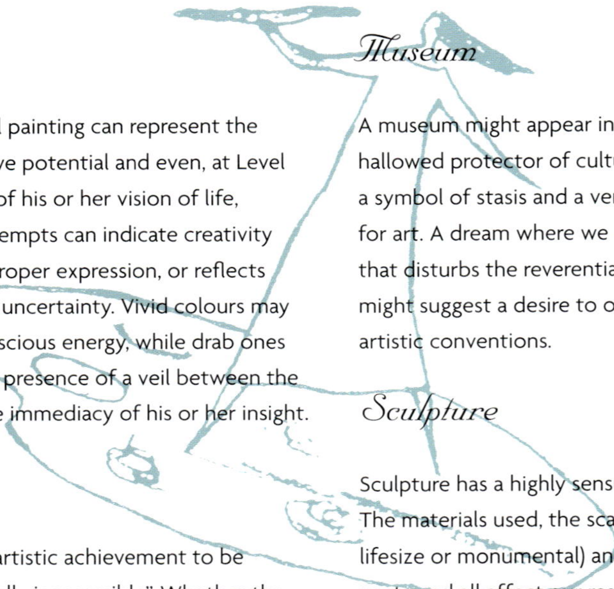

Painting

While successful painting can represent the dreamer's creative potential and even, at Level 3, the rightness of his or her vision of life, unsuccessful attempts can indicate creativity that still seeks proper expression, or reflects inner turmoil or uncertainty. Vivid colours may stand for unconscious energy, while drab ones can indicate the presence of a veil between the dreamer and the immediacy of his or her insight.

Artist

Freud declared artistic achievement to be "psychoanalytically inaccessible". Whether the medium is paint, stone, words or film, the artist represents expression by intuition rather than by reason or logic.

Exhibition

When an artist holds an exhibition, he exposes himself to the critical gaze of the general public. A dream where we put the products of our creativity, real or imagined, on display may represent feelings of vulnerability connected to a dearly held ambition, valued talent or cherished personal project.

Museum

A museum might appear in our dreams as a hallowed protector of cultural treasures or as a symbol of stasis and a veritable mausoleum for art. A dream where we create a great ruckus that disturbs the reverential silence of a museum might suggest a desire to overthrow existing artistic conventions.

Sculpture

Sculpture has a highly sensual, tactile quality. The materials used, the scale employed (whether lifesize or monumental) and the subject matter portrayed all affect our response to a piece, both in the dream world and in waking life. A sculpture that comes to life in a dream might recall the Greek myth of Pygmalion, who carved a statue representing his ideal of womanhood, only to fall in love with it. Luckily for Pygmalion, Aphrodite, the goddess of love, took pity on him and brought the statue to life. In all likelihood, a dream that explores similar themes represents a warning about the dangers of idealizing either one particular individual or the

opposite sex in general. Ultimately, we will tend to be disappointed in the end if we have placed someone on a pedestal.

Portraiture

Freudians would suggest that the phallic symbolism of a pen or pencil gives the dream activity of sketching a portrait a sexual quality. We may be attracted to the one whose likeness we are taking. The expression on the face of the subject can indicate how we imagine they feel about us. If we are creating a self-portrait, the face we draw or paint will reflect our own mood.

Art auction

If we feel anxious about the true value of our creative projects, we might experience a dream scenario where our work is put up for auction. The people bidding might represent those whose approval we most desperately crave

Fancy dress ball

A dance or a ball in which everybody is in disguise might represent our perception of the public personas of people we work or socialize with. Their costumes could give us clues about either their true nature or the image that they are trying to project. Our own costume may be similarly telling.

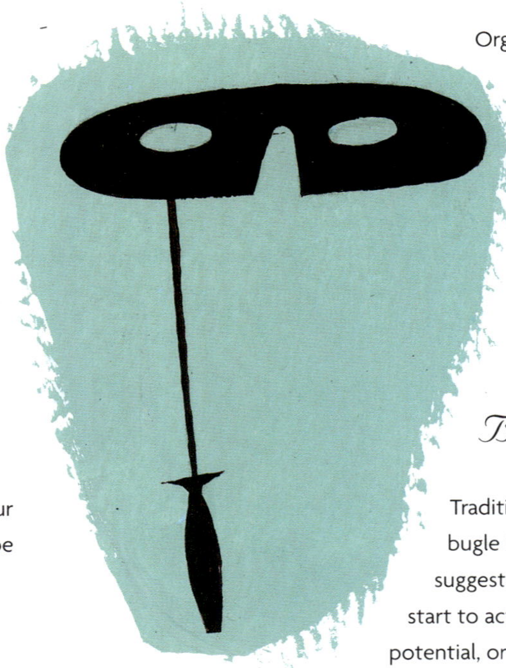

Harp

Harps were known in Egypt at least 5,000 years ago. They produce sound as if from nowhere, coaxed from the strings without the help of breath, and may be images of the spiritual side of the self. They are traditionally associated with the gods and heaven, from the lyre carried by Apollo, the Greek god of music, to artistic depictions of angels carrying harps.

Organ

Organs are associated with churches and with ceremonies such as weddings or funerals. Their appearance in our dreams might suggest that we are ready to make a major commitment, or perhaps that we are scared of death.

Bugle

Traditionally, the sound of the bugle is a call to arms or action, suggesting that the dreamer must start to activate his or her hidden potential, or must become more alert to the pressing necessities of life.

Whistling

Surprisingly, whistling sometimes carries magical overtones, as when a sailor whistles for the wind. Another possible connotation is the link between humans and animals, as in a master's call to a dog.

Sports and Play

To the small child there is no difference between play and work: all is simply activity, and the only distinction is between enjoyment and boredom. The dreams of adults retain this lack of differentiation. Thus, in dreams, play and games may symbolize work and other serious issues, just as work dreams may relate to more personal aspects of our lives.

The symbolism of dream play resides sometimes in the objects used, sometimes in the nature of the play itself or its outcome, or in the other people who accompany the dreamer as playmates.

Dreams about sports are similar: the type of sport, the prowess of our opponents, the role we have on the field – all contribute to the significance of the experience. Sports are essentially a type of game but with winners and losers and a formal set of rules. They can be used to represent our progress through life, especially in situations where we are involved in some form of competition.

Play symbols are open to a wide range of interpretations. Freudians, for example, link the rhythmical motion of playing on a swing to sexual intercourse, while others maintain that this dream symbol is more likely to be reminding the dreamer of the excitement and freedom of childhood.

Dreams of play often emphasize that creativity carries a non-serious element, and that the best ideas come when the mind is in a playful, relaxed mood. Conversely, such dreams may suggest that the dreamer is taking serious issues too lightly, or that what seems an innocent diversion may be to others a matter of profound concern. Playfulness may also indicate that we are breaking certain rules upon which a relationship or some other important issue depends.

In Level 3 dreams, play may be linked with the archetype of the Trickster, or the Divine Child (see pages 104 and 106), or may convey the message that there is an element of play in the universe itself, or that from one perspective the world is in essence what Hindus call *leela*, the divine play that constitutes life.

Chess

The game of chess is a rich mine of symbolism representing the fundamental dualities of life: black and white; life and death; male and female. Sexual rivalries and schemes of the utmost cunning are played out on the board as each player attempts to checkmate the other's king. It is a battle between light and dark, and we should examine the pieces that we play – humble pawn or deadly queen, devious knight or defensive rook (castle) – for insights into our unconscious.

Lottery

A dream in which we win the lottery may simply be a wish-fulfilment of the desire for wealth. Freudians understand money dreams to be connected with anal preoccupations, and a lottery win might represent a desire to move away from retentive hoarding toward sharing what we have with others.

Wager or bet

A bet placed with a bookmaker or a wager made with a friend might stand for a risky venture that we are undertaking. Have we fully considered the implications of this gamble?

Fortune-telling

The significance of a dream in which a prophecy is made or a destiny foretold may depend on our attitude to fortune-telling. Sceptics might be experiencing a change of heart about something, and may be more willing to consider a point of view that they would characteristically have rejected. To those for whom crystal balls and palm reading are not immediately associated with bogus magic, a dream featuring fortune-telling might suggest concerns about our prospects – professional, financial or romantic. The prediction that is made may be an expression of our hopes or fears about the future.

Sports arena

Sports can symbolize personal achievement or social interaction. The formal setting of any kind of sports arena – a football or baseball pitch, a tennis court or an athletics track – lends itself to the suggestion of competition, possibly in an institutional setting such as a school or the workplace. A dream in which we court the admiration of an arena full of spectators might suggest a deep-seated need for the approval of others.

Boxing

A violent sport, boxing may represent feelings of aggression and anger. If we find ourselves boxed into a corner, the dream might convey anxiety about a situation in waking life – perhaps we feel as though events have slipped out of our control or that we are being forced into a decision we would not otherwise make. Receiving a knockout blow might stand for a guilt-ridden desire for self-punishment.

Baseball

Baseball involves a wealth of sexual symbols, from the phallic bat and long-peaked cap to the gloves which are a female sexual symbol. Freudians would perhaps emphasize the sexual significance of the game still further and highlight the Oedipal competitiveness between the players and the father figure of the umpire.

Cricket

Similar to the equipment used in a baseball game, the bat, gloves and stumps used to play cricket have a strong sexual resonance. In its amateur capacity, this quintessentially English game is more relaxed than many other sports and its appearance in our dreams may convey a wish to swap a fiercely competitive work or home environment for something less stressful and more laid back.

Regatta or yachting

To Jungians, sailing in a regatta is most likely to symbolize the exploration of the collective unconscious. Freudians see the activity as representing our inaugural journey out of our mother's womb.

Soccer

The excitement of a game of soccer brings to mind a state of sexual arousal. A goal might symbolize orgasm, while a near-miss could represent feelings of sexual frustration or even fears of impotence. As with other sports, Jungians might interpret a dream win or loss as a reflection of our spiritual progress.

Fencing

The sexual symbolism of fencing is apparent, from the phallic connotations of the sword to the thrusting and parrying against an opponent. The fencers' masks hide their identity, and the most significant moment of the dream may be when they are removed. With what or whom have we been duelling? A partner? A sibling? Or our own unconscious urges?

Horse race

The rhythmic movement of riding a horse is a Freudian sexual symbol. The whipping action of the rider might signify unexplored sado-masochistic urges, while the hurdles that we jump can invoke the obstacles we must overcome in order to fulfil our sexual desires. There is also the added dimension of winning or losing: the euphoria of triumph can suggest orgasm, while a bitter failure might indicate anxiety about our sexual prowess. Alternatively, because horse racing is often the subject of gambling, there may be a hidden reference to good or bad luck, or to risk-taking.

Skating

The dream image of skating might recall the phrase "skating on thin ice". Perhaps we are involved in some venture that risks our personal integrity or financial security? Skating can also be a liberating activity and may convey a sense of freedom and exhilaration, especially if we find ourselves performing moves we would not consider attempting in waking life. Perhaps now is the time to step outside our comfort zone and try something new?

Role play

A dream involving childlike role play (mamas and papas, cops and robbers or cowboys and indians perhaps) might imply that the persona we adopt in our waking life does not represent the true self. We may have experienced a personal transformation, yet the image that others have of us has not changed accordingly.

Skiing

The descent down a mountainside is a classic Freudian symbol of sexual intercourse, to which the exhilaration of skiing adds a delicious thrill. Our enjoyment of skiing is usually accompanied, and perhaps heightened, by a frisson of danger, perhaps suggesting a sense of guilt accompanying our sexual urges or the fear of being caught in an illicit sexual act.

Hide and seek

The significance of the childhood game of hide and seek depends on which role we play. If we are hiding, then our dream might be an expression of anxiety. Maybe we fear that some past misdemeanour might return to haunt us, or perhaps there is an issue in our present lives that it is necessary, but distressing, to address. Jungians might interpret dreams in which we are the seeker as embodying a quest for spiritual enlightenment.

Transactions

Even the most trivial dream transactions can reflect profound truths and important issues. Some may be direct interactions with other people, the classic example being shopping – stores can symbolize the array of opportunities that we encounter in our lives. Other transactions may be less obvious – a dream scenario involving an examination may at first seem to involve only us, the protagonist, but on closer inspection we find that there is an exchange with the examiner going on. When one person performs some kind of action upon another, all kinds of obligations and emotions may be stirring below the surface.

Conflict

Violence in dreams is often strangely abstract, happening as if on film. Even if the dreamer commits an act of violence, the emotional charge may remain curiously neutral, which suggests that the dream is simply using physical violence as a metaphor for battles of other kinds – between theories or ideas, differences of opinion, or conflicting possibilities within the dreamer's own mind.

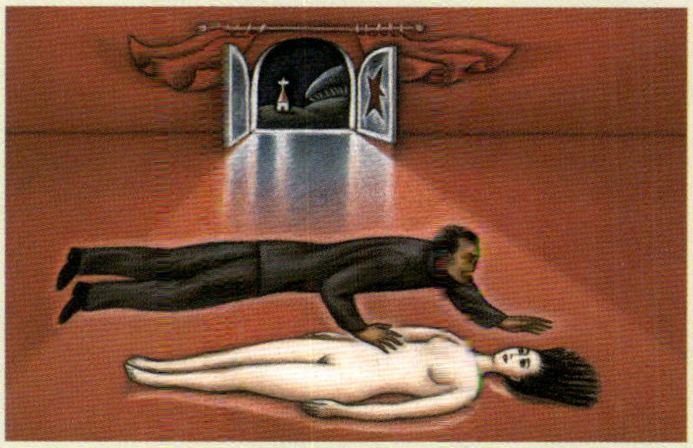

When the dreamer is the victim of violence, and the emotional charge is high, the dream may represent an assault upon status or relationships, or a threat to finances, health or general welfare. If the subject enjoys watching violence in dreams, this may be linked to unacknowledged aggressive impulses within the self. In Freudian psychology, dream violence toward the father or mother is often associated with a wish to throw off authority.

Violence toward the self

Violence toward the dreamer often represents a sense of guilt and a desire for self-punishment. This may be related to the ending of a relationship or the death of somebody close to us. Perhaps we feel, consciously or unconsciously, as though there was something that we could have done to prevent this difficult event. Alternatively dream violence may represent a lack of self-esteem and maybe even a sense of self-loathing. Whether the destructive urges that result from negative self-regard erupt into waking life or fester within our unconscious, it is important to address them before they cause us serious harm, physical or psychological. Dreams in which we are hurt or attacked can also indicate that the dreamer is too vulnerable or apprehensive in the face of the outside world, as if violent outer forces are battering him or her into quiet submission.

Violence toward others

This often represents a struggle for self-assertion, or a fight against unwanted aspects of the dreamer's inner or outer life. Violence against a child can represent failure to accept the child in oneself, while violence toward an older man or woman may indicate a refusal to listen to the wisdom of others. Lashing out indiscriminately at those around us might represent a struggle with the mutinous urges of our unconscious mind.

Wars and battles

Jung saw wars and battles as a sign of major conflict between aspects of the dreamer's conscious and unconscious minds. Such dreams are likely to reflect a struggle between deep instinctive forces and the rules of conscious conduct. The battle classically pitches a conscious demand for order against the instinctive urge of the unconscious to rebel. This may indicate a need for reconciliation rather than victory, and acceptance of our darker side rather than a futile attempt to drive it out.

Wrestling

A dream in which we wrestle a formidable opponent suggests that we are grappling with a problem in our personal or professional life. Facing a sumo wrestler might signify a sense of being dwarfed by the difficulties we face.

Jungians might highlight a connection to the biblical story of Jacob wrestling with the angel of God: we may be resisting the difficult path of enlightenment.

Killing

Killing can be a remarkably positive dream symbol and may have nothing to do with violent or aggressive urges. For dreamers who have been undergoing a process of psychotherapy or self-discovery, the image of people or animals being killed can represent painful memories or destructive habits of mind that we have decided to exorcise. The murder of an authority figure might suggest a desire to escape the moral or social constraints of our present lives, or it might represent an unresolved grudge against a parent, boss or schoolteacher.

Fist fight

The immediacy of a fist fight suggests a desperate struggle, perhaps with elements of ourselves or with someone or something that is oppressing or trying to control us. If we find ourselves paralyzed and unable to throw a punch, the dream may indicate a feeling of helplessness or lack of self-esteem.

Enemy

When the dreaming mind casts as an enemy someone with whom we have no quarrel, it could be time to examine that relationship more closely. The dream may be an alert from our unconscious that, despite appearances, this person is not to be trusted. A bitter foe may also represent the Shadow, the Jungian concept of the darker side of ourself.

Bruise

When the dreaming mind presents us with an image of a bruise, this might be a reflection of our current emotional state. Perhaps somebody has verbally lashed out at us and left us feeling hurt and vulnerable? The area of the body that has been injured may be significant.

Punchbag

A dream in which we see or violently pummel a punchbag may suggest that we are looking for an outlet for our frustrations. It is important to consider who or what the punchbag might represent and to ensure that we do not make an innocent individual, or ourselves, the victim of our unexpressed anger.

Tests and Exams

Examinations can be among the most stressful experiences in life, so it is hardly surprising that they crop up in our dreams long after our school and college years. Among the most anxious of examination dreams is that in which we arrive to face a test without having done any revision, or must search frantically for the examination room long after the bell has rung to indicate that the start is imminent.

Even when we have grown up and left school, life is full of tests. From job interviews to meals with prospective in-laws, sometimes it feels as though our performance is constantly being assessed, and for some of us, perhaps, that we are being found wanting.

Facing an interview panel

Oral examinations can be even more anxiety-provoking than written ones. The interviewers facing the dreamer on the panel may represent aspects of the self, suggesting self-rejection. To be tongue-tied in the face of the panel may suggest that the dreamer has no convincing answer to the voice of conscience or that he or she refuses to confront feelings that demand to be expressed. Such dreams might also suggest a difficult relationship with a parent or other authority figure who would be classed as an "interrogator" by psychologists. These people constantly probe and question us, and, although they often have good intentions, their behaviour can constitute an invasion of our privacy and may seriously undermine our confidence.

Examinations

A dream in which we run, often late, down corridor after corridor trying to find an examination room might evoke a sense of powerlessness over our own destiny. Dream examinations may also stand for a sense of being on trial in any area of our personal or professional life. Failure in a dream test can be a highly uncomfortable experience, encouraging the dreamer to face up to shortcomings that he or she may otherwise have been unwilling to see. Particularly when taking place in cold, impersonal surroundings, an examination can represent the remote powers of bureaucracy and authority that sometimes seem to control the dreamer's life, making arbitrary decisions that have a profound effect upon our future.

Forms and applications

A dream in which we find ourselves required to fill in an unintelligible questionnaire may convey feelings of helplessness in the face of seemingly insurmountable problems. An application form might suggest that something is missing from our life – it can help to consider whether the dream specified what we were applying for.

Giving and Receiving

Giving is a symbolic form of social interaction and, as a dream image, provides clues about the nature of our relationships with others. Of course, whether the gifts are welcome or unwelcome is crucial to their meaning. Receiving many gifts on a festive occasion such as a birthday emphasizes the esteem in which the dreamer is held by others, but if the gifts arrive at less appropriate times, they can indicate the bombardment of unwelcome advice to which the dreamer may be prone.

Buying a present can suggest our wish to make a special effort for the person concerned, or, more nebulously, can represent our feelings of generosity toward them. If the present is particularly expensive, this may be a symbol of the dreamer's wish to make special sacrifices, or to help or serve the other person in an especially important way. On the other hand, showering presents on others, particularly if they are rejected, may indicate that the dreamer is being too insistent in their gift of advice, lavishing attention where it is not wanted, or making inappropriate attempts to become acceptable to others. As with any dream image that appears exciting and attractive on the outside but turns out to be intrinsically defective, a gift that goes wrong suggests disappointed expectations, some kind of hidden agenda, or evil masquerading as good. An entirely empty gift box might represent hollow promises – perhaps with a warning from our unconscious that the promised financial reward or personal gains from a lucrative-seeming scheme may never materialize. Often a present that is never fully unwrapped relates to hidden mysteries, which the dreamer has started to unravel but for the moment remain at least partially unknown: the message is that with further perseverance we might eventually understand their true meaning. A popular dream interpretation book of the nineteenth century suggested that to give a present in a dream foretells adversity; and that if the recipient is a partner or a lover, the action may indicate that they are inconstant in love, or else unwell.

Incongruous gift

A gift that appears inappropriate to the dreamer, or causes other feelings of unease, may indicate the unwelcome attentions of another person – or praise or esteem of which the dreamer feels him- or herself to be unworthy. If the dreamer is the giver rather than the recipient, the dream may be a reminder to present our weaknesses – or our true nature – more accurately to others.

Box of chocolates

A box of chocolates may stand for the multitude of opportunities and varied pleasures that life offers us. In Freudian terms, it might either evoke the oral pleasures of infancy or represent excretion – and therefore perhaps an anal fixation that might lead us to be overly controlling or mean-minded about money.

Bouquet of flowers

A bouquet of flowers is an almost universally recognized symbol of love or appreciation. The beauty and transience of flowers speaks across cultures as an external expression of our innermost feelings. The colour and type of the blooms in a dream bouquet can be especially significant: while daisies might suggest innocence and playfulness, red roses could perhaps convey high passion and sexuality. Like a dream gift package that turns out to contain an unpleasant surprise, a decaying bouquet of flowers can imply disappointed expectations.

Gift-wrapping

Gift-wrapping an object in a dream can suggest that we are trying to disguise something, perhaps rather desperately. We may be hiding feelings of distress behind an optimistic veneer, or we may be more selfish than we seem; or perhaps we need to face an uncomfortable truth that we have hitherto repressed.

Letters and Packages

Receiving goods or messages through the mail in a dream often heralds something unexpected, such as a new opportunity or challenge. The dreamer's response to the contents of the package may give clues to the meaning. For example, failure to take a letter out of the envelope may suggest that full use will not be made of the chance on offer, while a sense of anticipation before opening it can indicate a more positive attitude. The identity of the sender (often an aspect of the dreamer's unconscious) may also be important. Perhaps this is a message from the intuitive understanding that is rooted in your unconscious.

Rarely do dreamers report actually reading a message received in the mail – dreams prefer to leave such obvious resolutions to the waking mind.

Sending a letter may also suggest that face-to-face communication is difficult for some reason.

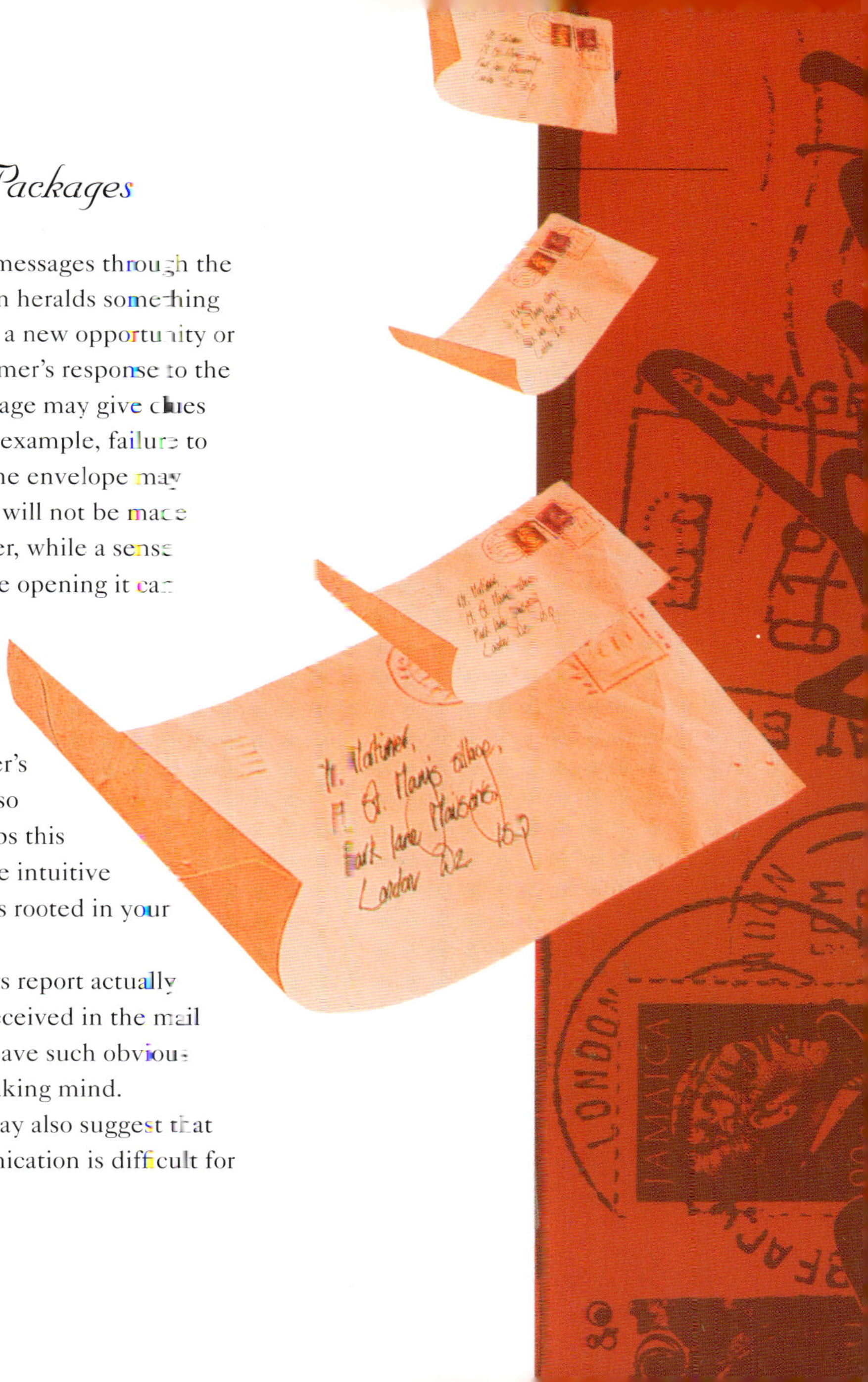

Stamp

A letter without a stamp may suggest an aspiration that cannot yet be realized, or perhaps a failure to attend to important details in life. An envelope covered in stamps may be a symbol of passionate enthusiasm or else the excessive efforts that can stem from insecurity.

Mailman

If the dreamer is acting as mailman, or is carrying a message for someone else, this may indicate a willingness to take responsibility, or to be entrusted with secrets. It can also relate to our power to give or withhold pleasure from others, or to a dawning awareness of our personal significance.

The mailman carries messages that often symbolize new opportunities, and so to dream that the mailman is passing our door without leaving a letter often serves to draw attention to the dreamer's disappointment, either over a particular issue or over the general direction of his or her life. If the dreamer runs after the mailman, this might represent a decision to take positive action and create our own opportunities.

Unintelligible letter

A letter that is written in a foreign language or in an indecipherable script can signify frustration with a seemingly unresolvable issue or a sense that our communication with others could be more effective. Alternatively, if we open

a letter to find only a blank page inside, then our unconscious may be prompting us to take more control of our life.

Anonymous letter

An anonymous letter can be an alarm signal from the unconscious. We may be experiencing a period of emotional turmoil and it may be time to take stock of the direction that our life is taking. Alternatively, we might feel that others know more about us than we would like.

Postcard

Postcards are generally a light-hearted means of communication. Open for anybody to read during their transit, their appearance in our dreams may suggest a desire for more laughter and openness in our life. The picture on the front of the card can also be significant – it might indicate a yearning for travel and adventure or, if it is of a place we have lived in or visited in the past, it might suggest nostalgia for that period of our life.

Envelope

Freud saw envelopes as a symbol of female sexuality. An unopened envelope might represent virginity or perhaps a woman's reluctance to enter into an intimate relationship. It can also represent an issue that we are reluctant to face. Opening an envelope or inserting a letter into one can signify the act of sexual intercourse.

Deeds and certificates

Deeds and other formal documents such as birth or marriage certificates often appear in our dreams during times of upheaval or transformation. They might suggest a craving for stability and certainty or they might be a response to an upcoming rite of passage. A dream in which we burn deeds and documents could signal a point of closure in our lives; or alternatively it could be an expression of a deep-seated desire for significant change.

Parcel

Like envelopes, Freudians understand parcels to represent the female sexual organs. Your response to receiving a dream parcel may be suggestive of your attitude to female sexuality, especially if you are a man. New love or anticipation of seeing our partner might inspire a dream where we tear open a parcel, eager for its contents. If, however, we are reluctant or even frightened to open a parcel, we may be afraid of the serious emotional commitment that can accompany intimate relationships.

Email

Most people today send more emails than letters, so it is not surprising when web-based forms of communication appear in our dreams. Accidentally sending an email to our entire address book might represent a warning from our unconscious about the dangers of being too public in our opinions. An anxiety

dream in which we click on "Send" before the message is ready could reflect concerns about communicating an idea that has not yet been fully formulated – perhaps, but not necessarily, in a work context. Clicking on the "Delete" button could point to a yearning to delete an undesirable person or situation from our life.

Contract

A contract might evoke a personal or professional commitment about which we are having doubts. Tearing up a dream contract might be a form of wish-fulfilment, expressing our desire to escape from an agreement that we are bound to or perhaps from a relationship, with a husband or lover, that is unwholesome.

Ink blot

Obscuring part or all of a letter or other form of verbal message, an ink blot can represent a miscommunication or ambiguity. A tear stain on a letter may conjure up feelings of guilt about a hurt that we have caused. Alternatively, if the tear was our own, it could evoke the emotional pain of bringing a relationship to an end. As with the psychological Rorschach test, the shape of the blot can also be significant.

Shopping and Money

Stores often symbolize the array of opportunities and rewards that are available to us in our lives. Our ability to use these chances may be signified by the amount of money we dream of having in our pockets.

The dreaming mind may concoct any number of shopping metaphors to symbolize our ability or failure to take advantage of life's opportunities, or to find solutions to particular problems. We may find ourselves in a store just before closing time, unable to find what is wanted before being shown the door; or the shelves may be too high and the dreamer unable to reach up to them; or the items on display may be so many and so various that the dreamer cannot choose between them.

For Jung, money represents power – the ability to achieve an objective. To find that we have insufficient cash to pay for what we want can symbolize a perceived lack of the abilities or qualifications needed to attain some particular goal. Freud, on the other hand, saw money as a symbol of excrement. He interpreted dreams of hoarding money as representative of anal fixation, perhaps as a result of mismanaged infant toilet training by overzealous parents. Anal fixation is a trait usually associated with people with obsessively orderly, highly controlling personalities.

Also, of course, dreams of money may simply reflect anxieties about our finances – especially in times of economic uncertainty during the Obama era.

Window display

To dream of seeing a window display full of attractive but somehow unattainable items often suggests that the dreamer feels excluded from the good things in life. The dream may also be reminding him or her to look elsewhere for more attainable, and perhaps ultimately more worthwhile, benefits. Jung believed that dreams involving a chemist's, or drugstore, often relate to alchemy and the processes of inner transformation.

Store interior

The dream image of a store might represent our view of the opportunities that life presents. How much we buy, and whether the items we purchase are the ones we were looking for, can reflect on the way we understand our ability to achieve our goals. A dream in which we cannot find the items that we intended to buy suggests frustration at not getting what we want out of life. If we are frantically rushing to the stores in a race against closing time, the dream may convey our concerns about life being too short to accommodate all the attainments we would like to notch up. A store can also suggest a materialistic approach to life.

Store counter

The display of tempting things at, for example, a deli or jewelry counter forces us to select from a wealth of different options. This may be pure wish-fulfilment, but there can also be an element of being overwhelmed by too much choice. If we are looking for a present, perhaps we feel we do not know the person (even our partner) well enough to choose wisely.

Trading

A trade can symbolize any form of interpersonal interaction. Our personal, professional and intellectual lives are full of trading: we unconsciously evaluate the qualities that every prospective colleague, friend or sexual partner has to offer us, and what they are likely to want in return.

Bill or check

Receiving a bill highlights the fundamental truth that it is necessary to invest our personal resources in order to progress. We may be shocked at how much we have to pay. However, a large bill is as likely to represent the extent of the opportunities open to us as it is to symbolize the personal cost. In an anxiety dream we might be unable to pay a bill, because our wallet is empty or our credit cards have been rejected. This could represent lack of self-esteem or fear of social humiliation; equally, however, it might simply be related to real-life money worries. A dream in which we write an invoice or receive a payment might suggest that we feel we deserve to be rewarded for our efforts in some sphere – personal, professional or spiritual. Scrutinizing a restaurant bill closely may reflect some mistrust of people in our life – even of friends or family.

Pedlar or hawker

Street pedlars conjure up images both of freedom and of inferior goods. Unfettered by rent and by the responsibilities of normal storekeepers, they work on the margins of respectable society, and hence may represent a yearning to escape the bounds of our everyday lives. Alternatively, we may be unsure about the motives of a new acquaintance or perhaps we are questioning the honesty of the other party in a business deal.

Selling

Selling is essentially the art of persuasion. We may be trying to "sell" an idea or project to our work colleagues or close family, or we could be deciding whether or not to "buy" somebody else's idea, explanation or excuse. Anything from the decision to move house to a proposal of marriage will involve some form of persuasion and a dream in which we are attempting to sell, or being sold, something (especially if we think that the item is of dubious value) is frequently an expression of anxiety about these transactions.

Rent

Jung famously postulated that the dream image of a house represents the self. Paying rent might suggest the importance of preserving the integrity of the self – giving our opinions their due even in the face of the disapproval of an overbearing parent or other authority figure. If, however, the dream highlights the fact that we do not own the house, then it may convey a lack of self-assurance. We may be experiencing an identity crisis or we might not feel comfortable with our body. Perhaps we have recently put on or lost a lot of weight and are finding the change difficult to accept.

Safe

Freudians would see a safe as a symbol of the female sexual organs or perhaps of sexual coldness. An item that we lock up in a safe could equally, however, represent a secret that we desperately want to conceal, or perhaps a hoarding instinct with all its implicit obsessiveness. In the Jungian understanding, money represents the power to achieve spiritual enlightenment and a safe may therefore represent a storehouse of wisdom.

Odds and ends

A store selling miscellaneous odds and ends – pens, pencils, spools of thread, buttons, ribbons, paperclips and the like – may represent all the quotidian details of life. It is important to strike a balance between the big picture and the small – but if we do not pay attention to the minutiae, and in particular to the little chores, the big picture may start to break up. We should also, however, be careful not to become so engrossed in the nuances of a situation that we miss its fundamental truths.

Bazaar

Heaps of spices, rolls of brightly coloured cloth, sizzling tureens of wonderful, fragrant stews – the sights, sounds and smells of a Middle Eastern bazaar might evoke a craving for travel or just a desire for new and exciting experiences. In our dreams as in waking life, however, the narrow streets and persistent hawkers of an exotic market may also feel claustrophobic and intimidating. We may be finding it difficult to adjust to a new job or to some other alteration in our circumstances. Trying to haggle with merchants might represent an interaction with a demanding friend, relative, neighbour or work colleague.

Pawnbroker

Visiting a pawnbroker might suggest a feeling of desperation. We may be worried that our spending has got out of hand, or perhaps that we are going to be forced to sacrifice some treasured ambition or ideal. The low price that we will get for our goods may also suggest that we feel undervalued in some respect. We may not be receiving the recognition we believe we deserve, either in the workplace or at home.

Stock market crash

A dream in which there is a disaster in the financial markets may involve an image of a banker or stockbroker throwing themselves from the window of a skyscraper. The dreamer may be expressing a feeling of intense disappointment – perhaps about a failed marriage or poor examination results in a favourite subject. The dreaming mind may use the concept of "investment" to symbolize any kind of emotional, intellectual or professional input. Our time and energy are precious and the drama of a dream stock market crash can reveal the frustration that we feel when efforts turn out to have been wasted.

Market

An open-air market is usually a colourful affair, offering a proliferation of goods for our perusal. In dreams, it may represent the possibilities open to us beyond the usual channels. Such a dream is especially likely to occur at a time of transit on or change – when we leave home as adolescents, for example, or upon retirement.

Communication

Good communication is the mainstay of our lives with others, in both personal and vocational settings, and poor communication, conversely, can prevent us from being happy or successful – indeed, it can drive us to despair. It is unsurprising, therefore, that many dreams focus on communication issues. When we feel that communication is poor, this may be for all kinds of reasons other than competent articulation of ideas – for example, it may be related to feelings of social inferiority. Interpretation often needs to look beyond the boundaries of the ostensible subject to understanding in the broader sense.

Typically, communication dreams portray the dreamer as unable to make him- or herself heard over the noise made by others, or desperately trying to attract attention, or trying to alert others to what the dreamer sees as an impending disaster of some kind. But we may also hear others dismissing us in various ways or making disparaging remarks at our expense. Listeners may turn away in contempt when we try to give opinions or advice, or to make pleasant conversation. Sometimes the dreamer may find others tearing up something that he or she has written.

Being tongue-tied in front of an audience, or being ridiculed by those present, suggests insecurity about ourselves or our beliefs or ideas.

Unruly audience during public speaking

An audience that refuses to be quiet while we are addressing them may relate not only to a lack of sympathy for the speaker, but also to a general confusion of ideas in waking life. The absence of an audience suggests a total neglect of the dreamer's ideas by others, or a complete lack of recognition of his or her achievements. A yelling and catcalling mob at our feet may reflect our own true feelings toward other people in general – are we guilty of believing ourselves to be "above the crowd"?

Alternatively, the dreaming mind may use the image of an unruly audience to disguise the identity of one individual whose behaviour toward us is unacceptably aggressive.

Disagreement

The airing of a disagreement can reveal your doubts about hitherto deeply held convictions – the dialogue that appears in the dream is a dramatization of your own inner conflict. However, this can signal a constructive moment in your personal development, an openness to testing new ideas in the light of experience.

Quarrel

A major quarrel in a dream may represent feelings of frustration in our waking life. If the other party refuses to listen to our point of view, or remains obstinate in the face of our arguments, we may feel insecure about our ability to communicate our needs or ideas.

Making a speech

A dream in which we frankly address an audience may represent a desire to have our point of view aired and understood. Perhaps there is some issue about which we would like to set the record straight. The rousing cheers of an adoring crowd might be a wish-fulfilment symbolizing our desire to be feted by those around us

Rules and Regulations

Rules carry associations of structure, compulsion, control. If, in a dream, we seem to be giving strict instructions to others or to ourselves, the unconscious may be drawing attention to a desire to make life less arbitrary and more predictable. If it is others who are making the rules, the underlying message may be the need for more discipline in life, or the need to be aware that our direction is being circumscribed by limits imposed from outside.

Dreams in which we stand accused of breaking rules of whose existence we were unaware emphasize the unfairness of many life experiences. Such dreams may help to release the dreamer's frustration, or else signify that we have not fully come to terms with injustice and are finding it hard to express ourselves.

Obeying rules can indicate that the dreamer is too easily led by others, but may also signify loyalty and integrity. For interpretation, it is often helpful to explore the nature of the rules obeyed. The unconscious may be encouraging us to look more carefully at beliefs or conventions we have allowed to go unquestioned.

To dream of arguing about rules may signify an inner conflict of some kind – perhaps a clash between instincts and conscience. Or it might reflect the adjustments that we need to make to our priorities within the context of a new or changing relationship.

Exposure to TV and the movies has given most of us sufficient knowledge of the courts to furnish a dream, even if we lack direct personal experience.

Rule-breaking

Dreams in which the dreamer defiantly breaks the rules – for example, by taking photographs in an art gallery or having a rowdy picnic in a public library – often hark back to early childhood. The dreamer's natural urge toward self-assertion and testing the limits imposed by others may have been restricted by parents or teachers, and his or her rebellious nature may still lie repressed in the unconscious, asserting itself by dream transgressions. Such dreams of misbehaviour can express a healthy creative urge. However, if the crime is more serious – for example, stealing a car – there might be guilt involved; or fear of others exploiting our weaknesses.

Lawsuit

A lawsuit might represent the dreamer's desire to punish people who oppose his or her actions or disagree with their opinions. Alternatively, it may suggest a deep-seated need to win the approval of our peers – perhaps represented by the jury.

Attorney or lawyer

The eloquent attorney who speaks for us in court could stand for a friend or relative who supports us in a time of stress. Alternatively, however, they may represent someone on whom we are overly dependent. Perhaps it is time to speak up for ourselves and voice our opinions confidently. Similarly, a dream in which we find ourselves in the role of the attorney could emphasize the importance of representing our own best interests.

Jury

Think carefully about the individuals who make up a dream jury: these are the people who will decide our future, and their identity may provide an important key to the inner workings of our psyche. The appearance of friends, family or work colleagues may be connected to some event in our lives, on which these people would be expected to have a view. Their opinion might have a significant impact on a decision about a job, say, or our choice of partner, or any other decision we might make. A dream in which we fail to recognize any of the jury can indicate a sense of being at the mercy of fate, or other forces beyond our control. To see our own face on the jury suggests that we might have some influence on our own destiny – or that we might be in the position of judging someone else, perhaps reluctantly.

Plaintiff

Acting as plaintiff in a trial and suing for some perceived injury or injustice might be an assertive act or it may stem from feelings of paranoia. If the dream is a product of a vindictive desire to see the other party punished, then losing the case could highlight the self-destructive quality of our anxiety. Winning the case, on the other hand, far from being a positive outcome, might point to feelings of self-righteousness or malevolence.

Cross-examination

A cross-examination in court could represent some aspect of the dreamer's life that is being subjected to intense and challenging scrutiny. The questions themselves may represent doubts – either the dreamer's own or doubts that he or she imagines in the minds of others. Alternatively, the dream may express our frustration at being expected to explain ourselves – perhaps because we feel guilt about something we have thought, said or done.

Subpoena or summons

An order to appear in court may represent guilt (as a cross-examination often does), but it could also be a call to stand up for an individual or cause that needs our help. A dream of being required to attend court could also reflect resentment at some obligation placed upon us.

Verdict

Although a judge may represent our father or another significant authority figure, a verdict, whether positive or negative, more often than not reflects our own judgment of ourselves.

Debt collector

A debt collector appearing at our door, or anyone else involved in the process of repossession (of a house, for example), might serve to draw our attention to some obligation we have been neglecting. There is also, of course, the obvious literal meaning of anxiety about personal levels of debt – a feeling that may be so strong it permeates the unconscious.

Thief or burglar

A dream in which we are mugged or burgled is likely to stem from anxiety, perhaps resulting from some aspect of a sexual relationship – in dreams, a real or imagined partner is often depicted in terms of possession. If our dream self is the thief, the object we are stealing may be significant to the overall meaning – phallic symbols, such as a gun or a car, or symbols of the female sexual organs, like a purse or a locket, might confirm connotations of adulterous or otherwise illicit inclinations. Robbery at gunpoint or knifepoint can express fears of violence, especially sexual violence. Similarly, a burglar breaking down a door or otherwise entering a house without permission can convey our fear of rape, of letting people get too close to the true self, or of emotional entanglement. The shadowy figure of a highwayman may represent the side of the self that craves freedom from social constraints.

Crime

A dream in which we commit a heinous crime is by no means an indicator of an inherently violent or anti-social personality. Rather, the dream may be expressing a sense of guilt, or perhaps a more general desire to escape from the social, financial or moral inhibitions placed on our waking life.

Trespass

A dream in which we enter another person's house or land without their permission

can convey a desire to venture into unexplored realms of emotional, intellectual or spiritual experience. The frisson of danger may be part of the satisfaction we gain. A dream trespass may also have a sexual dimension. If we are the trespasser, this may suggest a desire to commit adultery or usurp someone's place in a relationship. If we are the victim rather than the perpetrator, we may fear betrayal or violation.

Deserter

The soldier who deserts his post is an ambiguous dream image. On one hand, he may represent the temptation to ignore a difficult psychological or personal issue and run away from rather than confront our problems. Alternatively, he may be a courageous figure, bravely negotiating a hostile environment. Perhaps we feel that a cause we have been fighting for is not our own, or perhaps it no longer seems like a worthwhile expenditure of our energy. The combination of fear, guilt and relief when we dream of being a deserting soldier may make the scenario particularly appropriate as an expression of the anxiety surrounding the act of ending a relationship.

If, on the other hand, we are a hapless soldier left at our post by a comrade in arms, the dream may invoke a feeling of abandonment or neglect. Years on, we may still resent an inattentive parent, or perhaps more recently we have been left to fend for ourselves after the death of a loved one or the break-up of an emotional relationship. Do not rule out the possibility of this being beneficial for you in the long term – the dream may mark the beginning of greater psychological independence.

Smuggling

Smuggled goods tend to be both desirable and fraught with risk. They could stand for aspects of the self that we prefer to keep private, or perhaps they represent valuable new insights that we wish to share with our friends.

Counterfeiter

A counterfeiter might represent a warning not to take the promises of others at face value. If the one pressing fake goods or money on us is someone we know, our unconscious may be urging caution in a personal or professional relationship that we would not otherwise have questioned. A dream in which we attempt to pass off fake notes for real may invoke a sense of frustration with our progress toward personal fulfilment.

Poisoning

Administering poison to somebody we know may reflect unacknowledged hostility, or else a desire to rid ourselves of some emotion that is "poisoning" our peace of mind.

Environments

Any of life's possible social situations or settings – from a humble classroom in a village school to the Oval Office of the White House – can appear in a dream. When a setting corresponds to an actual memory, we know that the dream might well be rooted in our past circumstances – for example, if we dream of a factory where we once spent an unhappy period of employment, it is possible that whatever troubled us there is continuing to affect us today, in a completely different environment. Situations, of course, all come with their own characteristic paraphernalia, which offer scope for symbolism.

The Home

Domestic events are among the most common subject matter for dreaming. Mostly, they occur in Level 1 and 2 dreams: these often incorporate apparently trivial events from the recent past (and especially from the previous day) which the dreaming mind has selected because it recognizes their value in symbolizing (and thus helping to access) significant material that is stored in the dreamer's unconscious.

When interpreting domestic dreams, it can be helpful to look for anomalies between the dream material and waking experience. Often the dream is set in the dreamer's own home, or involves familiar domestic routines, yet some of the details may be strangely inaccurate. Items of furniture may be in the wrong place, domestic implements or appliances may have grown or diminished in size, ingredients for cooking or materials for cleaning are nowhere to be found, and total strangers may suddenly appear and treat the house as if it belongs to them.

Since the home is where we conduct such a major part of our lives, and since the activities we perform there are so richly varied, there is a wealth of available domestic symbolism. Every room of the home is laden with potential significance, and every implement – from the shower or stove to teaspoons and chopsticks – can be seized upon by the dreaming mind for its own purposes.

Whitewash

Whitewash can stand for a cover-up of potentially embarrassing or damaging misdeeds. These hidden truths may be our own, or our unconscious mind might suspect that others are concealing something about their character or their past.

Cooking

When food is being prepared for other people, this may indicate a wish to influence others, or make them dependent. As a symbol of togetherness, preparing a meal can suggest a quest for love and affection. If the emphasis is on the food itself, the underlying meaning may be the dreamer's desire to mould some truth or insight into a more palatable form, or to synthesize the disparate elements of our life into something nourishing for the soul. The cooking fire is traditionally the focus of the household (indeed, *focus* is Latin for "hearth") and thus can symbolize the deepest centre of our being.

Carpet or rug

The precise significance of a dream carpet may depend on its hue or on any pattern that embellishes it. A floral design may be a symbol of a garden, and perhaps of the Garden of Eden. More universally, it may evoke the Tree of Life, a concept that appears in a multitude of belief systems and mythologies all over the world. In accord with the idea of the house as a symbol of the self, a carpet covering up access to a lower floor may signify that we are smothering impulses from our unconscious.

Pots and pans

Cooking vessels are often sexual symbols. Whether the handle or the pot appears more obvious in the dream may indicate whether male or female sexuality is intended. The meaning has much to do with what is going on inside – a nutritious broth or something more self-indulgent or cooked to impress others?

Dish

A dish of freshly cooked food is usually served hot to be eaten immediately. In our dreams this may represent inspiration or ideas that should be acted on right away, or a problem we should tackle as soon as possible. A dish of cold leftovers may imply attitudes that we should leave behind us in order to progress.

Kettle

The protruding spout of a kettle gives it phallic connotations and makes it a predominantly male symbol. The boiling contents might represent passion. As with very hot water and steam, the image should alert us to the potential damage that strong emotions can cause to people who come into contact with them.

Table

The image of someone hiding under a table probably has its roots in childhood – a tablecloth can create a tent-like enclosure that may be a suitable place for children to conceal themselves. What makes the hiding-place precarious, in an anxiety dream, is the fact that it is impossible to get away from the shelter of the tabecloth without being seen by people at the table. Dreams may also feature a table as a surface on which to display objects. Interpretation could explore the idea of the table as a metaphor for openness – anything on the table surface is going to be visible to anyone nearby.

Cutlery

Collectively, a set of cutlery may represent the dreamer's domestic ambitions. Individually, each component can have very different connotations. Knives and forks are essentially scaled-down versions of weapons and may suggest either tamed aggression or the tensions within a seemingly harmonious domestic situation. Spoons have a female symbolism on account of their rounded shape and capacity to contain. If we feel vulnerable or overstretched, then a dream image of a spoon might express a desire to be "spoon-fed" or nurtured. A teaspoon or sugarspoon could resonate with us as a sign to take things slowly or in small doses, while a soup spoon or ladle might encourage us to drink deeply of the pleasures or values that life offers.

Teapot

As with a kettle, the spout of a teapot may give the object phallic connotations. An ornate teapot might suggest the beauty that we could find inherent in our daily routines if only we were to look for it.

Doing the dishes

Like washing hands, washing dishes may suggest a desire to wash away guilt or shame, perhaps caused by some sexual experience.

Cracked household objects

Cracked objects suggest flaws in the dreamer's character, or in certain of his or her arguments, ideas or relationships. Although Freudians would understand a broken bowl, vase or cup to be a female sexual symbol, Jungians would be more likely to interpret it as a representation of the dreamer's disillusionment with the world.

Alternatively, a cracked or broken vase or cup may symbolize a broken heart. A dream where we storm around a house breaking things usually indicates anger or disillusionment with whatever is symbolized by the item that we smash.

Vacuum-cleaning

Vacuum-cleaning is a very thorough means of ridding a house of dirt and may indicate a desire to completely erase a bad memory or past action. Vacuuming dust or ashes may convey a wish to move on from our grief after the death of a close relative or friend.

Spring-cleaning

A dream where we thoroughly clean our home (especially in springtime) may symbolize a need to purge ourselves of uncomfortable memories and bad habits. Now may be time to look deep inside ourselves and to cast aside those aspects of the self that are not constructive in order that we can make a fresh start.

Window-cleaning

A dream in which we wash and polish the grime from the windows of our home can stand for a desire to gain a clearer view of life. Our view of the outside world may be obscured by too much introspection or by an inability to see past our own preconceptions.

Laundry

The swirling waters of a washing machine can sometimes evoke the womb. Or perhaps it is time to deal with past issues including even deep-seated childhood hurts, that need to "come out in the wash" in order for us to lead a healthier psychological life.

The dream image of clothes may draw attention to the nudity they are meant to conceal. The action of hanging clothes on a publicly visible washing line might suggest a subliminal yearning for the lost innocence of childhood or alternatively it might indicate exhibitionist urges.

Colander or sieve

Water, flour or sugar draining through the holes in a colander or sieve may represent our life-force or energy draining away. Is there someone or something in our life that is sapping our strength? A sieve may also stand for the process of developing a new attitude to life, sifting or rinsing away outdated or unhelpful modes of thought or behaviour.

Furniture polish

Varnish or polish can both protect and enhance the appearance of furniture and floors. In our dreams it may symbolize a desire to gloss over our failings or it may signify a need to harden ourselves against criticisms directed by others. Or perhaps we want to cover up the cracks in a relationship.

Cookie jar

The cookie jar or biscuit tin of our childhood was probably a source of treats and rewards. A dream in which we find ourselves looking longingly at a cookie jar on an impossibly high shelf may be redolent of a craving for praise or recognition which never seems to materialize. The variety of cookies or biscuits in a cookie jar could represent an important choice that we have to make.

Architecture

Houses in dreams usually represent the dreamer, and can symbolize his or her body or the various levels of the mind. Like bodies, houses have fronts and backs, windows that look out onto the world outside, doors through which food is brought, and other openings through which waste is later expelled.

It was from a dream of a house that Jung formulated his theory of the collective unconscious. The house seemed unfamiliar but was undoubtedly his own, and after wandering its various floors he discovered a heavy door that led down to a beautiful and ancient vaulted cellar. Another staircase led down to a cave, scattered with bones, pottery and skulls. He interpreted the cellar as the first layer of the unconscious, and the cave as the "world of primitive man" within himself – the collective unconscious. Freud, however, interpreted Jung's dream as a form of wish-fulfilment, and found in the image of the bones and skulls a symbol of *thanatos*, the death-wish, possibly toward Jung's wife.

Other buildings can also represent aspects of the self. Courts of law may symbolize our powers of judgment, museums may stand for the past, while factories or mills often relate to the creative side of the dreamer's life.

Library

A library typically represents ideas, and the ready availability of knowledge. Books on a shelf out of reach may represent ideas beyond the dreamer's present understanding. If in the dream we are unable to concentrate on what we are reading, the ideas we are entertaining may not be productive for us. A library can also signify the dreamer's inner knowledge: consider looking inside the self for answers – the extent of our intuitive understanding may be surprising.

Rooms and floors

Like the mind, a house consists of different levels and compartments, all performing different functions and connected to each other by stairs and doors. In dreams, each room and floor can stand for different aspects of the personality or mind, which should be connected (integrated) but often are not. Jung saw the different floors as symbolizing the unconscious, the conscious, and higher spiritual aspirations. Locked doors or precarious stairs may suggest the difficulties we can face when we plumb the depths of the unconscious.

Given the phallic symbolism that Freud attributes to steps and stairs, a dream in which we ride passively between floors on an escalator may suggest an emotionally detached sex life.

Attic

Situated on the uppermost floor of a house, an attic usually represents our higher aspirations or creative ambitions – the garret was the traditional workplace of the artist or writer. Often a confused jumble, the contents of an attic may reflect feelings about the disorder in our life. As in a real attic, we will need to sort through the clutter diligently to arrive at a plausible interpretation. A chest full of paraphernalia may hint at projects and preoccupations unwisely abandoned. If, however, the chest resembles a coffin, it may be time to let go of aspirations that are ultimately unrealistic. An excessively orderly attic may indicate a doctrinal or otherwise formulaic approach to our spiritual life or an over-reliance on logic and reason in our pursuit of creative endeavours.

Window

Freud interpreted both doors and windows as feminine sexual symbols; Jung associated them with the dreamer's ability to understand the outside world. Looking into others' windows (voyeurism for Freud) can suggest the dreamer is too curious about others' lives, perhaps using this curiosity as a substitute for self-examination.

Balcony

A balcony is a classic Freudian symbol for a woman's breasts – *balcon* is in fact a colloquial French term for breasts, while a *balconette* is a bra. A dream of standing on a balcony may express our desire to return to the mother's breast. Freudians would suggest that for male dreamers it has overtones of the Oedipal rivalry felt by a son toward his father.

Door

A door opening outward may indicate a need to be more accessible to others, while a door opening inward can be an invitation to self-exploration. If a locked door proves frustrating for the dreamer, this may suggest that he or she should search for a new skill or idea to serve as a key. A door that is lacking a handle is a common dream symbol that can reflect a range of frustrations – from lack of advancement at work to being denied fulfilment within a marriage.

Ceiling

Modern usage refers to a "glass ceiling" as a metaphor for the obstacles hindering the advancement of women in the workplace. Anybody who feels that there is something preventing them from achieving their professional or personal goals may experience a dream in which they bang their head on the ceiling, perhaps after they have started to rise from the floor.

Walls

There is a duality inherent in the dream symbol of walls, in as much as they can both imprison and protect. We can surround ourselves with emotional walls, or even walls in the form of a hectic timetable or overbearing commitment to our work. Although we may successfully insulate ourselves from hurt by building walls, it is important to remember that we also cut ourselves off from many good experiences.

Basement or cellar

The basement or cellar of a building often relates to the unconscious. A dream of walking down a set of cellar stairs may represent determined or tentative self-exploration. The items that we find in a cellar may evoke different impulses – food and wine may suggest sexual passion, while scattered bones may reveal repressed homicidal tendencies.

Chimney

A powerful sexual symbol, a chimney can be either female or male depending on whether we view it from inside or outside. A chimney that has collapsed may represent fears of impotence. Traditionally, witches were believed to exit hell through a chimney on the way to their Sabbat gatherings and we may associate this symbol with black magic and the dark arts.

Furniture

The furniture in a house may represent our thoughts and emotions. A dream in which we are wandering around an unfurnished house may point toward an unsatisfied emotional life, with blocked feelings. Alternatively, it might symbolize a fresh start and our readiness to furnish our lives with new experiences. Mending, cleaning or rearranging furniture could imply a craving for emotional healing or a desire for more order in our personal lives.

Curtain

Curtains may express a desire to cut ourselves off from the outside world. While ostensibly a symbol of modesty, they can also represent exhibitionist urges – think of the classic image of a velvet curtain lifting to show a bright stage.

Wardrobe

Clothes frequently represent the Persona (see page 103) – the face that we present to the world. A wardrobe containing a number of different outfits may suggest the different "faces" we adopt in different situations, and within the dream our reactions to these different outfits can suggest which one we feel most truly represents the inner self. An overflowing wardrobe may represent exuberance or even exhibitionism. A locked wardrobe may suggest a desire to hide from public scrutiny.

Living room

Jung understood the different rooms of a house to represent different compartments of the self. As the room that we are most comfortable revealing to others, a living room or lounge may signify the conscious mind.

Kitchen

The kitchen is the room in the home associated with love, nourishment and creativity. A wealth of male and female sexual symbols exist in the food and utensils we may find there, and the environment is rich in maternal associations. A warm oven or glowing hearth may be a vivid symbol of the deep-seated love that the dreamer has for his or her family or friends. If, however, we dream of something burning in the kitchen, this may point to some conflict with the people we are closest to.

Utility room or scullery

As the room used for storing utensils, washing clothes and doing other necessary backroom chores, a scullery or utility room in a dream may be associated with the unconscious mind and the processes that go on there.

Bedroom

We associate the bedroom with birth, death, sleep and sex. In a shared or family house, the bedroom may be the only space we have that is truly private, and so for some people it might represent seclusion, safety and the innermost self. The bedroom can also appear in our dreams as a last resting place. Dreaming of parents asleep in their beds might reflect memories of their death, or express our fear of losing them. An empty bedroom may evoke our own death.

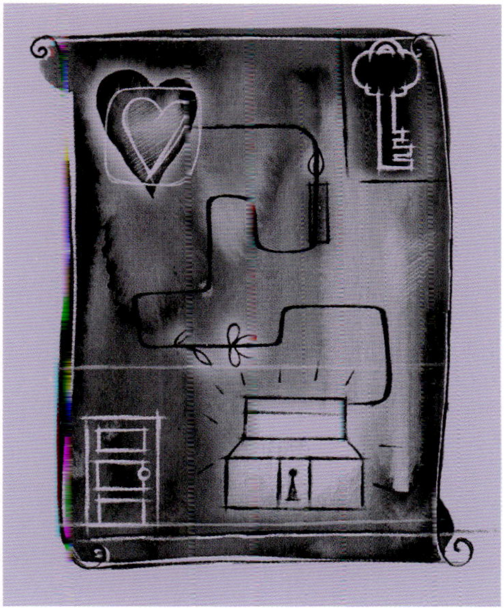

Bathroom

Although relaxing in a long bath is a popular way to relieve ourselves of the tensions and worries of the day, a bath in a dream may go a step further and evoke the safety of life in the womb. If there is a window open, our unconscious may be reminding us of the responsibilities attached to our life out there in the real world.

The appearance of a toilet or lavatory in a dream may represent a desire to flush away unwholesome thought-patterns or emotions. If the toilet is blocked then it may be proving difficult to break free of unhelpful habits.

Farm

The dream image of a farm may convey a desire to return to a simpler, more pastoral way of life. Or perhaps, even in an urban setting, we seek to feel more connected with our roots or with the practical realities on which we depend. We may not necessarily wish to move to the country – only to live by more traditional values within our town or city. Alternatively, a farm may suggest a particular form of career frustration: a yearning for a job that is more socially responsible.

Barn

A barn is a classic image for the good things we have harvested in our lives – whether as home-makers or professionally. There might also be a hint of our moral "harvest", or karma. Seeing a rat or spiders in a barn may indicate a guilt nagging away at our well-being.

Fence

Recalling the saying, "Good fences make good neighbours", a fence can suggest the steps we take to protect ourselves from the intrusion of others – often at the risk of ignoring our social responsibilities and the possibility of rewarding relationships. A fence in need of repair may suggest a deep-seated desire for privacy.

Garage

Despite being associated with traditionally masculine activities, a garage containing a car can be a symbol of female sexuality. A dreamer who is working in the garage fixing a car may be experiencing sexual problems in a relationship.

Fountain

Fountains are imbued with a rich mythic symbolism identifying them as the source of life, knowledge and eternal youth. For an artist suffering from creative block, the dream image of a fountain may herald fresh inspiration. As the source of life, a fountain might represent our mother, or perhaps a new rush of energy after a period of inactivity, depression or unhappiness.

Shed

A garden shed can be a place of retreat or it may be a storage place for a jumble of things you want to keep tidied away out of sight. A dream in which we visit a shed used for storage in this way can represent a project that we abandoned, perhaps prematurely. A shed that shows signs of regular use – for example, as a study – may be yet another symbol of the workings of the unconscious mind. Think carefully about the objects that you find there.

Greenhouse or glasshouse

A riot of exotic growth in a greenhouse might remind us of the unacknowledged instincts suppressed within the unconscious.

Factory

A factory may represent the dreamer's creativity viewed from the perspective of hard work. Depending on the context, the dream may emphasize either the productivity of the factory, or its mechanical, stereotypical nature. Workers on strike might represent some obstacle to our creativity – lack of time or resources perhaps, or writer's block. An endless production line can suggest boredom and frustration, and it may be time to look for a new job or career path or for new sources of inspiration.

Gasworks

The sulphurous smell of natural gas and its flammable properties link a gasworks to the Christian conception of hell. Symbolically, hell in turn can be synonymous with the dark chaos of the unconscious, and a dream set against the background of a gasworks may have a sinister or frightening feel. The darker sides of the psyche are often difficult to confront, and our response to the gasworks in a dream may be connected with our attitude to the daunting task of exploring our unconscious. When the dreamer senses an imminent explosion, this usually relates to bottled-up emotions.

Bar or pub

A bar or a pub can be a place where we socialize, or it may be the setting in which we drown our sorrows. As somewhere associated with overcoming inhibitions, a dream pub might be the arena in which we express our truest emotions. We may find ourselves telling a stranger our darkest secrets or dancing with wild abandon on the tables. The convivial atmosphere of a bar might also convey a craving for company – highlighting feelings of loneliness. If, however, we become embroiled in a brawl, the dream may be pointing to dangerously repressed emotions that are close to spilling over into destructive, uncontrollable anger.

Drunkenness in a dream might represent intoxication with life – a powerful sense of well-being and joy. However, if the experience is not pleasurable but uncomfortable or even frightening, then the dream might be a warning that we are losing control – perhaps we are in danger of developing an addiction to alcohol or drugs, or perhaps we feel as though our life is at the mercy of chance or the manipulations of other people. A dream of being a lone drinker in a dark bar may reveal a desire to obliterate difficult memories or to run away from our problems.

Tower

A tower is a powerful phallic symbol. For male dreamers the strength and sturdiness of a tower may reflect their sexual confidence or lack thereof. Many European folktales feature young women imprisoned in towers by tyrannical kings or fathers. These stories, and similar scenarios in our dreams, may resonate with women who are subject to the oppressive influence of masculine authority, whether in the family, in the workplace or in society. Towers are also significant for their impregnability and may represent somebody who is important to us but remains emotionally distant and detached.

Law court

Dreams set in a court of law may reflect conflicts within the self or between people we are close to. It may be that our capacity for judgment is being stretched by a major, life-changing decision, or by a complicated power struggle between family members or work colleagues.

Clock tower

From major landmarks such as London's Palace of Westminster to more commonplace examples appearing on a town hall or village church, clock towers act as markers of time and geographical position.

A ticking clock is a common dream symbol for the heart and for the passage of time or of our life. Clothed in the phallic form of a tower, the clock may be an image of masculine drive and the courage it takes for us to pursue our true ambitions. The chimes of a clock tower ringing the hour may herald a major event or personal watershed such as a wedding or the birth of our first child.

Eiffel Tower

The Eiffel Tower, in Paris, is a powerful phallic symbol and presents the dreamer with a probable image of male sexuality. The tower may also stand in for the popular view of Parisian life – perhaps the heady brew of revolution and romance, with overtones of art and the cancan. The movie *Moulin Rouge* may have helped to implant this image in a cinema-going audience.

Lighthouse

For Freudians a lighthouse is an unmistakable phallic symbol, rising out of a maternal sea. More modern interpretations look to its function as a beacon and a guide. Just as the beam of a lighthouse warns ships away from dangerous rocks, so a lighthouse in a dream may represent a warning about a potentially hazardous situation. A fog-probing lighthouse beam will indicate an area to avoid rather than one to navigate toward.

Windmill

A windmill grinds the flour that is needed to make bread and may represent the dreamer's role as the main provider for his or her family. The "daily grind" of work may be tiresome but it is usually essential.

Castle

A castle is a form of house and may appear in the guise of a fortress, a fairytale palace or a prison. To dream of being inside a castle suggests security, but may also remind us that the very strength of our psychological defences isolates us from others. The defences represented by a castle's thick outside walls can protect us from pain, but at the expense of meaningful relationships and emotional maturity. If we envision ourselves lowering the drawbridge of a dream castle, then perhaps we are ready to embark on a new emotional attachment. A ruined castle may represent the destruction of the masks, or personas, we might have worn in the past.

Palace

The elegant façade of a beautiful palace may represent the persona that we present to the world. If the interior of the palace seems shabby in comparison with the outside, the dream might be a warning about aspiring to levels that we cannot plausibly attain.

Place of worship

A church, cathedral or temple can represent the spiritual side of the dreamer, or else a longing for peace, wisdom or perhaps, more vaguely, a clearer sense of purpose. To feel that we are a stranger inside a church may remind us of the distance we have yet to cover if we are to become more adjusted spiritually or gain a more respected place in our community. A spire has obvious phallic connotations, while a dome may suggest feminine roundedness – in both the physical and the psychological senses.

A church spire may also be important as an obvious place for a lightning rod, and if one features in our dreams, this might be a reference to a feeling of vulnerability to sudden disaster.

Ruined or burning house

Our house in ruins may be an exaggerated image of some nagging problem – perhaps quite a trivial one, that has no connection with our domestic circumstances. However, the same image can also suggest a sense of personal dysfunction. Areas of the building that need repair may convey our concern about a specific failing. A burning building, although an image of destruction, may have positive connotations as a symbol of catharsis. Sometimes we need to purge the self of attitudes and ideas that are no longer appropriate.

Unfinished building

A house is a classic symbol for the self – the body, mind and emotions. The dream image of an unfinished building reflects the fact that we continue to change and develop all through our life. Careful interpretation of the specific symbolism might provide us with unexpected insights about what aspects of the self we should work on – better access to the basement of the unconscious perhaps, or more windows to the outside world. If we dream of an architect's plan, that might suggest some major project that we are keen to embark on.

School

School experiences are among the most formative in life, and can appear frequently even in the dreams of the elderly. Sometimes the dream relates to specific happenings remembered with pride or embarrassment, or repressed. However, a dream will often use a generic school to convey its message. Dreams of finding ourselves back at school, but demoted to a lower class, sent out of the room in disgrace or stripped of some coveted responsibility, can symbolize childhood insecurities that have still not been resolved.

As well as the school setting, school personnel may also be manifest. The teacher is a classic symbol for authority, and may represent the father or mother, an elder sibling, or others, held in love or fear, who have determined the course of the dreamer's life. Alternatively, a teacher may stand for that censoring aspect of the dreamer's personality that keeps our more unruly impulses in check.

Dreams in which the subject is summoned to the principal's study may signify inferiority, guilt, or simply a dread of having one's misdeeds found out. Being publicly praised by a teacher, or being awarded a school prize, or winning a school sporting fixture, may illustrate the dreamer's belief, or need for belief, in his or her abilities as a pupil or as a person.

Carrying a school bag

A school bag full of books, pens and paper may, if carried happily, relate to the dreamer's accumulated knowledge, and desire to continue learning. If the bag is heavy or uncomfortable, this may signify that some aspect of the past, present or future is a burden.

Ruined or dilapidated school

A dream that returns us to childhood only to witness decay or desertedness in the schoolhouse suggests that we are still carrying disappointed childhood expectations, or disquieting memories. Sometimes there is an added sense of the passing of time, the impermanence of life, and the need to look forward rather than dwell in the past.

Bullying

We usually identify with the victim rather than the bully in a bullying dream. Often this will relate to some painful childhood experience. Alternatively, it may point to a desire to dominate or be dominated, perhaps in a sexual or sado-masochistic way. If both the bully and the victim are the same sex, then the dream may be a complicated response to a homosexual relationship or a homosexual urge, perhaps a repressed one.

Teacher

Our teachers have a formative effect on our lives, whether for good or evil. Their authority over us is comparable to that of our mother or father, and they can in fact figure as dream symbols of our parents. If the teacher who appears in a dream is one whom we revered and respected, we should take careful note of their advice, for the wisdom they pass on to us may represent a missive from the unconscious.

Punishment in class

When we dream of being punished at school, there is often an implied reference to submission to an authority figure. Corporal punishment may reveal a desire for sado-masochistic sex. A punishment doled out for not doing our homework often suggests a sense of guilt at not meeting personal or professional obligations. Being forced to stand in a corner, which used to be a common school punishment, may reflect a feeling of social exclusion; copying out lines may reflect a dissatisfaction with routine.

End of term

Celebrating the end of a term and the start of a vacation may be tinged with regret for loss of friends who become less accessible as they return to their various homes. Or the dream may be expressing optimism about a new phase in our life – or relief at the ending of a difficult or unrewarding period.

Ink

If we dream of spilt ink staining our desk or books, this may suggest that we have committed some offence against our own moral standards or those of others. Black suggests a heinous misdeed or perhaps a misdemeanour conducted under the shadow of night, while red may signify blood or sexuality.

Classroom

Typically, the classroom represents learning, and its lifelong importance. It can also stand for competition, public esteem or censure, or the need to rethink aspects of our personal, social or professional concerns. The classroom can also symbolize nostalgia, or the dreamer's need to rekindle the passion of an earlier stage of

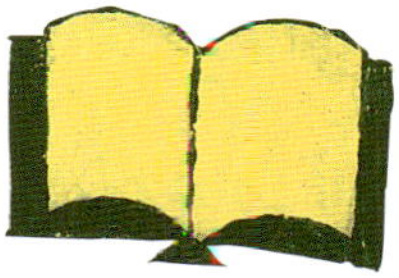

life. Sitting at the back of the classroom to escape the teacher's attention may suggest a tendency to shirk responsibility. Eagerly raising our hand to answer a question, however, may imply a desire to prove ourselves.

Exercise book

The state of an exercise book or notebook can convey the state of the dreamer's psyche. A notebook covered in scribbles and doodles may suggest either creativity or confusion,

or possibly a mixture of both. A neat, ordered notebook can reflect an organized approach to life, or a wish for more order in a disordered state of being. If we look at a notebook and discover sketches where there should have been lists of vocabulary or rows of sums, then perhaps the dreaming mind is drawing our attention to an inner seam of creativity waiting to be discovered.

School desk

Freudians would see a traditional school desk, with its lid and storage compartment, as a symbol of the female sexual organs. Rummaging around inside a desk can therefore relate to sexual intercourse, either experienced or desired. Another way of seeing the same dream would be to focus on the desk as representing the dreamer's personal domain in a classroom full of people. Echoing our need for individuality and personal space, carving our initials into a dream desk might reveal a preoccupation with establishing our identity in the eyes of the outside world. The desk, being a place for concealment, may also suggest the unconscious itself – perhaps the youthful unconscious, before adult experience impinges.

School bell

An alarm clock ringing in the waking world may feature in a dream as a school bell. Dreaming of the bell may herald the ending of classes and symbolically of a difficult episode in our life. If the bell rings for the end of a recreation break, the dream may be expressing regret at the ending of some pleasurable experience, perhaps a romantic or sexual one.

Playground

A playground may represent the need for more leisure. If we are watching other children play while refusing to join in ourselves, the dream may be pointing to our self-imposed isolation. If we have been excluded from the games, we may be suffering from low self-esteem and a fear of rejection. Reluctance to file back into class once the bell rings may be a response to an unpleasant situation in our professional life, or a preference for distraction over hard toil – a failure to look our responsibilities in the face.

Blackboard

The white letters we inscribe onto the dark background of a blackboard can reflect the power of knowledge to vanquish ignorance. The writing that the dreaming mind projects onto a blackboard may be symbolic of the principles and ideals that have guided our path. Although it is important to stick by our principles, we should also remember that cherished ideas, like chalk, are not necessarily permanent: wiping away the text may clear a space for something new.

College or university

Higher education can symbolize our nobler intellectual or spiritual aspirations. There may be an element of abstraction or impracticality in the course we are studying: could this reflect guilt over our self-indulgences?

Graduation ceremony

A graduation ceremony is usually a highly significant rite of passage and in a dream can relate to other landmark events, especially those that confer a sense of achievement, such as the birth of our first child.

Theatres and Circuses

The dream world is a kind of stage, a theatre in which magical transformations take place, images leap from the depths of the imagination, and the drama of life unfurls. Some dreams take this metaphor to its natural conclusion, using actual theatres, cinemas or circuses as their setting. Such dreams are usually characterized by a particular clarity and vividness, sometimes reminiscent of the qualities of a "grand" dream (see pages 65–70). The atmosphere of excitement and expectancy in the dream may mirror the feelings we experience in such settings in our waking life.

A dream theatre is an illusion within an illusion, and may appear to offer the dreamer an understanding of the mystery that lies behind the world of appearances. However, the dreamer may at times find the theatre or circus ring empty, or the cinema screen blank, and experience a haunting loneliness, as if he or she is excluded from the revelation that is

about to appear to others. This might reflect a sense of disconnectedness from our friends and family.

If we actually find ourselves on the stage, or in the circus ring, participating in the drama, it may be that we are enacting some inner tension or impulse, and have something to learn from the character or performance on display. But if the dreamer is an onlooker, this may indicate the danger of being taken in by the powers of illusion or else perhaps an unfulfilled wish to throw off the conventions of ordinary existence and become part of a more instinctive, colourful and exciting world.

Actors may represent other people of importance in the dreamer's waking life, or they may invoke the archetype of the Persona, the mask that we assume to confront the outside world. The interplay of humans and animals may carry particular significance, relating to the interaction between the conscious, rational mind and the unconscious, instinctive mind.

Stage

A dream stage is one illusion inside another, and represents our efforts to understand appearances. A dream in which we, the dreamer, appear on stage may reveal a preoccupation with the image that we project to others.

Stage play

Dreams involving a theatrical production often reflect the dreamer's darker unconscious urges. The events unfolding on stage can give us vital clues about the emotions that we repress in waking life. Is the play a comedy or a tragedy? A farce or a fantasy? What profound impulses are dramatized? How well do the actors play their parts? All of these questions may be relevant to the dream's meaning.

Actor or actress

Often a representation of the dreamer's chosen public image, an actor or actress can evoke our highest aspirations. More blatantly, it can reveal our basest urges. The reception that the audience gives to the performance may signify how convincingly the Persona disguises the dreamer's true self. A famous actor or actress may represent the Animus or Anima archetype, or perhaps our mother or father.

Comedian

Comedians are a version of the Trickster. Though often mild in their rebellion against society, they nonetheless poke fun at established norms and perhaps at the dreamer's pretensions and self-image. Consider whether the comedian provokes well-being, outrage or jealousy – sometimes we may find ourselves envying their subversiveness.

TV talk show

A talk show might suggest a yearning for exposure or celebrity. Alternatively, it might express a desire to air our opinions. Perhaps some issue that we feel strongly about has not been adequately discussed.

Movie

The glamorous world of the movies may evoke a desire to add a glossy veneer of acceptability to our more difficult unconscious urges. Given that movie stars are globally adored, there may be an element of wish-fulfilment. Particular movies inevitably seep into the unconscious. When interpreting a movie dream, do not forget the fact that the cinema is two-dimensional.

Stunt performer

This dream image may express a concern that excessive demands are being made on us in our waking life. Jumping from a burning building, for example, may be a fantasy escape from a relationship. A sense of the unjustness of the demands made on us can be highlighted by the lack of recognition that the stunt performer receives for his or her bravery: ultimately it is the star who gets all the credit.

TV game show

The big-money prizes available on a TV game show may be an indication of financial worries. Or the dream may point to low self-esteem (we need luck to bring us success) or a fear of public humiliation.

Circus

A dream circus may be an exhilarating whirl of performances, with tumbling clowns, daredevil acrobats and feats of strength or bravery. The multitude of acts and entertainers performing within the ring can be a reflection of the multi-faceted nature of a busy life. Perhaps we fear for someone's safety – could it be our own? Or perhaps there are concerns that one of the acts will fail, reflecting our own fears.

Juggler

A juggler may convey anxiety about the number of tasks that we must juggle to keep abreast of our responsibilities. A dream in which the number of juggled balls or spun plates keeps increasing may represent a cry for help in the face of a seemingly never-ending to-do list.

Clown

The clown is an aspect of the archetypal Trickster, making a fool of him- or herself to mock the posturings of others – and perhaps also the dreamer's own pretensions or inflated sense of self. Alternatively, a clown may reflect anxiety that our behaviour is incompetent.

Acrobat

The acrobat represents a combination of strength and grace, and thus the union of male and female. Trapeze artists may signify spiritual courage, demonstrating to the dreamer that only by risking our own safety can true inner progress be made. If the dream features you and your partner as a pair of acrobats, then it may be expressing a sense of deep harmony. Trust, communication and coordination are implicit in the acrobats' performance and only by working together can they succeed in their act. More obviously, an acrobat dream may reflect a fear of falling from the heights we have gained.

Lion-tamer

The lion-tamer symbolically triumphs over his baser instincts, not by repressing them but instead by bending them to his will. In Jungian terms, tamed animals indicate the impressive results that people can achieve when working on their primitive urges.

If you believe the lion might stand for someone you are close to, perhaps you desire unrealistically to control their character or their passions. Or the tamer's whip may express sado-masochistic desires.

Fire-eater

The fire-eater may represent the fierce, angry aspect of the self – the inbuilt resentments and frustrations. By ridding himself of destructive power, the performer indicates the possibility of controlling these impulses. He often stands for effectiveness, mastery, the outrageous action that overcomes difficulties.

Conjuror

The stage conjuror is the master of illusion, performing by trickery acts of transformation that might take the genuine magician a lifetime to achieve. He is thus the master of the shortcut, and of unexpected solutions, but also of cunning and deceit. Winning admiration not for his mystic powers but for his human skills, the circus magician may impress upon us the need to be wary of someone whose charisma might only be superficial.

Performing animal

For Jungians, performing animals at the circus, such as horses, elephants and seals, represent a dreamer's base instincts, and the extent to which we can work with our more primitive self to produce results that the conscious mind might not have thought possible. Freudians see training animals to perform tricks for humans as an expression of a desire for sexual domination.

Ringmaster

The ringmaster commands the skills of both humans and animals, yet performs no acts himself. He thus feeds upon others, and his presence in a dream may indicate the ultimately barren nature of power that comes from status or position, with limited skill. A ringmaster in a dream may be also identified with an authority figure, such as our father or boss. It is also possible that a ringmaster will be seen as exerting genuine powers, like the conductor of an orchestra – without his central point of focus, the whole show might collapse. In this respect there may be a suggestion of the Wise Old Man.

Tightrope-walker

A tightrope-walker precarious on a high wire may be a warning that we must proceed with extreme caution, or he may represent a general feeling of being required to do the impossible.

Snake-charmer

A snake-charmer luring a cobra from its basket may indicate a danger of being taken in by gaudy promises or insincere flattery. The exoticism of the snake-charmer might also evoke a craving for travel or excitement, or perhaps for an initiation into Eastern mystic or religious practices.

Town and City

Just as the house stands for the self in Jungian psychology, so the town or city represents the community, the social environment beyond the self, including family and friends, and the whole network of responsibilities which inevitably enfolds us (like a network of streets radiating from a square or market place).

A busy town, or one with doors and windows open, or bustling cafés, may represent the warmth of the dreamer's relationships with others; while a town with wide, empty streets or vast, desolate squares can indicate a sense of isolation or of rejection from society.

A large, impersonal city in a dream may suggest that the dreamer is conscious of having many acquaintances but few close friends, and may be pointing to the need to establish more intimate relationships. The city's vast size can be intimidating, and one tendency for anyone who is overwhelmed by this might be that they retreat into themselves. Another approach, of course, would be to try to make a personal mark within the concrete jungle.

If the houses themselves are vague and shadowy, the dreamer may lack self-knowledge or understanding of other people. A city beneath the ground or the sea typically relates to the dreamer's unconscious, and points to the common links that all of us share with others – an antidote against isolationism.

Freud, characteristically, sees in the image of the town an all-embracing archetype of woman – inviting us or forbidding us according to whether the streets of the town are brightly lit or dark and empty.

Village

Suggesting a slower pace and smaller scale of living, a village may appear as a pastoral idyll to dreamers disillusioned with the big city. There might also be suggestions of surveillance, since in a village it is difficult to be anonymous.

Walled city

A wall around a city (or individual house) suggests a wish to keep others out, but also to protect treasured possessions. A walled city may also signify an urge to resist change and to keep out new ideas. The dream may be suggesting that such a wall is necessary if personal values are to be maintained, or it may be inviting you to recognize that a wall already exists and to ponder its implications.

Ruined city

Ruins tend to suggest neglect and decay rather than deliberate destruction. A ruined town or community may be drawing the dreamer's attention to a neglect of social relationships, or of aims or ideals in life that were formerly more steadfastly kept in mind. Or if the ruins are ancient rather than recent, we may be yearning for a never-to-be-recovered – and perhaps over-idealized – past. A moonlit ruin may be a romantic wish-fulfilment – a yen for adventure and intrigue.

Metropolis

When a futuristic city appears in a dream, it may have been influenced by science fiction movies. Sometimes the implication is the dehumanizing effect of high-tech machinery – the loss of the personal touch.

Town on a Hill

Typically, a town or city on a hill, particularly if it appears in a Level 3 dream, suggests wisdom, heaven, the home of the gods, the stronghold of the righteous. The image may suggest a goal or ideal toward which the dreamer is striving, and may provide reassurance that such ambitions are ultimately attainable – or as a reminder, perhaps, to keep our feet on the ground in a spirit of humility, however lofty our aims.

Slums and Favelas

The dilapidated part of town with dirty streets and ramshackle houses may represent social, or family relationships of which we are ashamed. Or we might be craving more honesty and openness in our relationships than we can find with people who are more concerned with keeping up appearances.

If the town represents the self rather than our interaction with others, then a dream set in a slum district can suggest low self-esteem. Wandering around the areas that most people avoid could also, however, reveal a willingness to explore the less attractive aspects of the self. The dream may stem from a submerged desire to confront whatever dark urges are lurking in our unconscious mind.

Natural World

Dwellers in towns and cities may feel far removed from the natural world, yet our rootedness in nature and our longing to reconnect with it are fully recognized by the unconscious. When interpreting a dream it is a common mistake to focus exclusively on the human content. However, if landscape features, animals or plants appear, even peripherally, these may carry an important cargo of meaning. While attending to specific symbolism, remember that nature has generalized significance too – as the life-force, the essential vitality of all living existence.

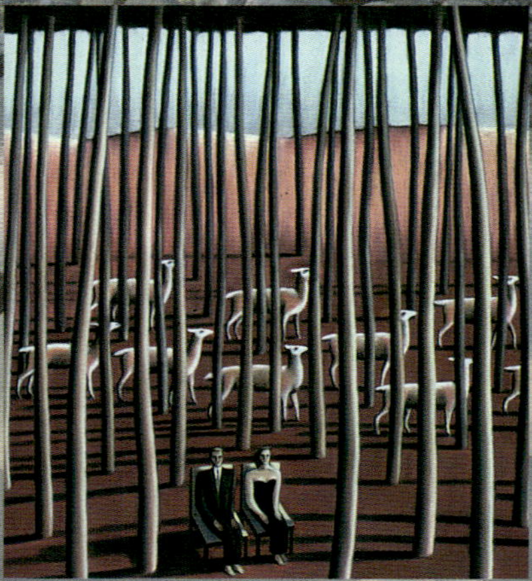

The Elements and the Seasons

The elements and the seasons are frequently associated with Level 3 dreams, because they relate to the natural energies and rhythms of life, and thus serve as powerful symbols both of the dreamer's own psychological make-up and of significant life changes.

Spring is an obvious signal of new beginnings, while high summer indicates achievement, and the need to savour the moment instead of always thinking about the past or future. Fall is the season of harvest, the reaping of what we have sown, as well as the time when we notice decay. Winter may be the unconscious, the darker, hidden side of the dreamer's self, but it may also indicate a fallow period – a time of reflection before fresh ideas burst forth.

Rivers and streams are particularly potent metaphors for the passing of time and the depths of the unconscious.

Rain, the fall of water through air, can suggest the imaginative and rational parts of the mind, which are complementary. It is also life-giving – it can spoil a picnic but enable long-term growth.

Earth

Dreams of sitting or lying on the ground may suggest realism, an end to extravagant flights of fancy. The earth can also symbolize fertility and, like water, can represent the feminine. Fallow soil can hint that new ideas are imminent: the old ground must be ploughed up and sowed with the seeds of new life which in time will grow and blossom.

Fire

Fire consumes but also purges. Evoking powerful emotions such as envy, lust and passion, fire is an ambiguous symbol – it destroys, yet in doing so purifies and clears a path for fresh growth. In dreams it can suggest the need for sacrifice, but at the same time promises to open up new opportunities. Fire is a masculine energy, and represents all that is overt, positive and conscious. Out of control, however, it may point to the need for the dreamer to take better charge of unbridled passion or ambition. It hints at the importance of clearing up troubling issues that have been cluttering a relationship – or perhaps of making a fresh start.

Air

Air is associated with freedom, the spirit and clarity of thought. We may find ourselves bounding in great leaps across the countryside, floating gently down to earth, or travelling in a balloon or on a cloud. This is the element that symbolizes otherworldly concerns, but the dream may also be warning of the dangers of losing contact with reality. Air may express self-confidence, an ability to think clearly and act decisively. The very breath of life, air may symbolize what is vital to our health and well-being – if we are being choked by pollution, something may be depriving us of this need.

Water

Water is the symbol *par excellence* of the unconscious, the depths of the imagination, the source of creativity. A dream of swimming suggests that the dreamer should venture into this realm, but if he or she struggles to stay afloat, this may be a warning that more caution and more careful preparation are required. Freud associated water with the womb. According to this interpretation, a dreamer floating happily in water may be expressing a wish to be "back home" with their mother. Like air, of course, water is indispensable to life, which means that it may carry similar symbolism.

Rainbow

A universally auspicious symbol, a rainbow stands for redemption, good news, promise and forgiveness. In Level 3 dreams it can be associated with the magical quest for the treasure of self-knowledge, or for the bridge between earth and heaven that awaits the enlightened mind.

Sky

The sky signifies spirituality and contemplation. A clear blue sky may denote pure and transcendent thought, while a cloudy or stormy sky shows an inability to think clearly or to perceive important truths.

Snow

Snow can symbolize transformation and purification – or, if it is melting, it can suggest fears and obstacles dissolving in the dreamer's path. Ice can indicate petrifaction, a halt to progress, or an obstacle impeding the creative flow of the dreamer's mind. Both snow and ice may represent a lack of emotional warmth, a suggestion that the dreamer has paid insufficient attention to his or her feelings.

Wind

A light, warm wind represents a welcome change; a high wind or gale, a threatening or dreaded change. If the wind blows away the dreamer's house or possessions, this may be a warning of tumultuous emotions or a tendency toward self-destruction.

Rain

By enacting the fall of tears, rain may symbolize sorrow, but of course it also has positive overtones of growth and regeneration. More specifically, rain can represent spiritual development. Freudians equate rain with urination, and dreams involving rain may occur when we have gone to sleep with a full bladder.

Storm

Stormy weather in a dream may indicate a wish to force things through to a definite conclusion, or to shake things up for the sake of a change. There might also be the implication of emotional crisis or catharsis. A hurricane flattening vehicles or ripping up houses may signify the fragility of the material or non-material world that we have constructed for ourselves.

Thunder

In many early belief systems, thunder was believed to be the voice or action of some powerful deity. The Greek god Zeus was the god of Thunder, as was the Norse deity Thor; and in the Judeo-Christian tradition God spoke to Moses in a voice of thunder when giving him the Ten Commandments. As children we instinctively fear thunder, although later in life most people overcome this. As such, thunder may represent the wrath of our father or another powerful authority figure. The fear from which a dream like this may originate could be buried way back in childhood.

Lightning

Lightning suggests inspiration, with the idea that flashes of brilliance are short-lived. There is also a destructive side, of course. Lightning and thunder can also be reminders of the awesome power of nature, and of the forces that lie beyond the dreamer's conscious control. (As the phenomenon that sparks fire on earth, lightning also has a sexual symbolism of sperms).

Hail

Accompanying a thunderstorm, hail may represent the pricks of a guilty conscience.

Flood

For many, a dream flood will have biblical overtones. It may be the necessary preparation for new life and a fresh start. This understanding fits both Freud's conception of the waters of the womb and the Jungian idea of the Deluge as simultaneously deadly and life-giving. A dream in which our house or town is submerged by a flood may convey a feeling that we are being overwhelmed by our responsibilities at home or at work. In the Freudian view of a flood as a mother-symbol, the dream might be interpreted as an expression of incestuous desire.

Sea

Jung believed that turning to face the sea indicates that the dreamer is prepared to confront the mysteries and the fears of the unconscious; while creatures emerging from the deep represent powerful archetypal forces. For Freud, the sea is a symbol of female sexuality, and tides express the ebb and flow of sexual union.

River

A river's steady flow represents the relentless march of time. Standing in a river suggests clinging to the present; crossing a river may represent the risks involved in changing course.

Dawn

The dawning of a new day may signal the end of a long period of grief, illness or depression. Like spring, sunrise suggests fresh hope and new energy. The dream may also relate to the dawning of an idea or understanding.

Daylight

Daylight streaming through a window is an optimistic dream symbol, full of energy. The dream may be encouraging us to stir ourselves and get out into the world, to make the most of the opportunities on offer. A shaft of daylight could also be drawing our attention to a specific object within a dream – think carefully about what it might have been.

Summer's day

A warm summer day may be a pleasant experience, reflecting optimism and contentment. Hot sun and dazzling light could also, however, represent a spiritual or intellectual shock or a sudden break with a long-held belief. If the sun feels oppressive, the dreamer may feel that the ideas of others are being foisted upon them.

Burnt wood

Charred wood might suggest the husk of a relationship or a crusade for which our passion has died, or it may indicate a fear of irreversible change, however caused.

Earthquake

To Jungians, an earthquake represents the eruption of the dark forces of the unconscious. Pent-up and powerful, they threaten to engulf the dreamer's conscious life. An earthquake may also represent the liberation of our creative energies or, to Freudians, the release of unexpressed sexual passion.

Fog or smoke

Fog or smoke can suggest confusion clouding our insight. We may be struggling to comprehend some new idea or feel overwhelmed by the implications of an important decision. A shaft of light breaking through the fog may suggest that the confusion is only temporary. Smoke has important spiritual connotations, as well as suggesting the fog of war. Native Americans believe that smoke is the vehicle upon which our prayers travel to the creator; and sweet-scented incense is an integral part of religious ceremonies all over the world.

Cloud

The appearance of a cloud in an otherwise clear blue sky reminds us that no state of calm contentment can last forever – perhaps we should enjoy the present while we can.
A cloud that passes over the sun may suggest the obscuring of insight, perhaps by emotion; while an image of a dear friend or relative floating on a celestial cloud may reveal a desire to make the thought of death more palatable. Clouds may also be a metaphor for unrealistic thinking – living with "our head in the clouds".

Twilight

Twilight is a time of transition or ambivalence – neither day nor night. Outlines blur and objects look less or more frightening than they are. A dream that takes place in twilight may occur at a period of change. Dusky light may allow us to look objectively at a situation that we would normally shy away from examining directly.

Falling leaves

Falling leaves can be an expression of the dreamer's anxieties about death and decay. Similarly, heaps of damp leaves lying in piles on the ground suggest the withering of hope, and may point to a pervading melancholy. The bright red and yellow hues of fall leaves may, however, inspire optimism – reminding us of the beauty that can be found even in decay and of the rejuvenation that will follow winter.

Darkness

Darkness can represent the repressive forces of the unconscious mind that prevent the dreamer from examining the uncomfortable thoughts that dwell there. Light in the dark may suggest a breakthrough in our personal development.

Sand

The body sinking into warm sand can suggest a desire to return to the womb. Sand is a common dream image of time passing – in an hourglass or slipping through the fingers. A sandcastle submerged by the sea is a symbol of transience.

Animals

Animals are particularly powerful dream symbols, and usually carry a universal meaning – although they can also appear as specific animals known to the dreamer, in which case their significance tends to be personal. As well as real animals (general or specific), dreams may also make use of animals encountered in movies, myths or fairytales. Sometimes, too, there may be a reference to animal associations embedded in the similes and clichés of idiomatic language (linking foxes with cunning, elephants with long memories, pigs with gluttony, and so on).

Animals have always signified our natural, instinctive and sometimes baser energies and desires. In dreams, however, they commonly draw our attention to undervalued or repressed aspects of the self, and put us in touch with a source of transforming energy deep within the collective unconscious. Devouring an animal can represent the assimilation of natural wisdom, just as in Nordic myth Siegfried learned the language of animals after eating the heart of the dragon Fafnir. Many native cultures also believe that eating an animal allows us to absorb some of its powers. Eating a deer, for example, is thought to make the hunter fleet of foot, while a cooked rabbit can encourage fertility.

Animals in dreams may be frightening or friendly, wild or tame, and their demeanour can help with interpretation. They may even speak or change their form. In the Native American tradition, the shaman seeks a power animal in dreams, who will then act as a wisdom guide and protector during the shaman's journeys to other worlds.

A dog can represent devotion, as symbolized by Argos, the first creature to recognize the Greek hero Odysseus when he came home from his epic wanderings; but a dog can also stand for the destructiveness of misused or neglected instincts (think of the hounds of the Greek hunting goddess Artemis tearing the mortal Actaeon to pieces after he invaded her privacy). Cats are among the commonest dream animals, and often stand for intuitive feminine wisdom and the power of the unconscious.

Wild beasts

Freud considered that ferocious, untamed animals represent passionate impulses of which the dreamer is ashamed – the more numerous and diverse the animals concerned, the more threatening and confusing these impulses may be. Wild beasts may also symbolize our deepest fears, especially about death.

Bat

To many people, bats are a demonic symbol representing blind folly and the darkest urges of the unconscious. In the Chinese and Native American cultures, however, bats are a symbol of good luck and rebirth. Remember, just as bats have the power to navigate in the dark, so we can use our instincts or intuition to guide us in times of uncertainty.

Dove

A dove is a symbol of peace, love and pacifism, as well as hope – as in the dove that Noah saw with an olive branch in its bill. A dove's presence in our dreams can reflect a desire to promote harmony and agreement or to foster love within our circle of family and friends.

Butterfly

Butterflies are often taken to symbolize the soul and its transformation after death. Taoist mythology preserves the story of sage Chuang-Tzu who was unsure whether he was a man who had dreamed that he was a butterfly, or a butterfly now dreaming it was a man.

Fish

Fish have commonly been used to symbolize divinity, and often stand for the spiritual abundance that feeds all men and women. In dreams they can also represent insights into the unconscious. Fish caught in a net and brought to the surface represent the emergence of such insights into the full light of consciousness.

Wolf

Wolves may symbolize the untamed impulses of the unconscious. Wild and savage, they can be a frightening spectre terrorizing our dreams. In some circumstances, however, a lone wolf may be an inspiring image, associated with self-reliance and with the courage and tenacity needed to pursue a path of spiritual development and self-fulfilment.

Insects

Insects, like many other small creatures, occur frequently in the dreams of small children. A dream of killing insects may be recalling a childhood hostility toward a brother or sister – perhaps one that has persisted into adult life.

Worm

Worms symbolize death and decay, and in dreams may symbolize threats to our financial prosperity or the affections of a loved one. They do, however, play an essential role in decomposition, and worms feeding on a corpse may evoke the continuity of life after death, or a metaphorical extension of that idea.

Mosquito

Mosquitoes can represent the tormenting instincts of the unconscious – on account of the waters where they breed.

Earwig

This is predominantly an anxiety symbol, since it used to be believed that earwigs crawled into people's ears while they were asleep.

Moth

The dreaming mind may use the image of a moth attracted to a flame as a metaphor for something that we are drawn to despite its negative effect on us. In its most severe form, this dream may even represent a death wish. Moth-eaten clothes full of holes might stand for a relationship that is slowly falling apart.

Fly

Valiant warriors in ancient Egypt were rewarded with golden flies that they wore on a chain around their neck. In a different vein, flies may be a dream image of annoying but relentless pursuit by nagging creditors, self-important advisors or persistent admirers.

Monkey

Monkeys often represent the playful, mischievous side of the dreamer, and may symbolize an undeveloped yet instinctively wise aspect of the unconscious that may require expression. A monkey is also one possible form of the Trickster archetype. In the East, it can also symbolize the untamed, chattering mind that needs to be stilled by meditation.

祖仙

Lion

The lion almost invariably appears in dreams as a regal symbol of power and pride, often representing the archetypal, powerful and admired aspect of the father. A lion hunting and killing its prey may conjure up resentment about our father's authoritarian tendencies. Jung, however, believed that the lion in the wild represents our latent passions – a dream of the creature may represent an urge to embrace our instinctive energies.

Bear

A bear is a powerful dream symbol recalling the ever-repeating rhythms of nature. During the coldest months of the year, many bears retreat into caves and enter a kind of hibernation. Not emerging again until spring, they may suggest that the dreamer needs to enter a phase of introspection and subsequent renewal, or they may simply act as a reminder that from death will spring new life. Female bears are also remarkable for the aggression with which they defend their cubs. Hence, a bear may appear as a symbol of protection – a spiritual guardian perhaps or a reminder of our duty to watch over those who are closest to us.

Toad or frog

As the warty familiars of witches, toads are often associated with the darker impulses of the unconscious. Frogs, on the other hand, are more likely to conjure up images of fertility and rejuvenation, on account of their prolific spawning.

DE TAVRO.

Horse

The horse generally symbolizes our harnessing of the wild forces of nature. A winged or flying horse can represent the unleashing of energy for psychological or spiritual growth. In Freudian dream interpretation, a horse is a symbol of sexuality, especially if ridden. Wild horses can represent the terrifying aspect of the father, or the untamed impulses of the unconscious. Occasionally, the centaur (half-man, half-horse) might appear, suggesting mind–body balance.

Bull or ox

A bull or ox is one of the most potent of all the symbols of male virility. When their great strength is harnessed to a plough, oxen represent the fertility of the earth and the rewards of hard work. This powerfully built animal evokes both the creative force of nature, and the ever-present threat of barely contained violence. The dream setting of a bullfight may suggest a need to harness the passionate aspects of our nature in order to make personal progress.

Cow

The milk, dung and meat of a cow are the essential building-blocks of human survival in many parts of the world. As a dream symbol, a cow presents a serene image of fertility and maternal femininity. Milking a cow, however, may be an expression of an incest-wish.

Rabbit

Rabbits are a common dream symbol of fecundity, pointing to pent-up sexual passions or a desire to start or expand a family. They may also suggest our inability to act when we are paralyzed by fear, like a "rabbit in the headlights". Alternatively, if we dream of a rabbit, perhaps the unconscious is pointing us toward a need to burrow away and conserve our energy.

Hare

In many folk traditions, the hare plays the part of the archetypal Trickster (see page 104). A dream hare may alert the dreamer to one or more of our more absurd pretensions.

Deer

The elegant deer may represent a delicate kind of femininity, perhaps stronger than it appears – perhaps even a version of the Anima archetype (see page 103). In our dreams a deer can invoke the gentlest aspects of our personality as well as our natural grace and beauty. A deer that is killed by a hunter can symbolize an innocent and instinctive spirituality destroyed by the darker urges of the unconscious.

Turtle or tortoise

The long-lived turtle or tortoise, with its robust shell, is a dream image of perseverance and wisdom. A glimpse of a turtle or tortoise poking its head from its shell has obvious phallic connotations, while the protective mobile home into which these creatures may retreat for safety may symbolize emotional withdrawal or defensiveness.

Beaver

Industrious and hard-working, a beaver can be a symbol of action and accomplishment. A dream in which a beaver's dam impedes a river may be a metaphor for a blockage in the flow of our creative inspiration or in our abilities to communicate or give.

Shark

Sinister circling sharks may represent the unconscious forces we most fear. Sleek and terrifying, they might also suggest "loan sharks" – creditors seeking to dismember our home, possessions or business. The gaping jaws, revealing razor-sharp teeth, can represent the female genitals in castration-anxiety dreams.

Whale

Whales may be associated with the biblical story of Jonah and therefore with spiritual rebirth. In the Freudian understanding, they can be a symbol of the womb and therefore suggest an incestuous desire for our mother.

Pig

One of the most intelligent farm animals, the pig nonetheless has a reputation for gluttony, ignorance and filth. Pigs can symbolize our most ignoble instincts and our propensity to pursue base, material pleasures. Pigs wallowing in muck may evoke an anal fixation.

Cat

Cats represent the mysterious, the intuitive and the feminine. Creatures of the night, they are not only soft and beautiful but also fiercely independent, and deadly to their prey. Like dogs, they may appear in our dreams as a guide or companion. Yet we should be careful where we follow them – as the accomplices of witches, they may be intent on letting our unconscious urges get the better of our higher aspirations. A black cat may also signify a presentiment of luck – whether bad or otherwise.

Goat

Goats have a dual symbolism. The idea of a scapegoat conjures up the image of an innocent victim taking the blame for another's misdeeds. More familar, however, may be the goat as a personification of the Devil, lecherous and leering, complete with cloven hooves, horns and stinking breath. In this manifestation a goat may represent a guilty conscience about our sexual urges or misdeeds.

Dog

Dogs usually appear in our dreams as faithful companions and guides. They may accompany us on our journey into the unconscious, warning us of danger and helping to keep our darker urges at bay. A bulldog symbolizes stubborn determination while a pack of wild dogs can represent the violent forces and untamed passions that lurk below the surface of the mind.

Mouse

A furry little mouse may conjure up an image of pubic hair and often implies a preoccupation with sex. A mouse darting in and out of a hole may be a male sexual symbol; a mouse caught in a trap might indicate castration anxiety or fear of being caught while performing an illicit sexual act. A mouse can also convey the dreamer's timid first steps toward spiritual awareness with traps and cats and poison representing the potential pitfalls awaiting us.

Rat

Rats are often a feature of anxiety dreams and of dreams expressing self-loathing or shame. The image of rats rummaging around in the bowels of the earth is both anal and phallic and can express feelings of guilt or even anger about our sexuality.

Sparrow

The sparrow too can have sexual associations (in China it was linked with the penis and eaten to boost virility, while in Greece it was associated with Aphrodite). However, like any other bird, it can also be a symbol of the spirit or soul.

Parrot

The parrot's bright plumage and talent for imitating human speech can make it a dream symbol of insincerity. The bird may represent someone (perhaps yourself) who clamours for attention yet fails to make a valuable or individual contribution. In Chinese folk tales, parrots inform on adulterous wives – hence a link with guilt and entrapment. Alternatively, a parrot may evoke the teeming jungle.

Owl

An owl is a powerful symbol of transformation, and its appearance in a dream may herald death and rebirth in some aspect of your life. Associated with the darkness that aids them in their hunting, owls represent the unseen and the unknown. In a dream the creature's ability to see in the dark could be significant – suggesting perceptiveness and intuition. "Owlishness" is a keen interest in study, sometimes at the expense of healthy social interaction. The sinister cry of the owl is sometimes the moment at which an owl dream ends.

Vulture

This bird is a harbinger of death, and the sinister image of vultures circling in the sky may suggest our forebodings about the future outcome of some enterprise. More obviously, vultures may reflect the dreamer's apprehension of death or illness, or perhaps concerns about an inheritance.

Tiger

Unlike lions, tigers tend not to be associated in Westerners' dreams with nobility or majesty. They are a terrifying image of violence, beauty and power. A tiger may symbolize the wild impulses that stalk the jungle of our unconscious or the fierce energy of the ego's will.

Panda

Tranquil and sedentary, the panda is the totem animal of peace and contentment. Its dependence on low-energy bamboo as a food source might reflect the dreamer's over-dependence on one particular source of income or emotional support.

Leopard

Just as the leopard does not change its spots, so we cannot change or deny our true nature. The dream image of a leopard may be a warning against trying to be something you are not.

Crocodile

This primeval predator lurks low in the water, disguised as an innocuous log or rock. In our dreams a crocodile may represent our unconscious fears or urges, waiting their chance to burst through into our conscious mind and seize us in their voracious jaws.

Elephant

An elephant in a dream may suggest robustness and indifference to pain, as well as insensitivity to the emotions of others. Perhaps we are thoughtlessly trampling over the feelings of people around us, wreaking havoc where we should be proceeding with tact. Long-lived and intelligent, elephants may also be associated with our grandparents or with the wisdom of older generations. Now may be a good time to seek the advice of someone more experienced than yourself. The trunk can be a penis symbol.

Swan

Swans are a preeminently sexual symbol, their white feathers evoking an ideal of feminine virginity, their long neck evidently phallic.

Snake

The snake in the Garden of Eden symbolizes temptation, yet we should also understand it as a representation of human sexuality, which in itself is natural and blameless. Freudians see snakes as inescapably phallic. In the Jungian conception a snake is a symbol of the dark, unseen, unfathomable aspects of the self that must be confronted in order to achieve personal growth and fulfilment.

Zoo

Different animals symbolize different aspects of the dreaming psyche. A zoo, in which all the animals are locked up together, is, therefore, a metaphor for control over the various turbulent and potentially conflicting aspects of the self. A zoo from which the animals are escaping signifies that the dreamer feels unable to keep control of the distractions in his or her life, or of his or her emotions.

Landscape

Landscapes frequently express the dreamer's inner nature or emotional life. As the theatre where we carry out our day-to-day activities, the habitual setting of our world can be mirrored or vastly upset in our dreams. Just as, in waking life, landscape has the power to move us spiritually, or drastically alter our mood, similarly the setting of a dream can inspire in us a sense of wonder, contentment, excitement or dread. A completely unknown landscape may be a composite of real places.

Countryside

A dream of looking out over an idyllic pastoral scene may represent a desire for a slower, more grounded pace of life. City-dwellers in particular may respond to such a setting as the image of the good life. If, however, the countryside of our dreams is drenched in rain or viewed at a distance through a window, the dream may be carrying a warning about the dangers of aspiring toward a utopian way of life. Freud saw the folds of a rural landscape as symbols of the female genitalia or a woman's curves.

Hill

Hills lack the intimidating aspect of mountains but they may also be less sublimely fulfilling to climb – though there may still be a wonderful view from the summit. They might appear in our dreams to reassure us that self-understanding is an achievable task and not one we should feel too overwhelmed by. Hills also have Freudian connotations of the female anatomy.

Mountain

For Freud, the primary significance of mountains (and hills) lies in the similarity of shape with a woman's breasts. A dreamer looking up at a daunting summit may be expressing anxiety about confronting their sexuality. Similarly, a dreamer standing proudly on a mountaintop might reveal a sense of sexual well-being or a desire for domination. Jung understood mountains to represent the self. A summit can give us a sense of perspective, while looking up at a peak from below may suggest the challenges we will face during the process of self-realization. There may also be suggestions of spirituality and transcendence, since a mountain is halfway to heaven.

Forest or wood

The dark forest, with its dense, seemingly impenetrable vegetation, may be an apt metaphor for the depths of the unconscious mind. According to Jung, a dream of being scared to enter the forest may express our anxiety about examining the unconscious closely. Freud understood the forest as a symbol of pubic hair and penetrating the tangled undergrowth as an evocation of the sexual act.

Olive grove

This is an optimistic dream image. Olive trees traditionally represent peace, prosperity and victory. An olive grove may stand for an end to strife or family conflicts or for triumph over adversity. Alternatively, the dream may signify the beginning of a new period of creativity.

Vineyard

A vineyard may evoke the exuberance, abandon and enjoyment that the wine made from its grapes will eventually bring. Harvesting the grapes can be an image of karma – the consequences of our actions or thoughts.

Orchard

An orchard heavy with fruit is a dream image of abundance and fertility. It may be a dream symbol of pregnancy or of phenomenal creativity. In the spiritual and intellectual sphere, an orchard containing only unripe fruit might act as a reminder of how much work we still have to do before we can attain our goals. Fruit rotting in heaps on the ground can signify that the dreamer is spoiling his or her chances of success by failing to recognize their potential or waiting too long before putting their ideas into practice. An orchard containing many different varieties of tree points to a rich inner life or possibly to a bewildering profusion of choices.

Garden

Analogous with the conscious self, a garden suggests a loss of control when it is overgrown; learning and the fruits of labour or study when it is well-tended. A walled garden may represent virginity or naivety. There is also a spiritual dimension to the garden embodied in the idea of Paradise. For all major religions, gardens represent the blessings given by God (the divine gardener) and the ability of humans themselves to achieve a state of harmony or grace.

Jungle

Wilder and more exotic than a forest, a jungle suggests an even deeper anxiety about what the unconscious may hold. Savage beasts, trailing creepers and poisonous creatures large and small evoke the dark urges that lurk in the deeper recesses of the mind. There may be implications of hidden treasure – perhaps the jungle contains a lost city? The movie *King Kong* as well as cinematic tales (or real-life experience) of Vietnam have no doubt rooted themselves deep in the mind.

Desert

Depending on the attitude of the dreamer, a desert may be an image of sterility and desolation, or an inspiring landscape with space for reflection, purification and rejuvenation. If the connotation is of a lifeless wasteland, it is important to consider what aspects of our life might feel barren – our career, home life, creativity, or spiritual self. Amplification around the Arthurian myth of the wasteland presided over by the wounded Fisher King can be productive. The flowering of the desert could be the gifts we take for granted in a habit-bound existence.

Island

An island may be a place of refuge and safety, or an open-air prison. Surrounded by sea it can symbolize the firm ground of the conscious mind, where the dreamer may instinctively prefer to stay, avoiding the murky seas of the unconscious. A dream of swimming toward an island to escape a rough ocean can express a desire to regain control of our life or a fear of hidden impulses we do not wish to acknowledge. The Isles of the Blessed in Greco-Roman myth and Avalon in Arthurian legend have a spiritual dimension – the island as heavenly reward and a place of refuge and peace to retreat to after death.

Riverbank

Like an island, a riverbank may represent a place of safety to which we return after swimming in the waters of the unconscious; or we may dream of ourselves by the side of the river contemplating the waters of the inner self. If the river appears to be bursting its banks, we might be afraid of being overwhelmed by our unconscious urges. An artificial embankment could suggest an emotional life that is overly constrained by reason.

Plains or prairie

The open plains evoke freedom and imagination, but crossing them may require courage and determination. This dream image may resonate strongly with dreamers who are beginning a new chapter of their life or embarking on a daunting new project. There may also be hints of the desert (see page 406) or of exposure – the self in the full gaze of the divine.

Stile or gate

These methods of transition may suggest an in-between state, crossing two worlds, or else the means to overcome an obstacle. Freudians see a stile as a sexual symbol because of the straddling action required to negotiate it.

Trench

For many dreamers, trenches will be associated with the death-traps of the First World War and therefore with feelings of siege and "entrenchment". The dream may represent a warning that our professional, social or financial situation may not be as secure as it at first appears, or perhaps our conscience or self-esteem is under siege.

Bog

A bog with its deceptively stable surface and sucking, water-soaked earth may be a dream representation of the Great Mother in her most possessive, controlling form. Trying to navigate a path across the mud can suggest the difficulty inherent in breaking free from energies that threaten to stifle our independence, or from intractable problems of various kinds.

Pit or quarry

Although Jungians see a pit as a symbol of our unconscious urges, Freudians would be more inclined to understand the image as an expression of anxiety about female sexuality.

Fields

Fields ready for harvesting can suggest ideas and inspiration waiting to be put to good use. They may also symbolize the rewards that we can reap after a period of hard work. A field that has already been harvested might convey that the dreamer has garnered all that is useful from a recent burst of creativity and is ready for something new. Lying in a meadow on a sunny day may be a wish-fulfilment dream of peace.

Valley

A valley is often an image of female sexuality. A steep gorge or ravine with trees hugging its sides and rapids raging across its floor suggests a dangerous or exciting sexual experience. For both male and female dreamers a valley may relate to a new relationship, or to an exploration of the feminine aspect of their sexuality. A lush, abundant valley with a wide river and grassy margins unites the elements of earth and water and is a symbol of fertility and plenty. This may feature in the dreams of people experiencing a fulfilling sex life.

Cliff

A sheer cliff wall may represent a seemingly insurmountable problem. The dreamer may have reached the end of the road in some way – a relationship that cannot be mended or a job in which they cannot progress. Standing at the top of a cliff looking down into a rocky gorge or angry sea may suggest that we are being forced into a decision we are reluctant to make; or it may herald positive change. Frightening as the prospect is, this could be the time to take a leap of faith. If a cliff looms above us, have we already fallen? Perhaps the only way is up.

Well

A well can represent the source of our creativity and of our most valued talents. A dream in which we try to draw water from a well that has dried up might indicate fears that our inner resources will fall short of what is required. A well may also stand for the unconscious mind. Dropping a stone into a well and listening for a splash might reveal a tentative desire to make contact with our latent instincts; drawing water from a well can convey a desire to bring our deepest emotions into the light of the conscious mind, whatever uncomfortable truths we might thereby discover.

Lake

A lake is a rich metaphor for the unconscious mind, and also a place of rebirth and enchantment (through the feminine symbol of water). Whether we value the unconscious as a storehouse of intuition, or fear it as the hiding-place of our least palatable instincts, will affect what we see when we peer into the water. The lake may be deep blue and teeming with fish or it might be murky, suggesting unknown horrors beneath the surface. A lake can be a place of recreation or it can hide a monster.

Dolmen

Dolmens and other prehistoric remains can suggest a desire to connect with our roots or to universal instincts and intuitions. Alternatively, they might indicate an aspiration to a way of life untainted by the superficial luxuries of modernity – reflecting an ascetic impulse, which is often motivated by a spiritual quest.

Cave

A cave can be an archetype of the unconscious, or an image of the womb, representing a desire to retreat from the hurly-burly. The dark interior may signify the mysteries of the self; the light outside, our spiritual aspirations. Traditionally, a cave is where the germinating powers of the earth are concentrated, where oracles speak and where souls ascend to celestial light.

Spring

The clear, fresh waters of a spring can represent maternity, purity and the source of life. Freudians would see the gushing water as an image of exuberant sexuality, while for Jungians the water of a spring is associated with the source of our inner being and spiritual energy.

Waterfall

The steep descent and turbulent water of a waterfall may evoke a significant and perhaps difficult change. We may feel as if we are being pulled along toward this change against our will, or we might be eagerly anticipating the exhilaration that will accompany going over the edge. The sudden drop and gushing, foaming water can also suggest orgasm (for men or women) or a major emotional release.

Hedge

Hedges may combine the female sexual symbolism of dense vegetation with the image of a wall or fence as a barrier that acts as both protection and constraint. The image of a hedge may suggest that you see a sexual or romantic involvement as a restriction on your freedom. In a social context, there are connotations of suburbia – its perceived uniformity, and perhaps strange goings-on behind curtains and topiary.

Plants

Plants are the lungs of the Earth and transform the sun's energy into a form that animals can consume. In dreams they can assume primal significance in connection with growth and harmony

Tree

Reaching from the earth up to the heavens, with roots spreading far underground, trees can be a symbol of the whole cosmos. For Christians trees may also evoke the cross on which Jesus Christ was crucified. Moreover, a tree can represent the dreamer's personal development – the roots may relate to the unconscious, or to our sense of stability; the trunk, to the material world and our physical strength or talents; the branches, to our highest spiritual aspirations.

Evergreen tree

In modern times fir trees are often associated with the celebration of Christmas, and their appearance in a dream may reveal the dreamer's attitude to this yearly festival or to family gatherings at this season. As a symbol of eternal life, evergreen trees can represent a powerful faith or an enduring love. Evergreen forests can be formidably uniform and cheerless, and hence can be seen as a kind of green desert. The pine, in the East, is a symbol of longevity or immortality. The yew, common in graveyards in England, is associated with death.

Oak tree

An oak often symbolizes majesty and wisdom, offering dreamers a sense of physical or spiritual protection. We might also associate an oak tree with male sexuality or an imposing male authority figure such as an unyielding father – for the Celts this tree was linked with male potency and wisdom. The dream image of an acorn can act as a reminder of the potential for something small and seemingly insignificant to turn into something great.

Plane tree

Commonly planted in cities, plane trees may represent the only natural element in a world of concrete, stone, brick, glass and steel. Their appearance in our dreams may remind us to remain in touch with our true feelings and innermost instincts, and to keep artifice and sophistication in their true perspective.

Nuts

Opening a nut to enjoy its kernel is likely to imply a reference to the female genitals. A nut that is difficult to crack may correspond to a problem that is difficult to solve.

Palm tree

Palm trees flourish in tropical climates, with their roots near water (feminine) and their tops in the sun (masculine) – thus providing a vivid image of sexual or psychic union. Extrovert and exotic, a palm may appear in dreams as a representation of a good life in a place of heat and abundance, or it may be associated with self-indulgent opulence. There is also a religious dimension, as palm leaves are linked with Christ's entry into Jerusalem – an event celebrated on Palm Sunday.

Blossom

Blossom can signify spring but it can also suggest female virginity, especially when it is pink or white. It may also indicate spiritual or intellectual potential – or else naivety.

Flowers

The petals, pollen and pistil of flowers make them an appropriate symbol of the female sexual organs. Wild flowers can suggest a desire for sexual freedom. Flowers also have spiritual connotations. (The symbolism of some particular flowers is given on the following pages)

Lotus

The lotus flower is a Buddhist symbol of spiritual awakening. Just as the lotus rises from the muddy depths of a lake or river up into the light, so we too can cultivate our awareness to transcend the physical and bloom in the full sunlight of enlightenment. This flower also suggests less elevated kinds of human growth – for example, the opening of the heart – as well as birth and rebirth.

Chrysanthemum

Orange and yellow chrysanthemums are autumnal flowers, seen by the Japanese as a symbol of happiness, long life, perfection and the sun. Their appearance in our dreams may signify any of these overlapping qualities.

Clover

The three leaves of a clover may appear to Christians as a dream image of the Holy Trinity (the Father, the Son and the Holy Spirit). For dreamers of other faiths or for agnostics it might instead evoke the union of mind, body and spirit. Finding a four-leafed clover is believed to be a symbol of good luck.

Orchid

Orchids are a symbol of virility or fertility – they take their name from the Greek *orchis*, meaning testicle. Their rare and delicate beauty has been prized for centuries and has come to symbolize luxury and artful splendour.

Sunflower

Sunflowers evoke happiness, optimism, openness and the life-giving sun they resemble. The sunflower turning its face to track the sun, however, might suggest that the dreamer is too easily led or distracted. In dreams, the sunflower can also indicate a memory of Van Gogh, who famously painted them – in which case the association might be with intense creativity or madness.

Mistletoe

In today's world we tend to associate mistletoe with kissing at Christmas, but for the Celts it was a healing plant, with power to ward off evil. Although a parasite, taking nutrients from the branches it lives on, mistletoe keeps the host tree green in winter and may denote the continuation of hope through hard times.

Cornflower

The cool blue petals of a cornflower may be linked to spirituality. A dream in which dried cornflowers appear may reveal a faith that is dessicated. Cornflowers can also imply surprising strength and determination – the flowers may be delicate but the stems are remarkably tough.

Daisy

We often associate daisies with the daisy chains we made as children. Their white flowers and nostalgic associations can make them a dream symbol of prepubescent innocence.

Iris

The iris evokes ambivalent sexuality, the upright, phallic stem adding a masculine dimension to the flower, whose form suggests the female genitalia.

Gladiolus

Named for the shape of its leaves, the gladiolus, from the Latin *gladius*, meaning “sword”, traditionally represents moral integrity and strength in the face of adversity.

Qualities and Myths

The Jungian concept of the collective unconscious puts special emphasis on archetypal dream symbols – those derived from the universal pool of experience that manifest themselves in myth and religion. These symbols will appear from time to time in our dreams, perhaps making us think initially that they have nothing to do with our own lives. Even if we are not spiritually inclined, we are likely to think in terms of values and responsibilities, as well as – to put it simply – happiness. We are all searching for fulfilment in some way, and it is the archetypes, with their universal freight of significance, that can act as helpful signposts along our pathway.

Numbers and Shapes

Popular dream interpretation has always placed great significance upon the occurrence of shapes and numbers.

Jung noticed the prevalence of archetypal shapes such as circles, triangles and squares in the dreams and doodles of his patients. As his clients began to progress toward psychological health, geometric designs, often with circles radiating from a central point, began to feature with increasing prominence in their dreams. Jung saw striking similarities between these patterns and the religious diagrams, or mandalas, that Tibetan Buddhists use as a focus for meditation.

Once Jung had identified this geometrical archetype, he found its equivalents in all the myths and belief systems of the world. The mandala seemed to him like a map of the integrated human mind, reflecting in its beauty and complexity the development of the psyche toward wholeness.

Numbers also represent archetypal energies of the collective unconscious, and play a major role in the world's symbolic, mythological and occult traditions. Most people also have a "lucky number" – one that has reoccurred significantly throughout their life. Various cultures subscribe to the idea that numbers such as three and seven are divine, and their appearance in dreams has been taken to be a revelation from a higher power. For Freud, dream numbers were usually "allusions to matters that cannot be represented in any other way".

Numbers in dreams may not be given directly (though this is by no means uncommon). In dream recall the dreamer may be aware that objects or characters were presented in certain numerical patterns, or that actions tended to be carried out a set number of times. Dream interpretation and amplification can then focus upon these numbers and identify the significance that they might carry for the individual dreamer.

One

One is the prime mover from which all manifest creation flows, the single principle from which diversity is born. In dreams it may represent the source of all life, the ground of being, the still centre of the turning world. One can represent the self ("oneself") or the erect phallus. It can suggest harmony and union within a family or other group, but may also carry connotations of conformity – the denial of diversity. It can have associations too with totalitarian authority.

Two

Two is the number of duality, divine symmetry, and balance. It represents the coming together of male and female, father and mother, and of the opposites that emerge from the one and define the created world. Two is a dialogue rather than a monologue, and may evoke the interaction between the conscious and unconscious minds. It also suggests ambiguity of meaning and the presence of doubt.

Three

Pythagoras called three the perfect number: it is the number of synthesis and the threefold nature of humankind, the union of body, mind and spirit. Three is also the symbol of the active creative force made manifest in father, mother and child and in the Holy Trinity. To Freud, three was a symbol of the male genitals. It is also a textbook complication in a relationship: "two's company, three's a crowd".

Four

Four is the number of the square, harmony, and the stability on which the world depends. It relates to the four seasons, the four directions,

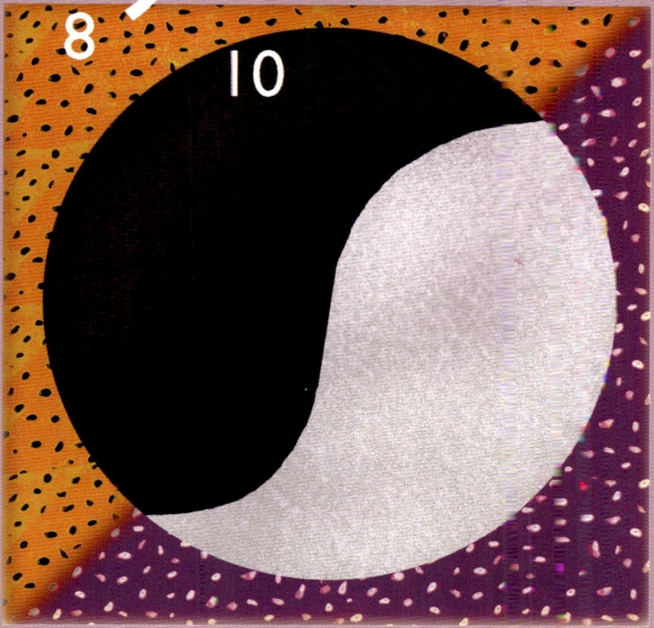

the four elements (earth, air, fire and water) and Jung's four mental functions of thought, feeling, sense and intuition.

Five

This is the number of the pentagram, the five-pointed star that represents humankind, the link between the heavens and the earth, with feet on the ground, arms reaching toward the horizon, and head in the skies (recalling Leonardo da Vinci's famous Renaissance image of the anatomy of a man).

Six

Six represents perfection. It is the number of love, and in dreams it stands for a movement toward new understanding and inner harmony. Six may stand for our intuition or our "sixth sense" or it may evoke the alchemical symbol of the battle between good and evil: two

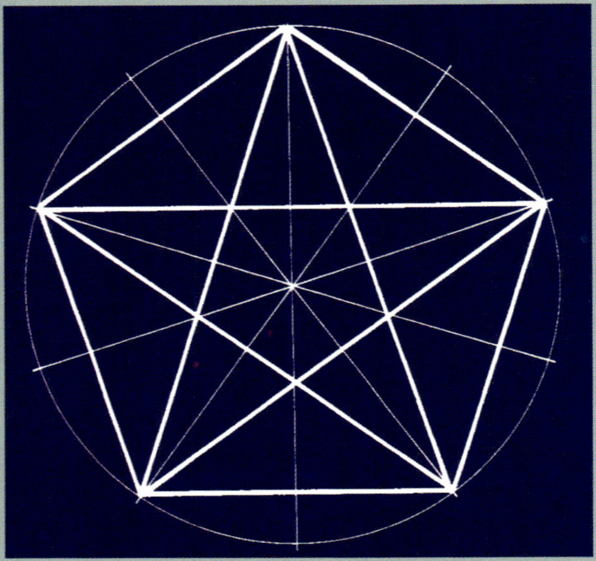

superimposed triangles, one pointing up to heaven and the other pointing down to hell.

Seven

In Christianity and Hinduism, seven is the number of God, the mystical number. In dreams, it is the number of risk and opportunity, and of the power of inner transformation. There are seven chakras and seven deadly sins. Seven echoes the rhythm of life (the seven heavenly bodies identified by ancient astronomers, the twenty-eight-day lunar cycle divided into four seven-day weeks), and life is said to pass in seven-year cycles. In the West a twenty-first birthday is a major coming of age celebration, while Jewish boys adopt adult responsibilities at the beginning of their fourteenth year.

Eight

This is the symbol of the initiate, of the Buddha's Noble Eightfold Path, and of regeneration and new beginnings. Eight symbolizes eternity – because, apart from zero, it is the only Arabic numeral to have no beginning or end. Turned on its side, it is a lemniscate – the mathematical symbol for infinity.

Nine

Nine is the number of indestructibility and eternity, of three multiplied by itself. It has the remarkable property that the digits of its multiples (up to a certain point) always add up to nine: 18 (9x2), for example, if added together (1+8), makes nine, as does 72 (9x8), 81 (9x9), and so on. Nine can symbolize gestation (the human gestation period is nine months) and, by extension, the completion of a creative task.

Ten

For Jews and Christians ten may be associated with the Ten Commandments that God gave to Moses, and therefore with moral judgments and the law. It is also the number of the incarnations of the Hindu god Vishnu, protector of good and destroyer of evil. In a dream, ten might be seen as the perfect score.

Eleven

Eleven is the beginning of a journey, reminding the dreamer that a new beginning (1) need not be an abandonment of what has already been learned (10). Broken into its constituent numerals (1+1), eleven can represent two.

Twelve

Twelve is the number of a new spiritual order. There are twelve disciples of Christ, tribes of Israel and signs of the zodiac. In dreams, twelve may suggest a vision of truth. Twelve months make a life-cycle in nature, perhaps prompting the dreamer to prepare for the future.

Thirteen

Thirteen is traditionally an unlucky number in the West – the treacherous Judas Iscariot was the thirteenth guest at the Last Supper. Despite this, its appearance may be a cause for optimism, since the thirteenth month is the first of a new annual cycle and thirteen is the number of the original twelve apostles, plus Paul.

Zero

Zero represents infinity, the void, the unmanifest. It might remind the dreamer of a Tibetan mandala or of the wholeness of a circle. When placed to the right of other numbers it multiplies them by ten and therefore has overtones of abundance and fertility. It can also signify the female principle, entry into the mysteries, or a sense of completion.

Thousand

A thousand symbolizes vastness and the great expanse of time and of the universe. It may bring to mind the millennium and the idea of completeness.

Circle

Without beginning or end, a circle symbolizes perfection, completion and the infinite. We may find protection within a circle, perhaps worn as an amulet in the form of a bracelet or ring, or we may feel imprisoned within its encircling walls. For Jung, a circle was an archetypal symbol representing the whole psyche, just as a square represented the body. Freud, on the other hand, understood circles to reveal a preoccupation with the vagina. In this interpretation, spheres can also be sexual symbols, suggestive of testicles or breasts.

Square

A square symbolizes the material world, evoking both its totality and its limits. Like the four walls of a house or castle, a square suggests stability but also restriction, stagnation and inhibition. For Jung, a symbolic image of a square inside a circle, or vice versa, suggested the union of matter and spirit.

Triangle

The triangle is a geometric representation of the number three and therefore of the associated trinities of the father, mother and child; mind, body and spirit; and the Father, the Son and the Holy Spirit. A triangle with an upward-pointing apex is believed to signify good, while a downward-pointing apex suggests evil. Freud saw the triangle as a symbol of the sexual organs – male if pointing up, female if pointing down.

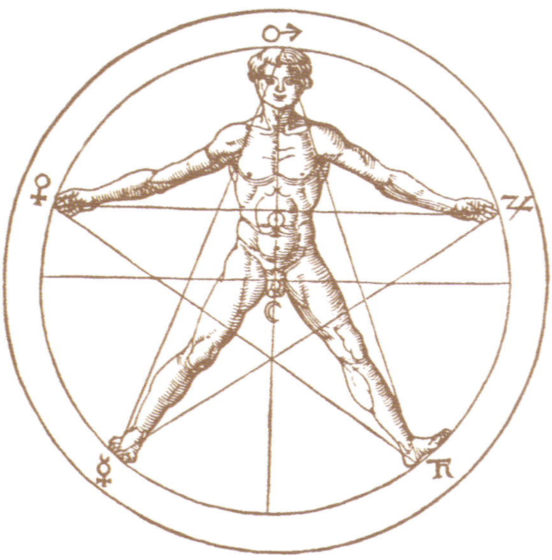

Rectangle

A rectangle in a dream may be a reference to the Golden Mean, a geometric figure of ideal proportions symbolizing a harmonious relationship between earth and heaven. Less grandly, in a Level 2 dream, a rectangle might be suggestive of a sports field or swimming pool. Rectangles can also carry some of the associations of a square (see opposite page).

Spiral

Spirals, a dynamic symbol of the life-force, suggest energy, movement and creative power. We may envision them as staircases, snakes or whirlpools, or perhaps as conical shells or celestial galaxies. Alternatively, they might appear simply as the churning of a void. Spirals are a symbol of sexual intercourse but they also represent spiritual progress. Some interpretations hold that a spiral rotating clockwise evokes our higher ideals and spiritual aspirations, while one that turns counter-clockwise signifies descent into the unconscious. More mundanely, a spiral may relate to anxiety about some situation in your waking life that appears to be spinning out of control.

Cross

Today the cross is primarily associated with Christianity. However the symbolism of this shape long predates Jesus Christ. We find crosses appearing in religious traditions across the globe from the ancient Egyptian *ankh* to the Hindu *swastika*. On a universal level the cross represents the union of earth and heaven, of humankind and the divine, and of the ground and the sky. It can also represent the four directions or four phases of the moon. For Christians the appearance of a cross in a dream might be a reminder of sacrifices that have to be made for one's faith – in parallel to the sacrifice Jesus made for the world.

Cube

A cube gives depth to the symbol of the square and accentuates its association with stability and completeness. If a cube appears to the dreamer to be particularly solid or weighty, this may suggest spiritual or intellectual immobility. The form may also evoke the shape of a die (the singular of "dice"), signifying the arbitrary forces of chance.

Star

A star shape may appear in our dreams with either five or six points. The superimposed triangles of the six-pointed Star of David suggest the dualities of good and evil or male and female. The five-pointed star, usually known as a pentagram or pentacle, may connote the five wounds of Christ or the four primal elements combined with spirit. Some people believe that a downward-pointing pentagram represents mastery of the physical world over the spiritual world, and therefore associate it with black magic. Medieval sorcerers associated the pentagram with Solomon's reputed powers over nature and the spirit world.

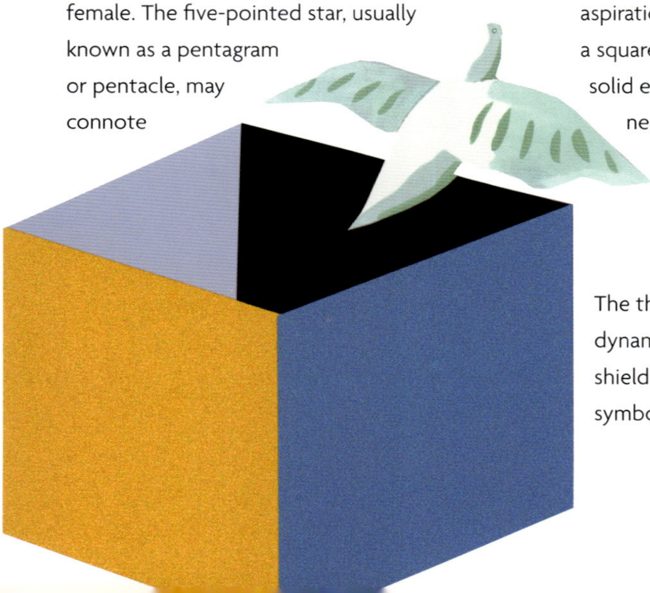

Pyramid

A phallic symbol in Freudian terms, a pyramid may also evoke the famous type of tomb built for Egyptian pharaohs – intended as a ramp to eternity, a portal through which the soul of the deceased king could travel to join the gods in the heavens. As well as hinting at otherworldly aspirations, pyramids combine the symbolism of a square base and peaked apex, suggesting the solid emotional or material base that may be needed if the dreamer is to pursue his or her spiritual aspirations.

Triskele

The three rotating limbs of a triskele symbolize dynamic energy. A common motif on the shields of Greek and Celtic warriors, this symbol may also represent martial prowess.

Colours

People woken during episodes of REM sleep almost invariably report that they have been dreaming in colour. The colours themselves are often one of the most revealing aspects of dream imagery, and colour is also a key element of all the major symbolic systems of the world.

As with other dream symbolism, the meaning of particular dream colours varies from one individual to another, depending upon the particular associations held in the unconscious, although universal meanings also come into play. The primary colours are usually most significant. Violet, a combination of the primaries red and blue, has an especially mystical, enigmatic quality, suggesting at one and the same time a union and a tension between the dual creative forces behind the universe.

Traditionally, gold and silver stand for sun and moon, masculine and feminine, day and night. For Jung, these hues represented the conscious and unconscious levels of the mind, and their juxtaposition suggested the path toward psychic wholeness.

Red

Red is the colour of vitality, passion, anger and sexual arousal. Red wine is often associated with excess and sensuality but at a deeper level can represent the altered states of consciousness associated with Dionysos, the Greek god of divine ecstasy. Red is also the traditional colour of demons and devils, representing the base urges lurking in the unconscious. The turbulent energy of red is not necessarily negative – fire and blood are, after all, symbols of life itself.

Yellow

In Chinese symbol systems, yellow was sacred to the Emperor, and in dreams this colour can represent the wise use of authority and power. Conversely, as in the saffron robes of the Buddhist monk, it can represent humility and the importance of service. Yellow can also be associated with sunshine, enthusiasm and joy, although pale yellow may sometimes suggest sickness and decay. In the West, yellow may be associated too with cowardice and deceit – think of the term "yellow-bellied" or the artistic portrayal of Judas Iscariot wearing yellow robes.

Brown

Brown represents soil, the earth and fertility, but may also evoke the autumnal melancholy of falling or rotting leaves. Freudians see brown as the hue of excrement and therefore suggestive of anal fixation and compulsive orderliness.

Green

Green is the colour of nature, the elements and the forces of regeneration, bringing new life from the death of the old. Leaves, grass and the green shoots of spring symbolize hope and a fresh start. However, when we say that someone is "green", we mean that they are naive or immature, and a dream that is strongly dominated by the hue may be an anxious response to a new responsibility or position. Green is also associated with jealousy and we may dream that we "see green" or are eaten up by a "green-eyed monster" when we experience this destructive emotion. To confuse matters further, green may suggest sickness and decay and evoke fear of death or ageing.

Orange

Orange combines the yellow of the spirit and the red of the libido: it can represent fertility, hope, new beginnings, and the dawning of spirituality. It is a hue that may stimulate activity and even the appetite. Orange is also the colour of fall leaves and as such may represent transition and a time of change.

Blue

Blue is often a spiritual colour when it appears in our dreams, suggesting the infinity of the sky and space, and the robe of the Queen of Heaven, the symbolic form of the Virgin Mary. Christ has also been shown wearing blue and Krishna is depicted as blue-skinned. On the other hand, a cool, celestial blue may symbolize the intellect and open-minded rationality. A deeper blue is more likely to signify the infinite depth of the unconscious mind. Blue may also suggest a mood of melancholy, as when we say that we are "feeling blue". As with green, there is considerable ambivalence here, and much will depend on context – trying to assess a dream by the particular shade of blue you remember is an unreliable process.

Black and white

Black, the void from which the universe was created, can represent infinite creative potential. Though linked with death, mourning, night and evil, it may also suggest glamour and mystery. The colour of clerical robes, it has overtones of renunciation. As the absence of colour, white may suggest ghostly desolation or sterility. In the East and especially China, it is the shade most commonly associated with mourning. More usually in Western society, however, it signifies purity and virginity.

Purple

The colour of royalty and imperial power, purple conveys magnificence and majesty. In dreams it may suggest a desire for opulence and luxury – or possibly a wish to control others.

Pink

Pink is linked to femininity and childhood, as well as human flesh. Being surrounded by soft pinks may suggest a nostalgic craving for the safety and comfort of infancy.

Sounds

Sounds in a dream should not be neglected during interpretation. Music especially tends to be meaningful. It may be that a melody has personal associations, or perhaps it is the title or lyrics of a piece that are significant. When the melody is unrecognized or not remembered upon waking, it could be that the music is carrying a more general message. For example, it can denote a beguiling danger, like the flute-playing of the Greek nature deity Pan, which enticed mortals from reason into the primitive world of nature. Strange, half-heard voices can suggest the promptings of inner wisdom.

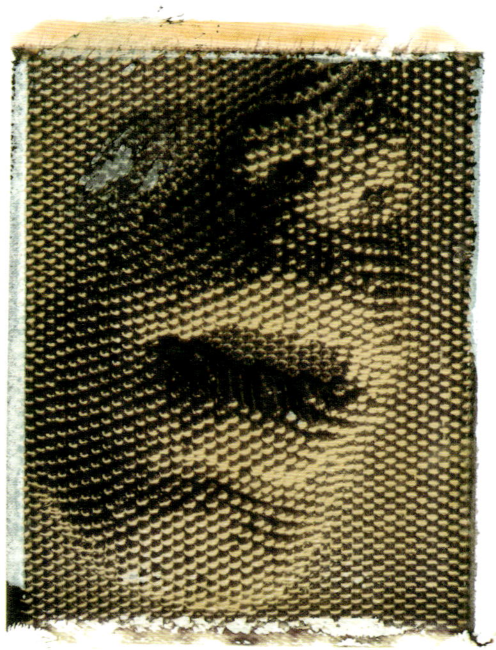

Babble

Unintelligible babbling, which may sound angry, can occur in our dreams at times of intense stress. We may be frustrated that we cannot make out the words, and this might tinge the dream with a mood of anger. Consider what might have caused this feeling, and see if you can take remedial action.

Hearing your name

Hearing someone call your name may suggest that you are about to enter the public spotlight – by making a speech at an important conference or a dear friend's wedding, for example. It may also be a signal to voice your support for a cause that you believe in.

Alarm clock

The intrusion of a ringing alarm clock into our dreams might be the result of a real-life alarm sounding to wake us up, or it may be imaginary, suggesting a preoccupation with time or deadlines. We might be worried that we are running short of time to complete an allotted task or achieve a personal goal, and perhaps we are experiencing stress and anxiety as a result.

Marching band

Hearing the sound of a marching band from afar may signify that we feel isolated – perhaps excluded from the community in which we live. The sound of the drum and the fife might also evoke the military recruitment bands of years gone by, suggesting the call of duty or a sense of looming conflict.

Laughter

Laughter can express many emotions – well-being, scorn, relief and embarrassment among them. If we laugh in awkwardness or fear, the dream may reveal a guilty conscience. If we are surrounded by people laughing at us, then we may suffer from feelings of persecution.

Voices

Disembodied voices may represent the inner self clamouring for attention. We may be too distracted by the demands of everyday life to listen to these deeply sourced promptings, but it is important for our mental and physical health that we do so. Voices from angels or heavenly beings might suggest a higher spiritual calling, while the voices of family or friends may resonate with a guilty conscience – perhaps we have failed to take these people seriously.

Melody

Music is a common symbol of personal creativity, and a melody that haunts our dreams, even if we cannot recall the tune, may represent an invitation to tap into our creative potential.

Gunfire

Gunfire can represent execution, violence, war or crime. We may identify a single shot with the starting pistol that signifies the beginning of a race, and therefore with a pressured situation or a fast-approaching deadline. Or gunfire might evoke the dreamer's wish to eliminate a rival: we may be vying with a competitor for the affections of a potential partner or for a promotion at work.

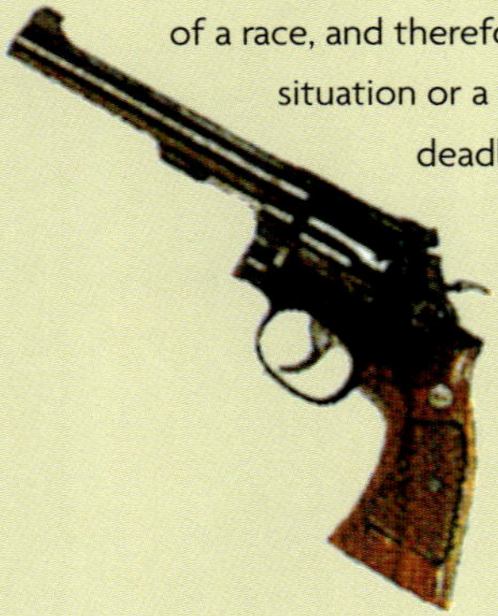

Swearing

Foul language is usually an expression of anger, fear or frustration, and so the dreaming mind may be drawing attention to unexplored feelings. If we do not swear in our everyday lives, the dream may be encouraging us to express ourselves more openly.

Cock-crow

A cock crowing can be a call to wake up, literally or metaphorically, and seize the opportunities on offer. It might suggest a spiritual awakening or else it could be an admonition from the dreaming mind that we should cast off our idle fancies and get down to the work in hand. Christians may associate the sound of a cock crowing with the denying of Christ by the apostle Peter, reminding us that people we rely on sometimes falter.

Whisper

A whisper is likely to represent our inner voice: the dream may reflect nagging doubts about some issue or planned action, or it might be urging us to act in accord with our instincts.

Air-raid siren

For dreamers who lived through the Second World War, the wailing of an air-raid siren might either conjure up nostalgic memories of a different era or be a fast-track to a nightmare. Even for generations who have no memories of the war, movies and TV programmes will have established an air-raid siren as an omen of death and destruction. The dream may act as a warning about an approaching emotional storm.

Baby crying

A crying baby may symbolize a part of the self that has been neglected. We may have set our creative talents aside to pursue a more lucrative profession, or we may have abandoned other ambitions. For female dreamers the sound of a baby crying could be a straightforward expression of maternal instincts, though perhaps with various forms of guilt mixed in.

Kettle whistling

The sound of a kettle whistling on a hob alerts us to the fact that the water has boiled. In a dream this sound may suggest that events have "come to the boil" and that the time is ripe for us to take action.

Shout

Shouting may be a warning or a call to action, or it might simply be a way of alerting us to someone's presence – for example, when a friend shouts to us in a crowded meeting place. There is no obvious symbolism in such a dream – but perhaps you are failing to give someone the attention they might deserve, or perhaps they are warning you to stop what you are doing.

Ghosts and Devils

The witches, vampires, werewolves and shadowy ghosts of children's dreams often symbolize those aspects of the self that the child is unable to understand or integrate into his or her world-view.

If childhood monsters persist into the dreams of adulthood, it could be that the work of comprehension and integration remains incomplete. The dreamer, fearful of forces beyond the reach of the conscious mind, may be still trying to reduce reality to safe and predictable dimensions.

As with all nightmares, such dreams serve the purpose of urging the dreamer to turn and face the pursuing dark forces, and see that it is only fear that turns them into monsters. By recognizing and accepting the many energies that make up our psyche, we may in time come to a closer acquaintance with our unconscious, where most of the mysteries of life reside.

The Tibetans often equate monstrous dream images with wrathful demons and guardian deities – the powers within the self that, properly used, can deter and destroy ignorance, illusion and false motivation. One nineteenth-century text on dream interpretation even suggested that to dream of ghosts and spectres was actively propitious, foretelling good news from distant places. To try to see a monster as a potentially beneficent force can sometimes help when more obvious interpretations fail.

Ghosts and spectral figures

The image of a ghost as an insubstantial being may suggest knowledge that now requires fleshing out and empowering by the conscious mind. Such images may also suggest fear of death or of an afterlife bereft of sensation and emotion. Dreams of ghostly figures hovering over the dreamer's sleeping body are related to OBEs (Out of Body Experiences), in which the dreamer's "soul" or dreaming body appears to shed its physical form. A dream in which a deceased friend or relative appears as a ghost may suggest that we are still mourning them: it may be some time yet before we fully recover from our grief. Ghosts can also symbolize dimensions of life that seem mysterious to us.

Monster

A monster often represents hidden impulses that fill the waking mind with disgust. By projecting them in the form of a strange and terrible creature, we are denying responsibility for them and separating them from the self.

The Devil

The Devil often represents the dark unconscious – our disturbing baser urges. Dreams about the Devil often have an archetypal quality, and tend to be vivid and dramatic. We may find ourselves locked in a desperate struggle between good and evil, running out of time and resources to save the world, or perhaps our loved ones, from domination by the forces of darkness. In the Jungian interpretation, the Devil is usually a manifestation of the Shadow archetype. It is important to integrate rather than reject those aspects of the self we judge to be "bad", for what we struggle against persists.

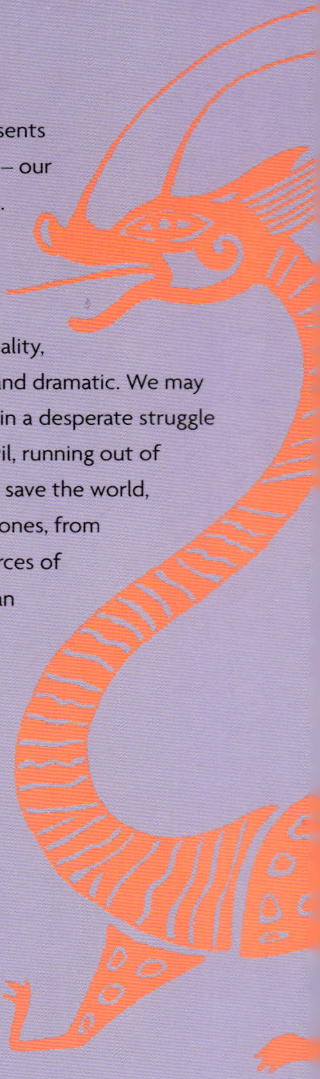

Fairy

In traditional folklore, fairies can be of either sex; however, in our dreams they tend to be female. For male dreamers a fairy may represent the Anima, or repressed homosexual urges.

Vampire

The dream image of a vampire suggests that someone or something is draining our energy. We may feel as though the responsibilities of our job are sucking life from us, or we may be trapped in a relationship that is exhausting us emotionally. Freudians would interpret the image of fangs piercing skin as a symbol of sexual intercourse.

Demon

Imps, spirits and fiends may represent our "inner demons" – the dark urges or unresolved conflicts in the unconscious that drive us to anger or addiction or cause depression. These demons may also represent a subversive inner voice that encourages the dreamer to transgress social norms – a voice that may have right on its side.

Zombie

Dreams in which we are desperately fleeing or fighting zombies can relate to any situation in our waking life that we want to escape or need to confront – even quite a trivial predicament since the dreaming mind often exaggerates.

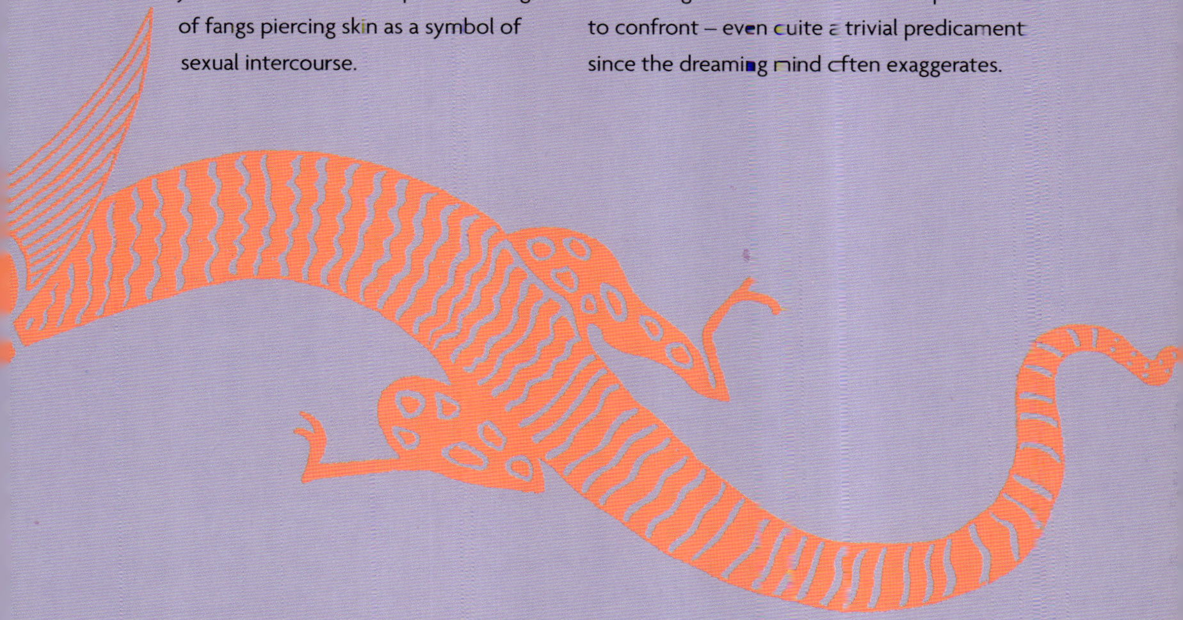

Metamorphoses

We live in a world where transformation is the norm – though its pace may be so gradual that we are unaware of it. The endless transition of the seasons, the cycles of Earth and sun, the young growing old, the present melting into the past, are the essential warp and weft of a human life.

Our perceptions of this constantly shifting world are as unstable as the world itself. Objects appear subtly different each time we look at them, depending on the angle of view, on our mood at that moment, on our level of attention, and on tricks of the light. The same pattern of change affects our perceptions of ourselves and others, and especially our apprehensions of people's characters and values.

In view of all this, it is hardly surprising that transformations also play a major role in our dreams. Often they serve as a kind of shorthand, a bridge passage between one dream subject and the next, linking images in the way a dissolve does in a movie. Equally, they can be meaningful in their own right, drawing attention to relationships between different aspects of our lives, and between the various preoccupations of the unconscious. Sometimes a whole scene will transform itself into another, like a vision conjured by an enchanter. It is relatively commonplace too for the dreamer himself or herself to change – for example, from young to old or from victor to victim. And settings may also be unstable – a place of security can become suddenly threatening, a tornado can sweep through a living room.

Words transforming into images

Freud once interpreted an elephant in a client's dream as a pun on the word *tromper*, the French for "to deceive", which sounds like *trompe*, the word for "trunk". Puns of this kind may enable the dreaming mind to give visual form to human qualities and preoccupations.

One object into another

Transformations can point to a desire to change ourselves, and may give us important clues about what specifically we would like to alter. A skateboard that turns into a house, for example, might express desire for greater stability.

Dreamer transformed into a plant

To become a plant (or a tree, like Daphne in Greek myth) is normally an image of nurture and integration, although for some dreamers the loss of mobility might be significant: the dream may be a warning against becoming too rooted in our ideas or in our routines. Conversely, to transform from a plant into a mobile being may signify a moment of awakening, when we shake off inertia and take positive action.

House transformed into a car

As we have seen, the house is the classic symbol of the self. Thus, a house transformed into something else is likely to be a comment on the state of the dreamer's psyche. A house changing into a car can indicate the importance of movement and progress, but it may also warn of the loss of firm foundations in life. Alternatively, such a dream could be suggesting that the dreamer is losing a sense of his or her own humanity, becoming mechanical, overbearing or ruthless in pursuit of personal or professional objectives.

Animal into person

An animal transformed into a human being can represent conquest over the dreamer's primal instincts; a human transformed into an animal can stand for descent to the more bestial levels of the psyche, or for the rediscovery of natural, spontaneous emotions. A hybrid, part man, part beast – with, say, a boar's head on a human body – may stand for the impossibility of casting off our animal instincts or baser urges. The dream may be encouraging us to stop denying these aspects of the self and work toward accepting them and integrating them into the whole self.

Agents of transformation

Agents of transformation, such as the wizard, magician or shaman, may appear as dream characters. They stand outside the rational, social world but have the power to change it. Such a figure may be a manifestation of the Trickster archetype (see page 104), who often appears when the ego is in a dangerous situation, through some misjudgment or moral lapse. A magician may also represent the means to effect a change, though we should be wary of relying on others to make things happen – perhaps we need to take action ourselves.

Seasons changing

A change through the seasons (such as we sometimes see in romantic movies) or from day to night or vice versa is often a message about our relation to time and potentiality. Winter turning to spring suggests new ideas or new hope, perhaps after a difficult emotional experience such as an episode of depression or a traumatic end to a relationship. When spring turns to summer the dreaming mind may be urging us to enjoy the present. The onset of winter may suggest that now is the time to take stock and conserve our energies.

Myths

In ancient Greek, *mythos* (from which the English word "myth" derives) originally meant "word", "saying" or "story", but later its meaning shifted to "fiction" or even "falsehood", as distinct from *logos*, or "word of truth", the currency of historians. However, we now believe that myth contains its own truths, and that many of these truths transcend time and place, resonating with profound meanings at a level deep within the psyche. If dreams and myths stem from the same roots in the collective unconscious, as Jung believed, then it is not surprising that mythical elements may be found in the dreams even of people whose last direct contact with myth is a distant schoolday memory.

Jung recommended the use of myths as a repertoire of parallels which would help a dreamer tease out the meaning of a dream – the process of amplification (see page 108). With Level 3 dreams, amplification is made easier by the fact that the dream material often contains explicit mythological themes: these represent the archetypal energies of the collective unconscious in personalized form, and may indicate the relationship of such energies to the particular life-circumstances of the dreamer.

Universalized figures in the dreams of Westerners often call to mind Greek, Egyptian and Christian equivalents – the mythologies with which we tend to be most familiar. The Resurrected God, the Hero, the Saviour, the Trickster, the Wise Old Man and the Young Girl are all recurring themes. Sometimes the mythic content is undisguised: a princess in a tower, for example, would be unmistakably a character of legend. However, more oblique references are also encountered, such as the Hero expressed as a movie star or as someone coming to the rescue in a modern context (perhaps, for example, to repair a broken-down car, truck or household appliance).

Mermaid

Combining the symbolism of fish and femininity, the mermaid is a powerful image of the mysterious otherness that haunts and fascinates the male psyche. In dreams, the mermaid typically embodies the Anima – a bringer of secret wisdom and, at the same time, a seductive temptress, luring the overt, active, male energies of the conscious mind into the uncharted depths of the unconscious.

Zeus or Jupiter

"The father of gods and men", Zeus (Jupiter to the Romans) was the supreme ruler of the gods in the Greco-Roman pantheon. He may be an uncompromising representation of our father or he may evoke the anxiety the dreamer feels in the presence of some other formidable authority figure. Enraged and throwing thunderbolts, he may stand for repressed feelings of anger or for the strictness of a parent. Famous for his sexual exploits, Zeus appearing in our dreams might also indicate a desire for adventurous sexual activity, perhaps with a new partner.

Odin

Like Zeus, the Norse deity Odin was the ruler of the gods, and may appear in our dreams as a representative of paternal authority. He is an ambivalent mythic figure: a poet, a wanderer, the god of war and of the wild hunt. One famous story surrounding him tells of how he sacrificed his right eye in order to drink from the well of wisdom – he may convey the price that the dreamer must pay in order to develop spiritually or intellectually.

Achilles

Like the Arthurian Lancelot, Achilles is a flawed hero. He is unashamedly human, given to fits of rage, jealousy and vindictiveness, yet he is half mortal, half god. His personal failings have their physical counterpart in the form of his vulnerable heel – the one part of his body that was not dipped in the River Styx when he was an infant. It is this weakness that eventually results in the hero's death in the Trojan war. In our dreams, the "Achilles heel" can refer to our fatal flaws and act as a warning against complacency.

Dionysos or Bacchus

The Greek god Dionysos, known as Bacchus in Roman myth, was associated with nature, wine, fertility and divine ecstasy. His followers, a wild roaming band of women known as the Maenads or Baccants, danced in ecstatic frenzy, tearing wild animals apart and eating their raw flesh. In dreams, Dionysos can stand for heightened states of consciousness or a recognition of our deeply instinctive primal energies. Dionysos expresses the need to take risks if we dare to explore our full potential. Pan, half man and half goat, serves a similar function: symbol of instinctive nature, in dreams he reminds us of natural beauty and of the forces of male potency and growth.

Herakles or Hercules

Another Greco-Roman hero, Herakles (or Hercules to the Romans) represents the strengths and weaknesses of brute force, and depending on the context of the dream may suggest that we proceed with greater or lesser aggression. Herakles is also notable for the series of apparently impossible tasks he was required to perform. The dream may express frustration with problems that never seem to end.

Minotaur

Half man, half bull, the Minotaur was a monstrous hybrid that lived in a labyrinth on the island of Crete until he was slain by the hero Theseus. In our dreams the Minotaur may represent the dark urges of the unconscious.

Poseidon or Neptune

Poseidon (or Neptune) was the Greco-Roman sea god. A stormy character carrying a trident, his appearance in our dreams can suggest disturbances in the deep waters of the unconscious. Alternatively, his tempestuous nature may reflect a tendency to mood swings or herald a sudden flash of creative inspiration.

Artemis or Diana

The Greco-Roman goddess of the hunt, Artemis conveys an image of proud and self-reliant, if vindictive, womanhood. For female dreamers she may evoke a desire to assert control and shake off traditional conceptions of femininity. Male dreamers might interpret Artemis as a dream symbol of an overbearing mother.

Medusa

One of the three Gorgon sisters, Medusa was endowed with snakes for hair and a visage so terrible that it instantly turned anybody who looked at her to stone. She may represent a negative self-image or the danger of uncovering destructive urges without attempting to understand them.

Aphrodite or Venus

Aphrodite, or Venus, was the Greco-Roman goddess of love and beauty. She symbolizes passion and lust and may encourage a female dreamer to be more at ease with her sexuality and her body. Male dreamers might find her desirable but perhaps also threatening.

Cupid or Eros

Son of Aphrodite, Cupid was the god of sexual desire, evoking playful concupiscence but also, through his arrows, the pain that love can cause.

Jason and the Argonauts

Jason's quest to find the Golden Fleece lends itself to a Jungian interpretation. An archetypal hero, Jason must slay the unsleeping dragon of his unconscious impulses if he is to achieve spiritual fulfilment and purity, represented by the Golden Fleece. He fails to kill the dragon however, only putting it to sleep with a magic potion – ultimately compromising his quest by letting his impulses lie dormant. The myth reminds us that spiritual fulfilment requires total commitment.

Narcissus

According to Roman myth, Narcissus was a handsome young man who fell in love with his own reflection and wasted away from pining until he died. The story warns of the dangers of vanity and may urge the dreamer not to become too attached to appearances.

King Midas

Granted a wish by Dionysos, King Midas asks that everything he touches should turn to gold. The gift turns out to be a curse, however, when it transpires that the spell covers food – he almost starves. The dream figure of King Midas may represent a warning about the danger of greed and of idealizing material things.

Unicorn

The unicorn is portrayed as pure white with a single horn protruding from its forehead, and it was believed that only virgins were capable of taming one. By the Middle Ages it had come to represent chastity and faithfulness in marriage. The unicorn is also a Christian symbol for the Virgin Mary, impregnated by the Holy Spirit, and is a common motif in religious art.

Dragon

Dragons are an archetypal symbol of power, dominance or creativity. In the East they are formidable but benign creatures, representing the emperor and the forces of heaven as well as primal energy and good luck.

Grail

The Holy Grail is the cup from which Jesus drank at the Last Supper; it was later used to catch his blood at the Crucifixion. Often the Grail will represent the dreamer's quest for spiritual perfection, but it can also refer to the heightened importance that we often attach to the quests on which we choose to embark. The Grail also has a Freudian connotation as a symbol of female sexuality.

Excalibur

Arthur's mythical sword could only be pulled from the stone in which it was embedded by the future king of the Britons – who had not yet been revealed. As a dream symbol the sword may stand for the evidence that should show the world that we are worthy of acclaim or heightened responsibility.

Superman

An archetypal hero, Superman is the alter ego of journalist Clark Kent. Reflecting his campaign to defend the world from evil, Superman remains chaste, keeping at bay the advances of Lois Lane, despite the fact that Clark Kent is in love with her. We may identify Clark Kent (there are parallels with the Arthurian Sir Lancelot) with guilt about allowing worldly concerns to distract us from our quest for spiritual enlightenment. Alternatively, the twin selves of Superman may reflect a duality we perceive in our own life – the part that we act with friends or colleagues may be at odds with our self-image.

Maiden in distress

A common symbol in myth and folktale is the rescue of a young maiden by a brave hero. Usually a prince or warrior, the hero may represent the noble, uncompromised side of the unconscious – the part that is not bound by conventional wisdom and dares to set out to seek the truth. The maiden herself is often imprisoned in a castle by an overbearing father or rejected suitor, her incarceration representing the repression of unconscious wisdom by the inflexibility of the rational mind.

Cerberus

Cerberus, the three-headed dog of Greco-Roman myth, guarded the gates of Hades, the Underworld. In dreams he may represent the disturbing instincts that lurk in the unconscious mind, discouraging us from exploring the unknown aspects of the self.

Chimera

Sister to Cerberus, the Chimera was a monstrous beast composed of multiple animals. Its three heads – a lion's, a goat's and a snake's – might represent character flaws such as pride, lechery and deviousness that the dreamer perceives within himself or herself. Less likely is a wordplay on the modern use of the word "chimera" to suggest an illusion or foolish fantasy – and perhaps a predilection for daydreaming.

Leprechaun

This mischievous Irish elf may be a permutation of the Jungian Trickster archetype. Attempts to catch a leprechaun or steal their pot of gold are rarely successful: the dream may be reminding us not to try to take shortcuts in the process of self-development.

Stars and Planets

Throughout history and across cultures, men and women have tried to read their destiny in the night sky. Fascinated by the motions of the heavenly bodies, every major civilization has developed its own way of associating them with the mystic powers that determine our fate.

Level 3 dreams about the heavens often convey a sense of the eternally unchanging nature of ultimate reality. We may feel ourselves to be at one with the stars, our identity absorbed into the far reaches of the universe.

Rarely, even in Level 1 and Level 2 dreams, do the stars and planets carry negative connotations, although some dreamers interpret them as emphasizing the insignificance of human life in the face of the vast impersonal forces of the universe.

Heavenly bodies normally appear singly in dreams, but if there is more than one it may be their juxtaposition that is important. The sun and moon together may represent the relationship between the conscious and unconscious, the rational and irrational; while Mars and Venus can stand for the relationship between male and female.

Dreams are riddled with paradoxes, and to look out is also to look within. Thus, gazing into the night sky can be a symbol for examining the unconscious where the infinite possibilities of the imagination make the everyday concerns of the conscious mind seem small and insignificant.

Stars

As well as representing fate and the celestial powers, the stars can stand for the dreamer's higher states of consciousness. A single star shining more brightly than the rest can signify success in competition with others, but may also serve to remind the dreamer of his or her responsibilities toward those of lesser ability. The brightest star could also be the one that is closest to destruction. Ever present in the night sky of the Northern Hemisphere, the Pole Star aids navigators and may act as a symbolic guide for those exploring personal or universal profundities.

Moon

The moon often represents the feminine aspect, as the queen of the night, and the mystery of hidden, secret things. It is also associated with water (because it governs Earth's tides), with the imagination, and with the passing of time. There may be an implication of natural evolution. A full moon may indicate serenity and stillness, signifying the dreamer's potential for rewarding contemplation, or it may be a symbol of emotional and spiritual completeness. A new moon is an obvious symbol of fresh beginnings.

Sun

The sun has strong connotations of the masculine, the world of overt things, the conscious mind, the intellect, and the father. In dreams, a hot burning sun can indicate the intellect's power to make a desert out of the dreamer's emotional life. Conversely, the sun hidden by clouds can suggest the emotions overruling rationality. A solar eclipse may suggest troubling events or emotions interfering with creativity or spiritual development.

Earth

A dream of leaving Earth may arise from fear of death or estrangement from our friends or family. Earth viewed from space might suggest feelings of isolation or loneliness.

Mars

Associated with the Roman god of war, the red hue of the planet Mars carries connotations of anger, passion and aggression. Alternatively, as the planet closest to Earth and the one on which many scientists hope to find life, its appearance in our dreams may convey a longing for, or preoccupation with, companionship.

Venus

Like its namesake the Roman goddess of love, the planet Venus has erotic associations. More generally, its brightness as the "evening" or "morning star" at twilight or dawn is often taken as propitious. Its appearance in a dream may signify our highest aspirations or most honourable ambitions – though without giving a sense of whether they are well-grounded.

Comet

Although comets were once interpreted as portents of disaster, a dreamer today is more likely to associate them with a warning of dazzling but temporary success, followed by rapid descent and eventual destruction. A comet can also represent ideas and insights flashing brilliantly from the unconscious, or a sense that our lives may take a turn toward the dramatic.

David Fontana

1000 Dreams

Discover the meaning of dream symbols, secrets & stories

Watkins
Sharing Wisdom Since 1893

1000 DREAMS

David Fontana

This edition first published in the UK and USA in 2015 by
Watkins, an imprint of Watkins Media Limited
Unit 11, Shepperton House, 89–93 Shepperton Road
London N1 3DF

enquiries@watkinspublishing.com

Editor: Elinor Brett
Managing Designer: Luana Gobbo
Designer: Gabriella Le Grazie
Picture Research: Emma Copestake
Commissioned artwork: Nick Dewar, Fabian Negrin, Heidi Younger, Alison Jay, Jamie Bennett, Grizelda Holderness, Leigh Wells, Sandie Turchyn and Marie LaFrance

A CIP record for this book is available from the British Library

B&N - ISBN: 978-1-78678-321-9
10 9 8 7 6 5 4 3 2

WEL - ISBN: 978-1-78028-040-0
10 9 8 7 6 5 4

Typeset in Agenda, Caslon and Nupital
Printed in China

www.watkinspublishing.com

"Those who have compared our life to a dream were right. ... We sleeping wake, and waking sleep."

Michel de Montaigne, *Essays*, 1580

Contents

Introduction

"What if you slept? And what if, in your sleep, you dreamed? And what if, in your dream, you went to heaven and plucked a strange and beautiful flower? And what if, when you awoke, you had the flower in your hand? Ah, what then?"

Samuel Taylor Coleridge (1772–1834)

I cannot remember a time when I have not been interested in dreams. As a child, they were an entry into a magic world which convinced me that there was more to existence than the commonplace experiences of daily life. When I talked to my young friends, I found they shared the same fascination with this inner world, and we often shared with each other our nighttime adventures (most of which probably lost nothing in the telling), spanning the gamut from fairytale happenings in which animals talked and wishes were granted, to the most blood-curdling and terrifying of nightmares. Probably I was lucky, in that most of my dreams were of the pleasant kind, taking me deeper and deeper into what I came to recognize in later years as the mysteries of my own unconscious.

The varied richness of my own dream life was such that even when I took up the study of psychology in my student days, nothing shook my conviction that dreams are a vital part of our mental life, carrying messages that help to reveal our hidden hopes and fears, and sometimes providing us with guidance and advice unthought of by the conscious, waking mind. I discovered the work of Freud and Jung and learned how dreams can help the psychotherapist understand the client's problems, and give valuable clues on what needs to be done in order to put these problems right.

Later, studying Buddhism, Hinduism and other Eastern traditions, I discovered the great importance that other cultures attach to dreaming, even seeing it as providing insights into what happens to consciousness after physical death. I learned that it is possible increasingly to take control of one's dreaming, to remember dreams in great detail upon waking, to influence the content of dreams, and even to dream consciously (so-called "lucid dreaming").

The more I've studied dreaming, the more I recognize the inadequacy of suggestions by some scientists that dreaming is merely analogous to a computer dumping unwanted data at the end of the working day. Nevertheless, it is important to recognize the advances that science has made in helping us understand, if not the cause and purpose of dreams, at least some of the mechanisms behind them. We thus know that everyone, from very young babies to the elderly, appears to dream every night, and those who claim not to do so are simply unable to remember their dreams. Modern researchers also teach us that dreaming appears to be important to our psychological health and that no single theory can account for its richness and variety.

My own experiences when running dream workshops and using dreams as an aid toward psychological understanding have shown me in addition that many people find dreaming is great fun. Dreams break all the laws of waking life. In dreams, the elderly can become young again, the young can become old. The failures and disappointments of waking life can be remedied. Flying and time travel become not only possible but absurdly easy. People and objects change shape and sometimes there are glimpses of scenes and places that resemble paradise. So although I hope you may learn from this book, I hope above all else that you will find it fun, and that it will help to enrich your journeyings into the strange, undiscovered country that beckons to us each nightfall.

David Fontana

For Reference

Further Reading

Ball, P. (2006) *The Power of Creative Dreaming.* London: Quantum; and New York: Foulsham.

Boss, M. (1997) *A New Approach to the Revelations of Dreaming and its Uses in Psychotherapy.* New York: Gardener.

Campbell, J. (1949) *The Hero with a Thousand Faces.* London: Paladin; and New York: Pantheon Books.

Castaneda, C. (1973) *Tales of Power.* London: Element; and New York: Harper Collins.

Castaneda, C. (1993) *The Art of Dreaming.* London: Element; and New York: Harper Collins.

Faraday, A. (1972) *Dream Power: The Use of Dreams in Everyday Life.* London: Pan Books.

Fenwick, P., and **Fenwick, E.** (1997) *The Hidden Door: Understanding and Controlling Dreams.* London: Hodder Headline.

Fontana, D. (1999) *Learn to Meditate.* London: Duncan Baird Publishers.

Fontana, D. (2007) *Creative Meditation and Visualization.* London: Watkins/Duncan Baird Publishers.

Fontana, D. (2008) *The New Secret Language of Dreams.* London: Duncan Baird Publishers; and San Francisco: Chronicle.

Freud, S. (1899) *The Interpretation of Dreams.* Leipzag and Vienna: Franz Deuticke; and London: Macmillan.

Garfield, P. (1976) *Creative Dreaming.* London: Futura.

Garfield, P. (1991) *The Healing Power of Dreams.* London and New York: Simon & Schuster.

Goodwin, R. (2004) *Dreamlife: How Dreams Happen.* Great Barrington MA: Lindisfarne Books.

Halifax, J. (1979) *Shamanic Voices.* New York: E.P. Dutton.

Hall, C.S., and **Nordby, V.J.** (1972) *The Individual and His Dreams.* New York: New American Library.

Hearne, K. (1989) *Visions of the Future.* Wellingborough: Aquarian Press.

Hearne, K. (1990) *The Dream Machine.* Wellingborough: Aquarian Press.

Hillman, J. (1989) *The Essential James Hillman.* London and New York: Routledge.

Holbeche, S. (1991) *The Power of Your Dreams.* London: Piatkus.

Inglis, B. (1988) *The Power of Dreams.* London: Paladin

Jones, R.M. (1978) *The New Psychology of Dreaming.* Harmondsworth and New York: Penguin.

Jung, C.G. (1963) *Memories, Dreams and Reflections.* London and New York: Routledge.

Jung, C.G. (1968) *Analytical Psychology: Its Theory and Practice.* London and New York: Routledge.

Jung, C.G. (1972) *Four Archetypes.* London and New York: Routledge.

Jung, C.G. (1974) *Dreams.* Princeton, NJ: Princeton University Press.

Jung, C.G. (1983) *Selected Writings.* London: Fontana Books (Harper Collins).

Jung, C.G. (1984) *Dream Analysis.* London and New York: Routledge.

Kleitman, N. (1939) *Sleep and Wakefulness.* Chicago: University of Chicago Press.

Lenard, L. (2002) *Guide to Dreams.* London and New York: Dorling Kindersley.

Linn, D. (2009) *The Hidden Power of Dreams: The Mysterious World of Dreams Revealed.* New York: Hay House.

Mattoon, M.A. (1978) *Applied Dream Analysis: A Jungian Approach.* London and New York: John Wiley & Sons.

Mavromatis, A. (1987) *Hypnagogia: The Unique State of Consciousness Between Wakefulness and Sleep.* London and New York: Routledge.

Mindell, A. (2000) *Dreaming While Awake: Techniques for 24-Hour Lucid Dreaming.* Charlottesville, VA: Hampton Roads.

Reading, M. (2007) *The Watkins Dictionary of Dreams.* London: Watkins.

Ullman, M., and **Limmer, C.** (eds.) (1987) *The Variety of Dream Experience.* London: Crucible; and New York: Continuum.

Ullman, M., and **Zimmerman, N.** (1987) *Working with Dreams.* London: Aquarian Press; and New York: Eleanor Friede Books.

Van de Castle, R. (1971) *The Psychology of Dreaming.* Morristown, NJ: General Learning Press.

Dream Index

The Dream Index, which refers to symbols, images, activities and the like, is intended to facilitate the interpretation of dream content. Page numbers in **bold** type refer to section headings in the Key to Dream Symbols.

W

XYZ

Subject Index

Page numbers in **bold** type refer to main entries; page numbers in *italics* refer to practical exercises in feature boxes.

Picture Acknowledgments

The publisher would like to thank the following people, museums and photographic libraries for permission to reproduce their material. Every care has been taken to trace copyright holders. However, if we have omitted anyone we apologize and will, if informed, make corrections to any future edition.

Key
l = left, r = right, a = above, b = below

Jamie Bennett: 90, 98, 110, 116, 117, 120, 125(inset), 131, 213, 431.
Nick Dewar: 16, 39, 50, 58, 66, 97, 128, 187, 212, 235, 242(inset), 243, 245, 249, 298, 302, 306, 360, 368, 434.
Hugh Dixon: 48, 74, 137 232, 271, 277, 294, 324, 333, 348, 350, 351(a), 354, 356, 378.
Grizelda Holderness: 1, 11, 30, 33, 37, 38, 46, 59, 68, 78, 86–87, 93, 100, 141, 146, 148, 172, 176, 182, 185, 189, 195, 206(inset), 209, 214, 219, 221, 229, 241, 270, 284, 292, 315, 316, 338, 339, 340, 343, 359, 373, 379, 382(inset), 386, 389, 398, 436, 438.
Alison Jay: 2–3, 25, 32, 47, 55, 60-61, 64, 81(inset), 82, 104, 126, 127, 134, 135, 144, 149, 152, 156, 159(inset), 160(inset), 161, 162-163, 165, 168, 193, 196, 226, 237, 246(r), 247, 253, 268, 279, 280, 282, 299, 301, 304(a), 342(inset), 369, 380–381, 388, 412.
Marie LaFrance: 5, 77, 423, 445.
Gabriella Le Grazie: 112.
Peter Malone: 10, 40, 42, 70–71, 75, 80, 91, 124, 151, 158, 164, 166–167, 177, 179, 198–199, 223, 225(b), 238–239, 272–273, 309, 318, 321, 335, 345, 352, 366–367, 370–371, 372, 429, 441.
Fabian Negrin: 6–7, 51, 69, 107, 111, 119, 121, 143, 153, 295, 308, 417, 448–449.
Jules Selmes: 62, 72, 95, 105, 170, 178, 186–187, 188, 215, 224(a), 234, 251, 252, 256, 257, 260–261, 265, 274, 281, 291, 311, 323, 326–327, 328, 330, 331, 341, 351(b), 363, 364, 428, 430.
Sandie Turchyn: 35, 76, 173, 174, 182, 264(inset), 329, 332, 355, 394, 419.
Leigh Wells: 44, 65, 102, 122, 139, 296.
Heidi Younger: 56, 85, 145, 162, 180, 134, 190, 192, 207, 210, 211, 230, 233, 267, 286, 288, 314(inset), 319, 322, 336, 424, 426, 433.
Eyewire Images: 115, 125, 382, 416.
Photos.com: 112, 159, 191, 242, 314, 342, 411.
Image Dictionary: 11, 81, 160, 206, 216, 283, 290, 404, 407.
iStock: 14 (Rzymu), 83 (Martin McCarthy), 205 (Quidnunc), 262 (Michelle Preast), 357 (Aimin Tang), 384 (Pawel Aniszewski), 402–403 (AVTG), 409 (Dimarmar).
Shutterstock: 96 (BasPhoto).
Mary Evans Picture Library: 21, 26 (Sigmund Freud Copyrights).
©BNN, Inc. "20's Kimono": 52, 53, 183, 222, 246(l), 307, 325, 376, 396, 397, 399, 414–415.